BEDROOM OF ADAM AND EVE

**BEDROOM OF ADAM AND EVE
CAUSE EFFECT AND SOLUTION**

OASIS AT MAGIC RANCH FLORENCE ARIZONA UNITED STATES OF AMERICA

Copyright © 2016 by Lungu Publishing Company Inc.

P.O. Box 2932 Florence Arizona 85132. All rights reserved. Unless permitted under the U.S. Copyright Act of 1976, no part of this publication may be reproduced, distributed, or transmitted in any form or by any means, or stored in a database or retrieval system, without the prior written permission of the publisher.

Lungu Publishing Company Inc.

P.O. Box 2932

Florence Arizona 85132 USA

www.lungupci.com

Library of Congress Control Number: 2016918740.

TABLE OF CONTENTS

INTRODUCTION 11

CHAPTER 1 12
WHAT IS SIN? 12
Sin is disobedience to God and God's law 12
Sin is rebellion against God 13
Sin is transgression 14
Sin is missing the mark 14
Sin is lawlessness 14
CHAPTER ONE. QUESTIONS FOR YOU TO ANSWER   15

CHAPTER 2 16
WHAT IS THE ORIGIN OF SIN? 16
Who was the Devil? What made him sin? 16
There is No longer pure and perfect will 17
CHAPTER TWO. QUESTIONS FOR YOU TO ANSWER   18

CHAPTER 3 19
ORIGINAL SIN 19
Irenaeus (and others) on original sin 19
CHAPTER THREE. QUESTIONS TO ANSWER   22

CHAPTER 4 23
NATURAL OF ORIGINAL SIN 23
Imputation of the sin of Adam 23
Total Deprived 23
Guilty 24
Corruption 24
Solidarity with Adam 25
CHAPTER FOUR. QUESTIONS TO ANSWER   25

CHAPTER 5 26
CONSEQUENCES OF ORIGINAL SIN 26
Total separation from God 26
Spiritual death 27

Physical death	30
Misery	34
Sufferings	34
Diseases	35
Lame	35
War	36
World catastrophe	37
CHAPTER FIVE. QUESTIONS TO ANSWER	38

CHAPTER 6 39
    ACTS OF SIN 39
    Addiction 39
    Depression 40
    Murder 41
    Lying 41
    Anger 42
    Suicide 43
    The Idol worship 44
    Witchcraft 50
    Abortion 51
    Sexual Harassment 52
    Adultery 54
    Fornication 56
    Divorce 57
    Hormosexualism 59
    Masturbation 61
    CHAPTER SIX. QUESTIONS TO ANSWER 62

CHAPTER 7 64
    WHAT DOES THE BIBLE SAY ABOUT SEX? 64
    Sex is a Good Thing 64
    What if I've Already Had Unlawful Sex? 65
    But It's So Tempting! 65
    CHAPTER SEVEN. QUESTIONS TO ANSWER 66

CHAPTER 8 67
    OMISSION AND UNKNOWN SINS 67

What does the Bible say about sins of omission?........................67
CHAPTER EIGHT. QUESTIONS TO ANSWER   70

CHAPTER 9..71
ORIGINAL SIN VS THE IMAGE OF GOD.........................71
Image of God in a broader sense 71
CHAPTER NINE. QUESTIONS TO ANSWER   73

CHAPTER 10..74
JESUS TOOK CARE OF ORIGINAL SIN AND ALL ITS FRUITS?......74
Jesus became truly man 74
Jesus Christ died..75
Double imputation in Christ................................75
CHAPTER TEN. QUESTIONS TO ANSWER   76

CHAPTER 11..77
RESULTS OF CHRIST FINISHED WORK.........................77
Reconciliation 77
Eternal Life 77
No Second death 78
Heaven for us 79
The Fulfillment of the Law 79
Jesus the Way to the Father 80
Living as Those Made Alive in Christ 80
Our true home is heaven 81
CHAPTER ELEVEN. QUESTIONS TO ANSWER   82

CHAPTER 12..83
THE TEACHINGS OF REFORMED THEOLOGY....................83
Two Sources of Knowledge of God..........................85
CHAPTER TWELVE. QUESTIONS TO ANSWER   86

CHAPTER 13..87
THE DOCTRINE OF GOD AND HIS CREATION...................87
Nature of God 87
God is ONE Spirit...88
Essence of God 88
One God in Three Persons 88

Attributes of God 89
God's Names 89
Works of God 90
Predestination 90
CHAPTER THIRTEEN. QUESTIONS TO ANSWER 92

CHAPTER 14 93
DOCTRINE OF MAN 93
CHAPTER FORTEEN. QUESTIONS TO ANSWER 95

CHAPTER 15 96
DOCRINE OF CHRIST 96
Who is Jesus Christ? What is His Nature? 96
CHAPTER FIFTEEN. QUESTIONS TO ANSWER 100

CHAPTER 16 101
DOCTRINE OF SALVATION 101
Regeneration 102
Conversion 103
Faith 104
Justification 105
Sanctification follows justification. 107
CHAPTER SEXTEEN. QUESTIONS TO ANSWER 109

CHAPTER 17 110
THE DOCTRINE THE CHURCH 110
CHAPTER SEVENTEEN. QUESTIONS TO ANSWER 112

CHAPTER 18 113
DOCTRINE OF THE MEANS OF GRACE 113
CHAPTER EIGHTEEN. QUESTIONS TO ANSWER 114

CHAPTER 19 116
THE DOCTRINE OF THE LAST THINGS 116
Second Advert of Jesus Christ 116
Nature of Christ return 117
CHAPTER NINTEEN. QUESTIONS TO ANSWER; 118

CHAPTER 20 . . . .**120**

THE DOCTRINE OF THE HOLY SPIRIT 120
1. The deity of the Holy Spirit. 120
2. Personality of the Holy Spirit. 121
3. The work of the Holy Spirit. 121
CHAPTER TWENTY. QUESTIONS TO ANSWER;   124

CHAPTER 21 . . . . **126**
BIBLICAL PASSAGES FOR PRISON MINISTRY 126
CHAPTER ONE. QUESTIONS TO ANSWER;   129

CHAPTER 22 . . . . **130**
SEVEN WAYS TEACHING REFORMED THEOLOGY IN USA PRISONS? . . . 130
A. Seminary Model 130
B and C Pod and Unit Model 131
D, E and F Chapel Model/Chaplain Model/Volunteer Model 132
CHAPTER TWENTY-TWO. QUESTIONS TO ANSWER;   134

CHAPTER 23 . . . . **135**
THE SIGNIFICANCE OF REFORMED THEOLOGY IN US PRISONS. 135
A. Among reformed theological seminaries in US prison 135
B. Among reformed prison chaplains. 135
C. Among reformed prison volunteers 135
D. Among US Prisons 136
E. Among prisoners that took the teachings of reformed faith. 137
F. Main Challenge for Prison Ministry 137
CHAPTER TWENTY-THREE. QUESTIONS TO ANSWER;   139

CHAPTER 24 . . . . **140**
CONFESSIONS OF CHRISTIAN CHURCH 140
APSTOLIC CREED 140
THE ATHANASIAN CREED. 141
THE BELGIC CONFESSION 143
CONFESSION OF BELHAR. 166
CANONS OF DORT. 170
HEIDELBERG CATECHISM 181
INTRODUCTION 181
PART I: MISERY 181
PART II: DELIVERANCE 183

GOD THE FATHER	185
GOD THE SON	186
GOD THE HOLY SPIRIT	191
THE HOLY SACRAMENTS	193
PART III: GRATITUDE	198
THE TEN COMMANDMENTS	199
THE LORD'S PRAYER	205
THE NICENE CREED	209
CHAPTER 24 QUESTIONS TO ANSWER	209
BIBLIOGRAPHY	**210**
ANOTHER WORK BY DR. EK LUNGU	**212**
CONTACT US	**213**
THE TARGET FOR THIS BOOK	**214**
ABOUT THE AUTHOR	**215**
DEDICATION	**216**
FRIENDS OF REFORMED THEOLOGY	**217**
HOW TO US THIS BOOK	**218**
WHAT YOU NEED TO DO	**219**

BEDROOM OF ADAM AND EVE

INTRODUCTION

Have you ever wondered how many times you have sinned in life? Has the blame game caught up with you whenever you fell in the act of sin? Or has sin become so normal life to you that you do not feel ashamed when you do it?

If the answer to these questions is yes, then you are not alone. Sin and blame game started in the Garden of Aden with Adam and Eve when they sinned against God. This proves the fact that all of us came from one man and woman, Adam, and Eve. All of us are one big family of Adam and Eve regardless of different color, tribe, and nation. We are all one race called human.

In this book, Bedroom of Adam and Eve, you will learn the origin and nature of original sin? You will learn how the original sin effected human race. All people in the world love the comfort of living in the bedroom of Adam and Eve. This has come to be known as total depravity. Humans are deprived of the will to come out of the self-made pit and live with God without the help of the Spirit of God Himself. Therefore, total depravity is the bedroom of Adam and Eve.

The best part of this book is that it also explains how human race can come out of the bedroom of Adam and Eve and start living in the bedroom of Christ Jesus through the grace of God. Bedroom of Adam and Eve also explains the teachings and confessions of those human beings that lived in the comfort of Christ.

Bedroom of Adam and Eve creates hunger in the lives of Christ, believers worldwide to go back to the bible and cultivate core Christian beliefs taught by early Christians.

I Edward Kavimba Lungu wrote this book under the supervision of the word and the Spirit of God for you and all your families. My hope is that God speaks to you as you read and study the truths of this book. Whatever you learn from this book practice and pass it on to generation.

BEDROOM OF ADAM AND EVE

CHAPTER 1

WHAT IS SIN?

One day, while teaching on the topic "Sin" in a chapel, I gave a good example of what sin was. In my hands, I had two small pencils. I showed them to the audience. I asked them one question, "What do you see in my hands?" They answered, "Two small pencils". Then I asked another question, "Why do you see these two small pencils in my hands?" Very few of them knew the answer.

The answer was obvious. The two small pencils were items or substance that could be seen and held in my hands.

Sin is not a substance or an item that we can see and hold in our hands. If sin was a substance, someone would have held and crashed it completely. In our generation, we have big sophisticated machines which were going to be used to catch and destroy sin if it were an item.

Unfortunately, sin is not an item or substance. What is a sin then? There are two ways to answer this question. One way, which is my way, is to let the holy bible help to answer the question. On the other hand, let human minds and religions that do not believe the Bible to be the word of God answer this question.

In this book, therefore, I will try to answer this question about sin, its origin, its effects, and solution based on the word of God.

I am convinced that after reading this book, you will have a good understand of what sin is and how it has affected human beings. You will also learn how the problem of sin has been solved through the finished work of Jesus Christ. In this book, you will also be able to study and even teach doctrinal beliefs the church has formulated and confessed in the Christendom.

Throughout generation, human beings have tried to answer and solve the problem of sin on their own but failed. When our First parents sinned against God in the Garden of Eden tried to solve one part of this problem by covering up their nakedness with leaves but failed. The bible says; "At that moment their eyes were opened, and they suddenly felt shame at their nakedness. So, they sewed fig leaves together to cover their nakedness" (Genesis 3:7).

For the first time, their eyes were opened and realized they were both naked. See how God solved this problem of physical nakedness finally. "And the Lord God made clothing from animal skins for Adam and his wife" (Genesis 3:21). It is not right for humans to go in public with no covering on their bodies.

If sin is not a substance, then what is it?

Sin is disobedience to God and God's law

There are many passages and verses in the bible that support this fact. I will only mention a few.

The writer of Psalm 78:10 says, "They did not keep the covenant of God and refused to walk in His law". They, meant the people of God in the Old Testament, which normally referred to the Israelites.

Moses did not enter the Promised Land with the rest of the Jews because he also disobeyed God. But still more Moses had to warn the Israelites not to disobey God once they were in the Promised Land saying, "But it shall come about, if you do not obey the LORD your God, to observe to do all His commandments and His statutes with which I charge you today, that all these curses will come upon you and overtake you (Deuteronomy 28:15).

Jeremiah the prophet had harsh words to the people of God when he said, "The Lord said, "It is because they have forsaken my law, which I set before them; they have not obeyed me or followed my law. Instead, they have followed the stubbornness of their hearts; they have followed the Baals, as their ancestors taught them." Therefore, this is what the Lord Almighty, the God of Israel, says: "See, I will make this people eat bitter food and drink poisoned water. I will scatter them among nations that neither they nor their ancestors have known, and I will pursue them with the sword until I have made an end of them" (Jeremiah 9:13-16).

Elsewhere in the New Testament, it is said, "They profess to know God, but by their deeds they deny Him, being detestable and disobedient and worthless for any good deed (Titus 1:16). And again, it is said, "For we also once were foolish ourselves, disobedient, deceived, enslaved to various lusts and pleasures, spending our lives in malice and envy, hateful, hating one another (Titus 3:3).

To sum up the fact that sin is disobedience to God and his law, let us go back to the book of Genesis chapter Three where sin begins. Eve revealed to God that she disobeyed God when the snake deceived her to eat the fruit from the forbidden tree. Then the Lord God said to the woman, "What is this you have done? "The woman said, "The serpent deceived me, and I ate" (Genesis 3:13). Eve was very much aware of the law of God, not to eat the forbidden fruit but want to do so anyway.

I like what Paul wrote to the Ephesian church saying, "Let no one deceive you with empty words, for because of these things the wrath of God comes upon the sons of disobedience (Ephesians 5:6).

Disobedience is a noun which comes from the verb 'disobey'. Per Oxford Dictionaries it means "failure or refusal to obey rules or someone in authority. Disobedience breeds defiance, insubordination or intractability to God and his law due to sin.

Sin is rebellion against God

When Eve had a discussion with the snake, Adam was right there. We do not know if he was listening or not, but it seems he was very close to his wife. When Eve got the forbidden fruit, and ate it Adam was present. Eve ate the fruit first and then gave some to her husband, Adam who ate them. We do not know how many fruits they both ate from that tree in the middle of the Garden. This is not the issue. The issue is now with Adam, who knew the law of God but chose to rebel against God and his law. Again, the problem was not in eating, but in choosing to rebel against the word of God.

The bible says, "When the woman saw that the fruit of the tree was good for food and pleasing to the eye, and desirable for gaining wisdom, she took some and ate it. She also gave some to her husband, who was with her, and he ate it (Genesis 3:6). The prophet Samuel said these words to a rebellious Israel, ""If you will not listen to the voice of the LORD, but rebel against the command of the LORD, then the hand of the LORD will be against you, as it was against your fathers." (1 Samuel 12:15). The prophet Isaiah echoed the same notion when he said, "For Jerusalem has stumbled and Judah has fallen, because their speech and their actions are against the LORD, to rebel against His glorious presence" (Isaiah 3:8).

Rebellion is refusal to obey the law or rules of a person, company, or any form of authority. The person knows the rule or acceptable normal standards, but willingly and knowingly decides not to follow or obey. This is sin in its entirety, especially if it is against God and his law.

Always rebellion must do with insurgence, insurrection, mutiny, revolt or uprising and up break against authority.

Sin is transgression

Transgression is a form of misdeed or wrong doing. It is a trespass, crime, infringement or violation of a law, command, or duty. When we sin against God and his law, we commit misdeeds which often is reliable for punishment. We need God's forgiveness just as the Psalmists said, "Blessed is the one whose transgressions are forgiven, whose sins are covered" (Psalms 32:1).

The prophet Daniel said, "Indeed, all Israel has transgressed your law and turned aside, not obeying your voice; so, the curse has been poured out on us, along with the oath which is written in the law of Moses the servant of God, for we have sinned against Him" (Daniel 9:10-11).

Adam and Eve did not follow through the law of God when they ate the forbidden fruits. Adam and Eve obeyed the devil and therefore violated the law of God. Both became transgressors.

Sin is missing the mark

God in the Garden of Eden already set the mark. The mark was to obey the law of God. God said to Adam, "The Lord God took the man and put him in the Garden of Eden to work it and take care of it. And the Lord God commanded the man, "You are free to eat from any tree in the garden; but you must not eat from the tree of the knowledge of good and evil, for when you eat from it you will certainly die" (Genesis 2: 15-17).

If Adam stayed on the mark of God, he was all right and upright. Adam was free to eat everything else in the Garden but not from the tree in the middle of the Garden. That was the mark. It was the absolute standard God put forth. But the moment, both ate the fruits from the tree in the middle of the Garden they missed the mark. They missed to live up to the standard God set for them. Both were no longer perfect in the eyes of God. Apostle Paul said, "For all have sinned and fall short of the glory of God" (Romans 3:23). The word 'all 'means all people starting with Adam and Eve have sinned and fall short of the glory of God Almighty. All people of all generations have missed the mark set by God.

Sin is lawlessness

The word lawlessness is made up of two words law and less. Law is a rule, canon or normal to be followed while less, simply means not enough, not complete, or not there. Therefore, lawlessness is a situation or a place without law. It is a chaotic condition. For example, we can say a lawless nation is a nation operating without laws. It is sometimes called a failed state.

Sin is lawlessness because it creates chaos or insanity in a person, nation, and the world. Where sin abounds, there is lawlessness. There is disobedience. No one pays attention to the law. In other words, there is a disregard for the law. Sin becomes the master and not the law of the land or stipulations of God. We can rightly state that lawlessness breeds anarchy, commotion, confusion, disarray, turmoil, and disorder.

Apostle John was right when he said, "Everyone who sins breaks the law; in fact, sin is lawlessness" (1 John 3:4). It is clear in the bible that there will be the final episode of lawlessness when the man of lawlessness is finally revealed and destroyed by of Our Master Jesus Christ.

Apostle Paul wrote this to the church of Thessalonians about a man of lawlessness;

"Don't let anyone deceive you in any way, for that day will not come until the rebellion occurs and the man of lawlessness is revealed, the man doomed to destruction. He will oppose and will exalt himself over everything that is called God or is worshiped, so that he sets himself up in God's temple, proclaiming himself to be God.

Don't you remember that when I was with you I used to tell you these things? And now you know what is holding him back, so that he may be revealed at the proper time. For the secret power of lawlessness is already at work; but the one who now holds it back will continue to do so till he is taken out of the way. And then the lawless one will be revealed, whom the Lord Jesus will overthrow with the breath of his mouth and destroy by the splendor of his coming. The coming of the lawless one will be in accordance with how Satan works. He will use all sorts of displays of power through signs and wonders that serve the lie, and all the ways that wickedness deceives those who are perishing. They perish because they refused to love the truth and so be saved. For this reason, God sends them a powerful delusion so that they will believe the lie and so that all will be condemned who have not believed the truth but have delighted in wickedness" (2 Thessalonians 2:3-12).

CHAPTER ONE. QUESTIONS FOR YOU TO ANSWER

What is Sin per Chapter One?

What is Sin per you?

Can you paint a picture of sin that is bothering you all the time?

Did God create sin?

In your own ways, can you explain the meaning of our memory passage in relationship to sin?

Who has the power to forgive our sins?

Have you ever tried to confess your sin or sins?

Have you asked Jesus blood to forgive those sins you have?

How do you know you 1 John 1:8-9?

How about John 3:16?

Romans 10:9-11?

BEDROOM OF ADAM AND EVE

CHAPTER 2

WHAT IS THE ORIGIN OF SIN?

The word origin has its origin in Latin. It means the source or beginning. The Bible is quite clear that the origin of sin is the devil known as Satan the father of all lies.

Speaking about the Devil, Jesus said, "You belong to your father, the devil, and you want to carry out your father's desires. He was a murderer from the beginning, not holding to the truth, for there is no truth in him. When he lies, he speaks his native language, for he is a liar and the father of lies (John 8:44). Sin has its root, foundation, and birth in the Devil. The Devil owns sins as its own baby.

Who was the Devil? What made him sin?

To answer these two questions, we need to read what the prophet Ezekiel in the Old Testament said, "You were in Eden, the garden of God; every precious stone adorned you:

Carnelian, chrysolite and emerald, topaz, onyx and jasper, lapis Lazuli, turquoise and beryl.

Your settings and mountings were made of gold; on the day, you were created they were prepared. You were anointed as a guardian cherub, for so I ordained you. You were on the holy mount of God; you walked among the fiery stones. You were blameless in your ways from the day you were created till wickedness was found in you" (Ezekiel 28: 13-15).

Ezekiel prophesied against an existing life style of a leader of the city of Tyre (Chapters 26-27). The leader of this city became very proud that he believed in himself to be God. Ezekiel warned the king of Tyre about the sin of pride.

But some of the phrases used by Ezekiel point to the Devil and not to king of Tyre alone. Phrases like "You were in Eden, the garden of God… You were anointed as a guardian cherub, and for so I ordained you… you walked among the fiery stones. You were blameless in your ways from the day you were created…" Who was in the garden of God? Who was this anointed guardian cherub? Who was this cherub that was created, but walked blamelessly in all its ways? The answers to all these questions do not point to the king of Tyre but to Lucifer.

This is what is deduced when the prophet Isaiah prophesied against the king of Babylon; "How you have fallen from heaven, O morning star, son of the dawn! You have been cast down to the earth, you who once laid low the nations! You said in your heart, "I will ascend to heaven; I will raise my throne above the stars of God; I will sit enthroned on the mount of assembly, on the utmost heights of the sacred mountain. I will ascend above the tops of the clouds; I will make myself like the Most High" (Isaiah 14: 12-14).

This prophecy in Isaiah was not just for the king of Babylon, but also for Lucifer, who was once a bright morning star in heaven. In Ezekiel chapter 28 it is said that God anointed and ordained Lucifer to a higher position than all the angels that were created. Lucifer was a powerful and shining angel next to God. He held a trustworthy position in heaven. Lucifer was full of pure and perfect free will as he performed his duties in heaven before the throne of God. But something in his heart started root secretly which only God Almighty knew because God knows all things even before we speak them. Now the pure and perfect free will is abused.

The Bible says, "You were blameless in all you did from the day you were created until the day evil was found in you… Your heart was filled with pride because of all your beauty. Your wisdom was corrupted by your love of splendor so I threw you to the ground" (Ezekiel 28: 15, 17). Lucifer sinned against God because of pride. He loved himself more than God. He wanted to be God himself. Look at the usage of the first-person pronoun I or self in Isaiah Chapter 14:12-14. The pronoun I am using five times. The meaning of I in this passage means personal or self-glorification. All that Lucifer was now planning to do would come from himself and not from God who gave him that position of authority.

Lucifer shinned brighter than all the angelic beings, God made. All other creatures admired him with adoration. This made his pride. And God rejected him and threw him down on earth from heaven. Not only from heaven, but from his highest anointed and ordained position. Lucifer was forced to be in a lowly position once he fell from his position. The name of Lucifer has now changed to Satan or the Devil father of all lies and deceptions.

There is No longer pure and perfect will

Some of you may ask, "Was there such a thing like pure and perfect free will? Remember the clue here is the verb 'was' in the past tense and not 'is' in the present tense. In the past tense, yes, there was pure and perfect free will and I can tell you why.

First, we know from the Bible that God is not the source of sin or evil. The Genesis creation story confirms this fact. All that God created he called it good which means pure and perfect with no sin. All things were made for him for his glory (Colossians 1:16).

Secondly, per Genesis Chapter One Verse One God made all things in heaven and on earth. Therefore, all that he made were pure and perfect. Lucifer as a created angel was purified with a perfect free will until sin was found in him.

Thirdly, our first parents, Adam and Eve exercised pure and perfect free will before they sinned against God in the Garden of Eden.

Pure and perfect free will helped angels and our first parents, Adam and Eve serve and worship God alone. There was a holy relationship between God and Angels, and between God and Adam and Eve before the fall. All of them could choose to fellowship with God. Both had the perfect free will to communion with God the Father until disobedience found root in them.

BEDROOM OF ADAM AND EVE
CHAPTER TWO. QUESTIONS FOR YOU TO ANSWER

What is the origin of sin?

Who was the devil and what made him sin?

Is there pure, perfect human free will?

Why do we sin?

Can we stop sinning on our own?

Who can help us not to live in sin?

Explain Ezekiel 28:13-17?

What does Ezekiel 26-27 mean to you?

Is the devil a spirit of human?

CHAPTER 3

ORIGINAL SIN

We cannot speak about the teaching of Original sin without discussing two thoughts of school taught by two prominent theologians Irenaeus and St. Augustine. Irenaeus was born in 130 AD in Smyrna now modern Turkey. He was a disciple of Polycarp, who was a follower of the Apostle John. Irenaeus died in AD 202.

St. Augustine was born January First in 354 AD in Tagaste in Algeria in Africa. He died at Hippo Regius in Algeria in AD 430.

Both these men were bishops during their time of serving the Lord Jesus, though they lived more than two hundred years apart. Both wrote influential theologies that shaped our Christian world view.

I am very certain that both men did not speak to our modern languages that some of what they taught may have been lost or misrepresented when translated them in our modern dialects.

Many writings have been published on the topic of the original sin between these two early writers that cannot all be included in this book. But I have some postings About Jon Garvey which may help shed light of what has been going on between the Eastern Church and the Western church on the doctrine of the original sin.

Irenaeus (and others) on original sin

Posted on 17/05/2012 by John Garvey

I had reason to dig around in some of the Patristic literature recently, and came across Irenaeus' (late 2nd century) teaching about Adam and sin whilst looking for something else. It reminded me that I haven't yet recorded in this blog what Irenaeus actually teaches, which is an oversight as many modern writers in the evolution/theology field, and outside it, question the traditional teaching on original sin, most often by attributing it to Augustine in the west. The Eastern Church, they say, never thought the idea of hereditary sin. Even John H Walton, much of whose excellent work, I have been reading of late, mentions this as a plain fact, in order to defend the concept that Adam need not be regarded as the physical ancestor of the entire human race.

Now I am open to alternative views of Adam's role as the author of human sin, since the relevant Scriptural passages are difficult to interpret dogmatically. Neither do I regard the Church Fathers as the fount of infallible gospel truth. But the Patristic writers do at least give us an idea of what "the Church has always taught", and if modern writers are misrepresenting their positions truth is not served.

Irenaeus wrote over two centuries before Augustine, and is regarded as an authority in both the Eastern and Western traditions. His main teaching on this matter, in Against Heresies Book III, is actually primarily against the heretic Tatian's teaching that Adam was not redeemed from his first sin. Irenaeus wants to prove how fitting it was that God should save him, and how the Scriptures support that assertion. In other words, his theme is tangential to our interest here, and it is likely that any teaching involving original sin merely reflects the prevailing belief of orthodox Christians then. So in #2 of chapter XXIII, he says:

For it is too absurd to maintain that he who was so deeply injured by the enemy [Satan], and was the first to suffer captivity, was not rescued by Him who conquered the enemy, but that his children were - those whom he had begotten in the same captivity.

See that Irenaeus says that Adam's children are beaten in captivity. But is that captivity to sin, or just to mortality? In the previous paragraph he has said that Adam became "a vessel in Satan's possession", in his power, because Satan wickedly bought sin upon him, and pretending to offer immortality instead made him liable to death. In other words, the captivity is both: death is the consequence of sin for Adam's children as for Adam. But he clarifies this by an illustration:

If a hostile force has overcome certain [enemies], had bound them, and led them away captive, so that they begat children among them; and somebody, compassionating those who had been made slaves, should overcome this same hostile force; he certainly would not act equitably, were he to liberate the children of those who had been led captive, from the sway of those who had enslaved their fathers, but should leave these latter ... the children succeeding to liberty through the avenging of their father's cause, but not so that their fathers, who suffered the act of capture itself, should be left [in bondage]. For God is neither devoid of power nor of justice, who has afforded help to man and restored him to His own liberty.

I think it's clear that the whole force of Irenaeus' argument is that Adam entailed bondage to sin and death on his physical descendants. He does not spell out whether that bondage consists of the tendency to sin, or guilt for

Adam's first sin, but the first seems more in line with his words and is usually the main point at issue in terms of discussing Adam's progeniture.

How is this different from Augustine's view? In the matter of the inheritance of bondage to sin not at all. Augustine's contribution was, firstly, to argue carefully from Scripture for the additional element of corporate human guilt for that first sin. But his most contentious offering, though frequently forgotten now, is merely a suggestion for the mechanism of the transgression of original sin. He suggested that sin was transmitted to the new life as it was conceived through the concupiscence (lust) now inherent in fallen sexual relations. This doesn't resonate with our modern mindset - but neither does it affect the nature of original sin itself.

What, then, has the Eastern Church rejected about original sin? Here's my reading, as an outsider to Eastern Orthodoxy, suggests that all is not as it is often portrayed. An article by Orthodox writer Vladimir Moss, unfortunately no longer online, argues strongly that the tendency in Orthodoxy to deny the transmission of sin down the generations is a recent change initiated primarily by publications of Metropolitan Anthony Khrapovitsky (1926) and Fr. John Romanides' (1957), who argued that Orthodoxy had fallen into its own bondage to the Augustan tradition by accepting his erroneous translation of Romans 5.12. Moss, as a traditionalist, disputes their modern translation of this verse, their conclusion and their re-writing of history, and says that their teaching itself is not Orthodox (remember the high regard given to tradition in Orthodoxy - one can draw such conclusions in a way impossible within Protestantism).

Moss gives a long paragraph of Orthodox authorities for his claim, which is worth posting here since the article itself is no longer available:

The Holy Fathers, on the other hand, contrary to the heretics just quoted and contrary to Metropolitan Anthony, stress the causal link between the sin of Adam and our death. Thus St. Athanasius the Great writes: "When Adam had transgressed, his sin reached unto all men". Again, St. Cyril of Alexandria writes: "[All men] have been condemned to death by the transgression of Adam. For the whole of human nature has suffered this in him, who was the beginning of the human race." Again, St. Symeon the Theologian writes: "When our Master descended from on high Him by His own death destroyed the death that awaited us. The condemnation that was the consequence of our forefather's transgression he completely annihilated." Again, St. Gregory Palamas writes: "Before Christ, we all shared the same ancestral curse and condemnation poured out on all of us from our single Forefather, as if it had sprung from the root of the human race and was the common lot of our nature. Each person's individual action attracted either reproof or praise of God, but no one could do anything about the shared curse and condemnation, or the evil inheritance that had been passed down to him and through him would pass to his descendants." Again, St. Anastasius of Sinai writes: "In Adam we became co-inheritors of the curse, not as if we disobeyed that divine commandment with him but because he became mortal and transmitted sin through his seed. We became mortals from a mortal…" Again, St. Gennadius Scholarius writes:"Everyone in the following of Adam has died, because they have all inherited their nature from him. But some have died because they themselves have sinned, while others have died only because of Adam's condemnation - for example, children".

To me, it seems that this Eastern tradition includes both the elements of original sin - transmission of the sin nature and guilt for Adam's sin. All very Augustinian. I wonder if the old rejection of Augustine by the ancient Eastern Church may merely relate to the question of transmission by concupiscence, because otherwise ancestral sin (as Orthodox writers prefer to call it) was alive and well until challenged in the twentieth century in the East, just as it has been in the west (often by claiming that the East never held it!). It is probably true to say that the Eastern Church inherits a less radical view of sin than Augustine's - Irenaeus' image of bondage because of Satan's deceit seems to predominate over Augustine's bondage to our own all-pervading corruption.

But the net result is the same - both primary traditions of the Church assume that sin is inherited by descent from Adam. Our attempts to accommodate historic Christian doctrine to modern scientific findings needs to take that into account, and to demonstrate clearly just why the Fathers were wrong about it, if we end up rejecting it. End of Jon Garvey post.

In my judgment, the doctrine of the original sin was not fully developed during the time of Irenaeus. Though Irenaeus mentioned the bondage of the will of man after the fall, he did not explain fully how that bondage affected the rest of humanity. During the time of Augustine, the church got it right when scripture became the verifying factor that all humans inherited guilt and corruption from Adams sin through imputation.

To me the original sin belongs to the Devil/ Satan first, the original manufacturer of sin. While in heaven, when he sinned, he had that original sin in and with him. That was the sin of pride which affected all fallen angels that are now called demons.

Secondly, that original sin (in and with the Devil) came to mankind through deception in the case of Eve and rebellion in the case of Adam. Throughout Christendom the original sin has been known as ancestral sin or the sin of our ancestors, which literally translated as ucimo wa makolo athu in my Zambian Nyanja language.

Both Satan and our ancestors (Adam and Eve) had original sin when they sinned against God. Humanity wished that the original sin stayed with Adam and Eve alone without spreading to everyone but it did not.

CHAPTER THREE. QUESTIONS TO ANSWER

What is original sin?

Who was Irenaeus?

What did Irenaeus believe about the original sin?

Who is the original manufacture of original sin?

What is UCIMO WA MAKOLO ANTHU?

CHAPTER 4

NATURAL OF ORIGINAL SIN

Imputation of the sin of Adam

Key verse or I can say the key passage in the bible that deals with imputation of the sin of Adam to the rest of the people is Romans 5: 12-21. In this passage, we see the problem that came through one man Adam and the solution that came through one man Christ sometimes known as the Second Adam. There is a transaction going on in this passage between Adam and the rest of us and between Christ and the few of us.

This transaction is spiritual though it can also be physical. We get physical and spiritual decay in body and soul through Adam and, we get spiritual and physical immortal body of Christ at the end of all things.

In this passage, especially Romans 5: 12b Adam is our example. He brought sin to us all due to his original disobedience to God. Everyone else individually commits sins and eventually dies. Sin and death come to us through Adam's sin. In Adam, we are all guilty before God. There is solidarity between Adam and human races. Apostle Paul consolidated this fact by saying that one man sinned (Romans 5:13-19) and therefore all sinned (Romans5:12). This solidarity points to the fall of humans. Now we can see that federalism view works very well. It shows that God appointed Adam representative head of humans. What Adam did is charged to all his posterity. Therefore, Original sin of Adam is imputed to all people.

Whatever happens in the spiritual world is very hard for our naked eyes to perceive. Imputation of the sin of Adam to the rest of us is done spiritually though its effects are seen with our physical eyes in this world. Whether we hold the immediate (direct) or mediate (indirect) view of imputation, we still do not understand how the guilt and corruption of Adam gets to us. Both the guilt and corruption are imputed to us due to Adam's Original sin.

But through faith in God and his written word and the help of his spirit, I know and declare that all people have a corrupt nature inherited from Adam. This is the effect of Adam's sin. Thus, hereditary depravity is imputed to all. All people have sinned because all have inherited natural corruption from Adam. To be precise Adam's first sin was imputed to every person directly. Therefore, in Adam as our representative all people were tried and declared guilty. The same punishment caused due to Adam's sin is waiting for all people unless they believe in Christ before death. The bible says, "For all have sinned and fall short of the glory of God, and all are justified freely by his grace through the redemption that came by Christ Jesus (Romans 3:23-24).

Total Deprived

How deep did original sin go into the spirit and soul of Adam and Eve when they sinned against God? Were there some parts of their bodies not touched by sin? Are children born with or without the original sin from Adam?

BEDROOM OF ADAM AND EVE

These are the questions we will try to answer in this section of total deprived. We have already discussed that the sin of Adam is imputed on all people everywhere in all generations. But the depth of original sin in man has been always questionable. Some schools of thought suggest that sin did not go far deep enough and therefore there are some good left in a person after a fall while others conclude that all parts of human beings have been infested with sin.

Deprived means lack of something or materials. Denying or refusing something or someone of getting or exercising certain privileges. For example, if the church deprived their pastor of performing duties, then the church denies the pastor of being their minister. Another good example is some of the children in Africa nations. Many of them suffer from malnutrition because they are deprived of nutrition food.

Total deprived therefore is the total lack of something or doing something due to sin. Man, is said to be totally deprived because he is incapable of doing what he used to do with God before the fall. Sin has deprived man of choosing to fellowship with God for himself without the help of the spirit of God. Sin has incapacitated man and all its effects have spread to all parts of the body and soul.

Man, created the hole too deep due to sin that he could not get out by himself without the help of God. Moreover, the man loves to be in that deep hole he has made because he loves the fruits of the sin. If there is one thing, humans love to do, is sinning. Man, does not need a trainer to sin due to total depravity which in this book is the bedroom of Adam and Eve. Pelagianism states that God makes the soul of man at birth without corruption. It says that children are born good but commits sins as they grow up. These sins can be forgiven through baptism. In other ways Pelagianism suggests that man has full volition.

On the other hand, Arminianism accepts that man is deprived but not total deprived because he still has volition to choose God without the full help of God. Both Pelagianism and Arminianism do not hold to the doctrine of total deprived taught in the bible followed by many Calvinists.

African church bishop Augustine started teaching the doctrine of total depravity, though the church in his time did not fully understand it until the time of reformation. Augustine taught that after the fall man became totally deprived that even his free will was no longer free but in bondage. Man, was incapable or unable to freely choose to worship and know God. Natural of man became corrupt through and through.

Guilty

The standing of Adam before God before he sinned was right, therefore we can say Adam was righteous in all his deeds. But the standing of Adam before God after the fall was not right, therefore, declared guilty by the court of heaven.

Adam our representative and the head of human race gives each of us the guilty inheritance even before we are born. We are all guilty before the heavenly judgment in Adam. Same punishment given to Adam is given to all his posterity due to sin. Paul in Romans 3:23 said "All have sinned and for, short of the glory of God" and in Romans 5: 12 said, "Therefore, just as sin entered the world through one man, and death through sin, and in this way death came to all people, because all sinned- "

We inherit the guilty judgment by God due to the disobedience of Adam.

Corruption

All human beings are by nature corrupt due to total depravity brought by Adam. We inherit moral and spiritual corruption from our first parents due to their disobedience to God and his law. Augustine taught that all men inherit natural corruption from Adam (Harrison, Everett, Ed., Baker's Dictionary of Theology, Grand Rapids: Baker Book House, 1960, p. 488.) King David sums up best when he said, "Against You, you only, I have sinned and done what is evil in your sight, so that you are justified when you speak and blameless when you judge. Behold, I was brought forth in iniquity, and in sin my mother conceived me. Behold, you desire truth in the innermost being, and in the hidden part you will make me know wisdom...." (Psalms 51:5-6).

Solidarity with Adam

All human beings are now in solidarity with Adam in sin, guilt and corruption. We are all born in sin because of Adam original sin. We are all guilty before our God because of the disobedience of Adam and Eve. We all inherit natural corruption due to the original sin of Adam. We all have formed a sodality with Adam because we share the same bag back and misery that came to the world through him. Consequently, we all experience death in life because of the disobedience of Adam. Therefore, just as sin entered the world through one man, and death through sin, and in this way death came to all people, because all sinned.

To be sure, sin was in the world before the law was given, but sin is not charged against anyone's account where there is no law. Nevertheless, death reigned from the time of Adam to the time of Moses, even over those who did not sin by breaking a command, as did Adam, who is a pattern of the one to come (Romans 5:12-14).

CHAPTER FOUR. QUESTIONS TO ANSWER

What is the nature of the original sin?

Define the imputation of Adam sin?

What is total deprived?

What is guilty?

What is corruption?

How are we in solidarity with Adam?

Which part of the human body is not totally deprived?

What does Roman 5:12-14 mean?

Explain the meaning of Roman 3:23?

What is the Will?

Is your will totally free?

Define freedom of the will?

CHAPTER 5

CONSEQUENCES OF ORIGINAL SIN

Total separation from God

Total separation from God is very true because of total depravity. Adam brought the total separation of all human beings from God due to rebellion. Separation is the opposite of togetherness. Where separation exists, there is no fellowship or relationship.

When Adam fell, he started running away from God. Together with his wife Eve decided to hide in the Garden of Eden. For the first time his rebellion caused him to alienate himself from his best friend ever.

Adam and his human race found it impossible to come into relationship with God the Creator due to internal separation.

A good example of separation from the father is the parable of the lost son. He asked wealth from his father and decided to go away from his him after getting what he wanted. This son did not bother of being in relationship with his father due to sin of separation from his deal home until the spirit of God came upon him. Hear what Jesus said in Luke 15:12-32;

Jesus continued: "There was a man who had two sons. The younger one said to his father, 'Father, give me my share of the estate.' So, he divided his property between them.

"Not long after that, the younger son got together all he had, set off for a distant country and there squandered his wealth in wild living. After he had spent everything, there was a severe famine in that whole country, and he began to be in need. So, he went and hired himself out to a citizen of that country, who sent him to his fields to feed pigs. He longed to fill his stomach with the pods that the pigs were eating, but no one gave him anything.

"When he came to his senses, he said, 'How many of my father's hired servants have food to spare, and here I am starving to death! I will set out and go back to my father and say to him: Father, I have sinned against heaven and against you. I am no longer worthy to be called your son; make me like one of your hired servants.' So, he got up and went to his father.

"But while he was still a long way off, his father saw him and was filled with compassion for him; he ran to his son, threw his arms around him and kissed him.

"The son said to him, 'Father, I have sinned against heaven and against you. I am no longer worthy to be called your son.'

"But the father said to his servants, 'Quick! Bring the best robe and put it on him. Put a ring on his finger and sandals on his feet. Bring the fattened calf and kill it. Let's have a feast and celebrate. For this son of mine was dead and is alive again; he was lost and is found.' So, they began to celebrate.

"Meanwhile, the older son was in the field. When he came near the house, he heard music and dancing. So he called one of the servants and asked him what was going on. 'Your brother has come,' he replied, 'and your father has killed the fattened calf because he has him back safe and sound.'

"The older brother became angry and refused to go in. So his father went out and pleaded with him. But he answered his father, 'Look! All these years I've been slaving for you and never disobeyed your orders. Yet you never gave me even a young goat so I could celebrate with my friends. But when this son of yours who has squandered your property with prostitutes comes home, you kill the fattened calf for him!'

"'My son,' the father said, 'you are always with me, and everything I have is yours. But we had to celebrate and be glad, because this brother of yours was dead and is alive again; he was lost and is found.'"

This young son wanted his share of wealth from his dad. He knew the law (Deuteronomy 17:51) that his father was going to give to him as an inheritance, though he should have waited until dad died. The main problem of this son was to go away from his father after he got the riches. This is what sin does, deceiving ourselves being God when we are not. Sin makes us feel as if we are in control of the situation, but we are actually not. Sin makes us run away from God and creating our own safe zones which always are detrimental. The young man in the parable learned a hard way.

Prophet Isaiah rebuked the people of God when they loved to sin than following his laws given to them through Moses; "surely the arm of the Lord is not too short to save, nor his ear too dull to hear. But your iniquities have separated you from your God; your sins have hidden his face from you, so that he will not hear" (Isaiah 59:1-2).

Isaiah said it again in Isaiah chapter 1: 15 saying, "When you spread out your hands in prayer, I hide my eyes from you; even when you offer many prayers, I am not listening. Your hands are full of blood!" Symbolically blood represents sins or cruel acts allowed to go on for many years among the Israelites. Sin causes separation of soul, spirit, and mind from our God.

Spiritual death

The moment Eve ate the forbidden fruit she died spiritually and the moment Adam got the forbidden from his wife Eve and ate it he died spiritually too. Instantly both our first parents became spiritually dead the moment they decided to eat fruit from the tree of knowledge of good and evil (Genesis 2:17). When Adam saw that his wife was not physically dead when she ate the fruits he decided to rebel against the law of God and ate the fruit anyway. They did not know they were now both spiritually dead. Now their actions spoke volumes. First time their eyes saw they were naked and then tried to run away from God. For the first time, they learned to hide and seek which became insanity of the human race.

When God pronounced judgement to Adam, Eve his wife, and the snake, Adam knew his spiritual life with God had been distorted forever. This time Adam had fear in his heart instead of peace and joy that he had before the fall.

This is how the fall of man happened;

Now the serpent was craftier than any of the wild animals the Lord God had made. He said to the woman, "Did God really say, 'You must not eat from any tree in the garden'?"

The woman said to the serpent, "We may eat fruit from the trees in the garden, but God did say, 'You must not eat fruit from the tree that is in the middle of the garden, and you must not touch it, or you will die.'"

BEDROOM OF ADAM AND EVE

"You will not certainly die," the serpent said to the woman, "For God knows that when you eat from it your eyes will be opened, and you will be like God, knowing good and evil."

When the woman saw that the fruit of the tree was good for food and pleasing to the eye, and desirable for gaining wisdom, she took some and ate it. She also gave some to her husband, who was with her, and he ate it. Then the eyes of both were opened, and they realized they were naked; so, they sewed fig leaves together and made coverings for themselves.

Then the man and his wife heard the sound of the Lord God as he was walking in the garden in the cool of the day, and they hid from the Lord God among the trees of the garden. But the Lord God called to the man, "Where are you?"

He answered, "I heard you in the garden, and I was afraid because I was naked; so, I hid."

And he said, "Who told you that you were naked? Have you eaten from the tree that I commanded you not to eat from?"

The man said, "The woman you put here with me-she gave me some fruit from the tree, and I ate it."

Then the Lord God said to the woman, "What is this you have done?"

The woman said, "The serpent deceived me, and I ate."

So, the Lord God said to the serpent, "Because you have done this,

"Cursed are you above all livestock and all wild animals!

You will crawl on your belly and you will eat dust all the days of your life.

And I will put enmity between you and the woman, and between your offspring and hers; he will crush your head, and you will strike his heel."

To the woman, he said,

"I will make your pains in childbearing very severe; with painful labor, you will give birth to children.

Your desire will be for your husband, and he will rule over you."

To Adam he said, "Because you listened to your wife and ate fruit from the tree about which I commanded you, 'You must not eat from it,'

"Cursed is the ground because of you; through painful toil you will eat food from it all the days of your life.

It will produce thorns and thistles for you, and you will eat the plants of the field.

By the sweat of your brow you will eat your food until you return to the ground, since from it you were taken; for dust, you are and to dust you will return."

Adam named his wife Eve, because she would become the mother of all the living.

The Lord God made garments of skin for Adam and his wife and clothed them. And the Lord God said, "The man has now become like one of us, knowing good and evil. He must not be allowed to reach out his hand and take also from the tree of life and eat, and has lived forever." So, the Lord God banished him from the Garden of Eden to work the ground from which he had been taken. After he drove the man out, he placed on the east side of the Garden of Eden cherubim and a flaming sword flashing back and forth to guard the way to the tree of life" (Genesis 3).

Spiritual death is caused by spiritual being which in the story Satan is. Man, was incapable in himself to turn against superior being (God) without the aid of a spiritual being (Devil). We must not be fooled here to put entirely our spiritually dead on Adam and his wife alone. It was the Devil who started it, though God was aware of these events.

Spiritual death is just as bad as being physically dead. Jesus did not entertain people who lived in this world spiritually dead. He called them hypocrites (Matthew 23).

Jesus Heals a Man Born Blind;

As he went along, he saw a man blind from birth. His disciples asked him, "Rabbi, who sinned, this man or his parents, that he was born blind?"

"Neither this man nor his parents sinned," said Jesus, "but this happened so that the works of God might be displayed in him. As long as it is day, we must do the works of him who sent me. Night is coming, when no one can work. While I am in the world, I am the light of the world."

After saying this, he spat on the ground, made some mud with the saliva, and put it on the man's eyes. "Go," he told him, "wash in the Pool of Siloam" (this word means "Sent"). So, the man went and washed, and came home seeing.

His neighbors and those who had formerly seen him begging asked, "Isn't this the same man who used to sit and beg?" Some claimed that he was.

Others said, "No, he only looks like him."

But he himself insisted, "I am the man."

"How then were your eyes opened?" they asked.

He replied, "The man they call Jesus made some mud and put it on my eyes. He told me to go to Siloam and wash. So, I went and washed, and then I could see."

"Where is this man?" they asked him.

"I don't know," he said.

The Pharisees Investigate the Healing

They brought to the Pharisees the man who had been blind. Now the day on which Jesus had made the mud and opened the man's eyes was a Sabbath. Therefore, the Pharisees also asked him how he had received his sight. "He put mud on my eyes," the man replied, "and I washed, and now I see."

Some of the Pharisees said, "This man is not from God, for he does not keep the Sabbath."

But others asked, "How can a sinner perform such signs?" So, they were divided.

Then they turned again to the blind man, "What have you to say about him? It was your eyes, he opened."

The man replied, "He is a prophet."

They still did not believe that he had been blind and had received his sight until they sent for the man's parents. "Is this your son?" they asked. "Is this the one you say was born blind? How is it that now he can see?"

"We know he is our son," the parents answered, "and we know he was born blind. But how he can see now, or who opened his eyes, we don't know. Ask him. He is of age; he will speak for himself." His parents said this because they were afraid of the Jewish leaders, who already had decided that anyone who acknowledged that Jesus was the Messiah would be put out of the synagogue. That was why his parents said, "He is of age; ask him."

A second time they summoned the man who had been blind. "Give glory to God by telling the truth," they said. "We know this man is a sinner."

He replied, "Whether he is a sinner or not, I don't know. One thing I do know. I was blind, but now I see!"

Then they asked him, "What did he do to you? How did he open your eyes?"

He answered, "I have told you already and you did not listen. Why do you want to hear it again? Do you want to become his disciples too?"

Then they hurled insults at him and said, "You are this fellow's disciple! We are disciples of Moses! We know that God spoke to Moses, but as for this fellow, we don't even know where he comes from."

The man answered, "Now that is remarkable! You don't know where he comes from, yet he opened my eyes. We know that God does not listen to sinners. He listens to the godly person who does his will. Nobody has ever heard of opening the eyes of a man born blind. If this man were not from God, he could do nothing."

To this they replied, "You were steeped in sin at birth; how dare you lecture us!" And they threw him out.

Spiritual Blindness

Jesus heard that they had thrown him out, and when he found him, he said, "Do you believe in the Son of Man?"

"Who is he, sir?" the man asked. "Tell me so that I may believe in him."

Jesus said, "You have now seen him; in fact, he is the one speaking with you."

Then the man said, "Lord, I believe," and he worshiped him.

Jesus said, "For judgment, I have come into this world, so that the blind will see and those who see will become blind."

Some Pharisees who were with him heard him say this and asked, "What? Are we blind too?"

Jesus said, "If you were blind, you would not be guilty of sin; but now that you claim you can see, your guilt remains.

In this story, Jesus healed the man born blind twice; First, Jesus healed the physical condition of the man born blind. He touched his eyes and made them see again. Secondly, Jesus healed the soul of the man born blind who now was able to see. Jesus revealed to the man that he was the messiah. The man believed in Jesus Christ. He now became a follower of Jesus Christ and in our terms, we can call him a Christian.

The moment we are born in this world we have a spiritual condition which needs spiritual cure. Jesus said to Nicodemus unless you are born again, you cannot see the kingdom of God. To be born again is to be made by the spirit of God from above. John 3: 3-5. A man in his spiritual condition cannot inherit the spiritual kingdom of God without regeneration by the Holy Spirit.

Physical death

Physical death is plain simple. It is the total separation of the body and the Soul (spirit). One is said to be dead when the soul departs from his body and returned to his maker and the body goes down to earth where it came from.

Physical death is the result of the fruit of disobedience caused by Adam. In the Bible, God said to Adam, "You are free to eat from any tree in the garden; but you must not eat from the tree of the knowledge of good and evil, for when you eat from it you will certainly die" (Genesis 2:16-17).

This was the first-time death was mentioned in the bible. We can ask some questions here, "Did Adam and Eve know what death met before they sinned against God? Was there the possibility of death among creation of God? For example, did Adam see grass or animals die before the fall?

These are some of the questions we may not fully grasp because the bible is silent on matters like these therefore we cannot speculate.

One thing we are sure of is that the moment Adam and Eve ate the forbidden fruit they did not die physically. They continued to live their lives as though they were outside the Garden of Eden. God drove them out of the Garden after clothing them with a skin of the animal that was killed. Now we hear about animal death.

The Lord God made garments of skin for Adam and his wife and clothed them. And the Lord God said, "The man has now become like one of us, knowing good and evil. He must not be allowed to reach out his hand and take also from the tree of life and eat, and live forever." So, the Lord God banished him from the Garden of Eden to work the ground from which he had been taken. After he drove the man out, he placed on the east side of the Garden of Eden cherubim and a flaming sword flashing back and forth to guard the way to the tree of life (Genesis 3:21-24).

The first-time physical death is associated with human beings is when Cain killed his brother Abel.

Cain and Abel;

"Adam made love to his wife Eve, and she became pregnant and gave birth to Cain. She said, "With the help of the Lord I have brought forth a man." Later she gave birth to his brother Abel.

Now Abel kept flocks, and Cain worked the soil. In the course of time Cain brought some of the fruits of the soil as an offering to the Lord. And Abel also brought an offering-fat portions from some of the firstborn of his flock. The Lord looked with favor on Abel and his offering, 5 but on Cain and his offering he did not look with favor. So, Cain was very angry, and his face was downcast.

Then the Lord said to Cain, "Why are you angry? Why is your face downcast? If you do what is right, will you not be accepted? But if you do not do what is right, sin is crouching at your door; it desires to have you, but you must rule over it."

Now Cain said to his brother Abel, "Let's go out to the field. "While they were in the field, Cain attacked his brother Abel and killed him.

Then the Lord said to Cain, "Where is your brother Abel?"

"I don't know," he replied. "Am I my brother's keeper?"

The Lord said, "What have you done? Listen! Your brother's blood cries out to me from the ground. Now you are under a curse and driven from the ground, which opened its mouth to receive your brother's blood from your hand. When you work the ground, it will no longer yield its crops for you. You will be a restless wanderer on the earth."

Cain said to the Lord, "My punishment is more than I can bear. Today you are driving me from the land, and I will be hidden from your presence; I will be a restless wanderer on the earth, and whoever finds me will kill me."

But the Lord said to him, "Not so; anyone who kills Cain will suffer vengeance seven times over." Then the Lord put a mark on Cain so that no one who found him would kill him. So, Cain went out from the Lord's presence and lived in the land of Nod, east of Eden (Genesis 4:1-16).

BEDROOM OF ADAM AND EVE

The Bible did not describe the emotional and physical expression of Adam and Eve due to the loss of their second son. It might be true that they both had the AHA moment when they saw death for the first time. Adam and Eve might have remembered what God said to them about the consequences of eating the forbidden fruit.

Physical death is a big brawl to our entire human race because it spreads to all and affects all, regardless of what sins we may or we may not commit. Physical death is the result of the original sin our first parents brought to all of us when they sinned against God. In the New Testament, Paul wrote, "The wages of sin is death". Romans 6:23a. It is not the result of the daily sins we commit though sometimes some sins we commit may seem to have a direct link to physical death. For example, when we commit sins that lead to death, we are faced with capital punishment which may lead to physical death as the result of our actions. But even capital punishment is directly linked to original sin because it is the result of sin. Whether small sin or big sin it is still sin in the eyes of God.

Not all sins that we commit leads to death, but all deaths are the result of Sin. Paul wrote a great message about the link between death and original sin when he said," therefore, just as sin entered the world through one man, and death through sin, and in this way death came to all people, because all sinned.

To be sure, sin was in the world before the law was given, but sin is not charged against anyone's account where there is no law. Nevertheless, death reigned from the time of Adam to the time of Moses, even over those who did not sin by breaking a command, as did Adam, who is a pattern of the one to come" (Romans 5: 12-14).

The word of God says that people died physically from the time of Adam to the time of Moses as the result of original sin and not as the result of breaking the law. God had not yet given the law that period.

Therefore, every one of us will experience physical death because the bible says all have sinned and for, short of the glory of God and it is written that the wages of sin is death. This proves that all of us human beings are related to Adam because we have strong solidarity with Adam in physical death due to the fall. We all will one day die whether religious or not, whether rich or poor, whether educated or not. Listen what Jesus said to the rich fool;

The Parable of the Rich Fool

Someone in the crowd said to him, "Teacher, tell my brother to divide the inheritance with me."

Jesus replied, "Man, who appointed me a judge or an arbiter between you?" Then he said to them, "Watch out! Be on your guard against all kinds of greed; life does not consist in an abundance of possessions."

And he told them this parable: "The ground of a certain rich man yielded an abundant harvest. He thought to himself, 'What shall I do? I have no place to store my crops.'

"Then he said, 'This is what I'll do. I will tear down my barns and build bigger ones, and there I will store my surplus grain. And I'll say to myself,' "You have plenty of grain laid up for many years. Take life easy; eat, drink and be merry."'

"But God said to him, 'You fool! This very night your life will be demanded from you. Then who will get what you have prepared for yourself?'

"This is how it will be with whoever stores up things for themselves, but is not rich toward God" (Luke 12:13-25).

Before Jesus told the parable, there was a man who came to him with a question. This man had issues with his brother over family affairs. Per the Law of Moses the elder brother was to receive a double portion of inheritance from his father (Deuteronomy 21:17).

It seems this man did not like this law and wanted Jesus to help in dividing the inheritance equally. Jesus Christ knew the man had a problem of greed. Jesus addressed this issue in the parable of a rich fool.

In the parable, the man was blessed with fertile land and lots of crops that he decided to destroy the old barns and make bigger ones. That was a great plan, but the issue this man had was that he did not include God in all his plans. The man talked to himself a lot and finally told his soul to be happy and rejoice the rest of the life. The man thought he had it all together without God.

To cut the story short the man died suddenly when God came and took his soul. The man was a fool and selfish. He was full of greed. He could not even last a night despite all that God gave him.

In the parable, the man died, though he did not get sick or ill. It seemed very unfair. Death came to this rich fool without a warning. Death is the result of the original sin brought by the disobedience of Adam. But in Christ we die no more. Death has been swallowed up in the victory of our Lord Jesus Christ. Christ died and rose again.

Internal death in Hell or in everlasting lake of fire

The destination of sin is hell. Hell, is a place where all its fallen angels will spend the rest of their lives. Hell, will also include a destination of ungodly people. This is a final impact of the original sin if not taken care of by the cross of Jesus before death.

Hell, is a place where all people that die without believing in Jesus Christ will spend their lives when the Parousia comes. In Hell, ungodly will be fully aware of their state of suffering, but will be unable to control or change it. In the parable of the rich man and Lazarus the rich man knew his state of mind and asked for help.

The Rich Man and Lazarus;

"There was a rich man who was dressed in purple and fine linen and lived in luxury every day. At his gate was laid a beggar named Lazarus, covered with sores, and longing to eat what fell from the rich man's table. Even the dogs came and licked his sores.

"The time came when the beggar died and the angels carried him to Abraham's side. The rich man also died and was buried. In Hades, where he was in torment, he looked up and saw Abraham far away, with Lazarus by his side. So, he called to him, 'Father Abraham, have pity on me and send Lazarus to dip the tip of his finger in water and cool my tongue, because I am in agony in this fire.

"But Abraham replied, 'Son, remember that in your lifetime you received your good things, while Lazarus received bad things, but now he is comforted here and you are in agony. And besides all this, between us and you a great chasm has been set in place, so that those who want to go from here to you cannot, nor can anyone cross over from there to us.'

"He answered, 'Then I beg you, father, send Lazarus to my family, for I have five brothers. Let him warn them, so that they will not also come to this place of torment.'

"Abraham replied, 'They have Moses and the Prophets; let them, listen to them.'

"'No, father Abraham,' he said, 'but if someone from the dead goes to them, they will repent.'

"He said to him, 'If they do not listen to Moses and the Prophets, they will not be convinced even if someone rises from the dead'" (Luke 16: 19-31).

Hell, is not oblivion state which deludes oneself of knowledge and consciousness. People in hell will be aware of themselves, but internally separated from the blessing hand of God. Call it the dark side of life forever.

Hell, is a place of fire for ever;

The rich man in Luke 16:24 cries: "...I am tormented in this FLAME."

In Matthew 13:42, Jesus says: "And shall cast them into a FURNACE OF FIRE: there shall be wailing and gnashing of teeth."

In Matthew 25:41, Jesus says: "Depart from me, ye cursed, into everlasting FIRE..."

Revelation 20:15 says, "And whosoever was not found written in the book of life was cast into the LAKE OF FIRE."

The only way for humans to avoid hell is to believe in Jesus Christ alone for redemption.

Misery

Misery is the absence of joy or happiness. It is a state or feeling of great distress or discomfort of mind or body. Adam and Eve did not experience misery before the fall. They both had a great relationship with God. Adam and Eve had joy with God and fellowshipped with him in the Garden of Even before they fell.

Adam and Eve did not experience anguish, anxiety, torment, pain, grief, heartache, heartbreak, despair, dejection, rejection, desolation, gloom sadness or sorrow before the fall. After the fall, all human beings experience misery as a result of sin. Paul in the letter to Roman Christians said, "Ruin and misery mark their ways" (Romans 3:16). This was a quote from the prophet Isaiah, who spoke against evil people who loved bringing ruin and misery on others. The word of God says there is no one righteous before God, therefore all love ruin and misery. This is the result of sin.

Sufferings

Misery breeds suffering. Suffering is a verb which simply means someone or something undergoes pain or distress. All human beings suffer at some point in life and this is the result of sin. Christ experienced suffering though his sufferings were a direct result of our sins, and not his since he did not have sin.

Many people have asked this question, "Why does a loving God allow suffering in the world which he created? To answer this question, we should always link suffering with original sin. Suffering does not happen on its own without sin. It is the result of sin. God is aware of it and neither is he surprised by it.

Job suffered a lot in his lifetime. All his children and animals died, yet he did not curse God or blamed him for his sufferings. Joseph was also a good example in the Bible who suffered by the hands of his brothers. Joseph was sold as a slave and even lived in prison before God intervened and exonerated him to a higher position in Egypt. David suffered as he was running away from his son because he sinned against God. Absalom wanted to kill his father and took over the kingdom ship. God head David prayer of confession and finally restored him on the throne as king of Israel. In the New Testament, all disciples of Jesus Christ suffered for their faith in Jesus Christ. Many disciples of Jesus Christ were killed brutally. Jesus himself suffered and died for our sins. Suffering is part of our living as fell on earth. I am sure there is no suffering in heaven.

Diseases

The Bible does not say anything about Adam and Eve experiencing disease before the fall. We do not even know if the animals got a disease and die before human sin against God. What is clear is that sin breeds misery which sometimes results in diseases.

A good passage in the Old Testament is where God warned his own people of the consequences of disobedience. The Lord will send on you curses, confusion and rebuke in everything you put your hand to, until you are destroyed and come to sudden ruin because of the evil you have done in forsaking him." The Lord will plague you with diseases until he has destroyed you from the land you are entering to possess. The Lord will strike you with wasting disease, with fever and inflammation, with scorching heat and drought, with blight and mildew, which will plague you until you perish" (Deuteronomy 28:20-22).

Both in the Old and New Testaments we read about people who had diseases. Some of these people died where others were cured of their diseases, though eventually they also died. Right now, there are thousands and thousands of different diseases in the world that make humans and animals sick and die. If there are no sufferings in heaven, we can say for sure there are no diseases in heaven too. Therefore, diseases came into this world when sin came into the world. Whether we are born with diseases or have them after birth, they are all due to sin. One day all diseases will be swept away. No more diseases in the new kingdom of God (Rev 21-22) and this include all forms of cancer.

Lame

In politics, a lame duck, is an elected official who is approaching the end of their tenure, especially one whose successor has already been elected. The official is often seen as having less influence with other politicians due to their limited time left in office. It means a person or a thing had all the powers and functioned before then ceases to function in its role though still in the same leadership position.

I do not suggest that origin sin causes a lame duck Congress, a lame duck president or any lame duck leader.

To be lame is to be born with a physical or mental dysfunction. It means one or more than one part of the body is not working normally. There is one proverb in the bible that says, "Like a lame man's leg, which hang useless, is a proverb in the mouth of a fool." Proverbs 26:7. In this proverb a leg of a person doesn't work normally. Though this leg is part of the body, it is useless because it does not perform its rightful function. The man in the proverb is said to be lame. The proverb equates the word lame to being a fool. A foolish person looks or walks normal, but his words or deeds are foolish. Thus, lame because the person does not function normal.

There are many examples in the Bible of people born lame. Some of the lame people received restoration through the power of God while others did not.

In the Old Testament lame people were disqualified to serve as priests (Lev. 21:17). Lame animals were disqualified to be offerings to God (Det.15:21). But there is a prophetic message through Jeremiah and Isaiah that said that time would come when the lame would be restored (Jeremiah 3:18; Isa 35:6).

When Jesus came into the world he brought with him new era 0f the kingdom of God. He demonstrated this new era by performing various miracles, including healing the lame. Look at this passage where our Lord Jesus performed miracles (Matthew11:5, 15:30, 31; 21:14; Lk 7:22; 14:13). And He said to them, "It is written, 'MY HOUSE SHALL BE CALLED A HOUSE OF PRAYER'; but you are making it a ROBBERS' DEN." And the blind and the lame came to Him in the temple, and He healed them. But when the chief priests and the scribes saw the wonderful things that He had done, and the children who were shouting in the temple, "Hosanna to the Son of David," they became indignant…

Jesus disciples continued performing miracles like the healing of a lame person at the beautiful gate. Read together with me the passage below;

And a man who had been lame from his mother's womb was being carried along, whom they used to set down every day at the gate of the temple which is called Beautiful, in order to beg alms of those who were entering the temple. When he saw Peter and John about to go into the temple, he began asking to receive alms. But Peter, along with John, fixed his gaze on him and said, "Look at us!" And he began to give them his attention, expecting to receive something from them. But Peter said, "I do not possess silver and gold, but what I do have I give to you: In the name of Jesus Christ the Nazarene-walk!" And seizing him by the right hand, he raised him up; and immediately his feet and his ankles were strengthened. With a leap, he stood upright and began to walk; and he entered the temple with them, walking and leaping and praising God. And all the people saw him walking and praising God; and they were taking note of him as being the one who used to sit at the Beautiful Gate of the temple to beg alms, and they were filled with wonder and amazement at what had happened to him (Acts 3:2-7).

In our generation, there are many people born lame, some are healed from their deformation while others not. All lame conditions are directly or indirectly linked to the sin of Adam. Sin brought misery to all mankind. One day this misery will be swept out by the coming of the new kingdom in Christ Jesus. All human beings will be restored to their original status Adam and Eve were before the fall.

That will be the day when Kanyuka Lungu the current headman of Kanyuka village will have normal legs. My elder brother Kanyuka Lungu has a lame leg. Since I have known him, he has been walking limping. God has blessed him with strength, though. He cannot run very fast or too far, though he can walk miles. There are other people like him and some in a worse state than Kanyuka. God understands and will one day restore their bodies. In fact, he will give each one of us everlasting body (I Cor. 15: 53).

War

War is the absence of peace (Shalom). For example, if the body is at war, then it has no peace within itself. Then the body is said to have issues or fights from within. It has war. If the nation is at war, then the nation has no peace. Its members are at war either within itself or against another nation. In the kingdom of God, there is no war but peace. In the kingdom of the devil there is no peace, but fights among its members. This is war. Any form of war is the result of sin, whether justified or not. Adam and Eve before they sinned against God did not experience war but Shalom with God all the times.

When God formed man, he breathed into him his spirit. The spirit of God is always peaceful. There is nothing strife in the spirit of God from God by nature is peaceful. No war is found in him.

It is fitting to say the devil who is the source of war tried to wage war against God in heaven and he was defeated. It is also right to say the devil tries to bring war among humans themselves and against God their creator.

Why do people go to war against their fellow human beings? If you see the underlining factor you will come back to say that sin brought all these wars. The cause of all wars is our human depravity. It all started with Adam and Eve. But when we fight against one another our eyes do not see sin as the root cause but ourselves. If we see sin as the cause of war, then we will be trying to find the solution to it. But when we see only ourselves in the fight, we justify killing each other as the solution to war. No right human being likes war, but due to our sinful condition and deprived world we live in, war has come to be part of our living. This is sad.

It is correct to say the war will be gone out of this world when the new kingdom comes through our Lord and Savior Jesus Christ. This prophetic message of Isaiah will then be fulfilled, "And He will judge between the nations, and will render decisions for many peoples; and they will hammer their swords into plowshares and their spears into pruning hooks. Nation will not lift up sword against nation, and never again will they learn war" (Isaiah 2:4).

In the New Testament, the apostle John saw a new heaven and new earth with no war. John also saw the old heaven and old earth gone from the presence of the Almighty God (Rev. 21-22).

No matter what we do or say we will never end this world. Wars or our man-made weapons will never put to the end of this world. Nuclear weapons will never end this world. God himself will put an end to all wars and sin. The devil will be dealt with finally. Satan will be put in the lake of fire forever.

But right now, before we die sinful desires within us go to war against the spiritual forces. Christians are always at war because sin fights against the law of the spirit of life in them through Jesus Christ (Romans 8:1-2). The good news is that the spirit of Christ in them ultimately wins.

A good example of the battle between sin (evil) and the spirit in our body is the passage in the book of Romans where Paul explains the dilemma we Christians sometimes have in our walk with the Lord as we fight against evil desires in our lives.

"In the Roman passage, Paul tries to do the right thing, but always ends up doing the wrong thing. The origin sin that came from Adam plays a major role here. The body is at war, though freed from the law of sin and death by the blood of our Lord Jesus Christ. God justifies all his people by his grace. But God's elect are not totally sanctified from the pollution of Adam's sin until Parousia. Hear what Paul said in this passage in Romans;

We know that the law is spiritual; but I am unspiritual, sold as a slave to sin. I do not understand what I do. For what I want to do, I do not do, but what I hate I do. And if I do what I do not want to do, I agree that the law is good. As it is, it is no longer I myself who do it, but it is sin living in me. For I know that good itself does not dwell in me, that is, in my sinful nature. For I have the desire to do what is good, but I cannot carry it out. For I do not do the good I want to do, but the evil I do not want to do-this I keep on doing. Now if I do what I do not want to do, it is no longer I who do it, but it is sin living in me that does it.

So, I find this law at work: Although I want to do good, evil is right there with me. For in my inner being I delight in God's law; but I see another law at work in me, waging war against the law of my mind and making me a prisoner of the law of sin at work within me. What a wretched man I am! Who will rescue me from this body that is subject to death? Thanks, be to God, who delivers me through Jesus Christ our Lord!

So then, I in my mind am a slave to God's law, but in my sinful nature a slave to the law of sin" (Romans 7:14-25). Justification is done once and for all but sanctification is a daily process. It is our walk with the Lord daily as we fight against sin and all its many parts till we die.

World catastrophe

There are many things in the world we fail in understanding; world catastrophe is one of them. For example, we see tornados without warning, falling on the nation or part of the nation killing thousands of innocent people. We see earthquakes destroying the land full of people or animals.

BEDROOM OF ADAM AND EVE

We see tsunamis causing water in the sea destroy the land full of creatures. We see the sinkhole on land and on the sea, that can swallow cars and even homes for both righteous and unrighteous people.

God made the world and it was good with no catastrophe. We do not know what God is doing with other galaxies, but we can only speak of ours. Our earth is full of catastrophes which cannot be explained. All we can say is that sin has bigger part of them.

These earthly disasters fall on all people regardless of their faith. Catastrophes in the world prove our human powerlessness when they happen. We cannot prevent them from happening.

But just like all misery that comes to humans in the world would end one day, world catastrophe will also end at the Parousia. Then I saw "a new heaven and a new earth," for the first heaven and the first earth had passed away, and there was no longer any sea (Revelation 21:1).

CHAPTER FIVE. QUESTIONS TO ANSWER

What are the consequences of original sin?

What is total separation from God?

How do you define spiritual death?

What is physical death?

Are we born spiritually blind?

What do you learn from the parable of the rich fool?

What do you learn from the story of Cain and Abel?

What is misery?

Define war?

Did Adam get sick before the fall?

Did Adam see animals and plants die before the fall?

CHAPTER 6

ACTS OF SIN

Sin is transgression against the law of God. The New International Version bible says everyone who sins breaks the law; in fact, sin is lawlessness while King James Bible says whosoever commits sin transgresses also the law: for sin is the transgression of the law (I Joh 3:4).

When we obey the law of God, we are living per what God wants us to be but when we do not follow the law of God we sin against God.

How can we follow the law of God without sinning? It is impossible on our own effort. God in Christ Jesus has fulfilled the requirements of the law through the death of his Son. God gives us the Holy Spirit that helps us receive the finished work of Jesus Christ in our lives. Therefore, by the grace of God through faith in Jesus Christ we become children of God. In Jesus Christ, we can keep and obey the law of God.

The Bible says," Therefore, there is now no condemnation for those who are in Christ Jesus. For the law of the Spirit of life in Christ Jesus has set you free from the law of sin and of death" (Romans 8:1-2). Christians are now living under the law of the spirit of life in Jesus Christ and not under the law of sin and death. No one can condemn us not even the devil and all its fallen angels. Sin can no longer completely enslave believers in the Lord Jesus Christ now and forever more. But the question remains, why do we commit sin?

We commit acts of sins because we are not yet fully received immortal and spiritual sinless bodies. We are still within reach of the devil and its fallen angels. We commit sin in thought, word, deed and even knowingly or unknowingly. Remember, there is no smaller or greater sin in the eyes of God. Sin is sin, whether we know it or we do not know it. We will reach perfection when we are with God in heaven and not when we are still here on earth. But we should bear in mind that in Christ Jesus, we have already attained this perfection, though not in totality (1 John 1:8-10).

Addiction

This word addiction is made up of two verbs *Add* or *to add* and *act* or *action*. When we add these two verbs we come up with a continuous action that is very hard to stop or break by our own efforts. This process of adding and acting, is always accelerated by sin.

Human beings are by nature born of sin and therefore are masters of addiction. We love to live in the addictive atmosphere. Addiction is the game we all like to play because it is easy and follows our deprived condition well.

When Adam and Eve disobeyed God, they dug a pit which became their bedroom. This pit has become our bedroom too, until we are called out of it in Christ Jesus through the power of his spirit. Since all of us are sinners, therefore all of us can be addicted of something at a certain period of our lives. Not all addictions are sinful in nature, but all addictions are treated as transgressions in the eyes of God. We should not be addicted to anything else, even our own self. We need to love God with all our minds, strength, power, and soul. Our soul is the seat of all emotions that make us get addicted to things of the world. If we love this world and the things of this world, then the love of God is not in us (1 John 2:15-16). Addiction becomes problematic because it always takes the place of God in our lives.

Addiction is a process of doing one thing repeatedly in a period of time. This process always seems good in the eyes of the person doing it that it becomes a master of his life. For example, a drunkard loves alcoholic water, which becomes the master of his life. A drug user loves drugs which are the master of his soul. But addiction on itself is not a substance that we can touch, but rather it is a way of life which is very hard to stop because it comes from a depravity heart. Listen what Jesus said to the Pharisees, "Again Jesus called the crowd to him and said, "Listen to me, everyone, and understand this. Nothing outside a person can defile them by going into them. Rather, it is what comes out of a person that defiles them."

After he had left the crowd and entered the house, his disciples asked him about this parable. Are you so dull?" he asked. "Don't you see that nothing that enters a person from the outside can defile them? For it doesn't go into their heart, but into their stomach, and then out of the body." (In saying this, Jesus declared all foods clean.)

He went on: "What comes out of a person is what defiles them. For it is from within, out of a person's heart, that evil thoughts come-sexual immorality, theft, murder, adultery, greed, malice, deceit, lewdness, envy, slander, arrogance, and folly. All these evils come from inside and defile a person" (Mark 7:14-23). Addiction comes out of the sinful soul and defiles the man.

This process of addiction is always lonely even when people seem to be in a family setting or a group. Therefore, addiction is isolating.

It is very hard to break the habit of addiction alone. We need God and one another to help reduce or even eradicate addictive behavior in our lives. It is not good to isolate an addict. Therefore, it is not good to laugh or criticize an addict because by doing so, we are judging and isolating him, which eventually makes his life hard to even receive counsel from anyone including God. When we isolate the addict, we let him live in the area of his own comfort called the bedroom of Adam and Eve. The addiction is in any form an act of sin. It must not be entertained in our lives. Let the blood of our Lord and savior Jesus Christ help us break any form of addiction in our lives (1John 1:8-9).

Depression

Depression is a state or mood of falling. There is nothing good that comes out of depression. Depression causes people to have low esteem. There are many factors that cause depression, especially mental depression. Depression causes isolation and a state of rejection among people. Depression is another act of sin, though in most of the time we do not choose to be depressed but due to situations around or within us we found ourselves depressed.

For example, when our dear ones die our mourning can turn into depression. Feeling sorry or being pitiful due to the loss of a friend can lead to depression. We sometimes blame ourselves since we could not help our family member get out of worse condition which made them die.

Whatever causes we may have that lead us into depression, we must be assured that depression of any sort is not from God. It is one of the acts of the bedroom of Adam and Eve. It is the product of our total depravity. The total cure of depression is in the blood and the spirit of Jesus Christ.

EDWARD KAVIMBA LUNGU PHD
Murder

Murder is taking the life a person or self willingly or unwillingly. Murder is deadly and is not welcomed. Cain was the first person to murder his brother Abel.

"Now Cain said to his brother Abel, "Let's go out to the field," while they were in the field, Cain attacked his brother Abel and killed him.

Then the Lord said to Cain, "Where is your brother Abel?"

"I don't know," he replied. "Am I my brother's keeper?"

The Lord said, "What have you done? Listen! Your brother's blood cries out to me from the ground. Now you are under a curse and driven from the ground, which opened its mouth to receive your brother's blood from your hand. When you work the ground, it will no longer yield its crops for you. You will be a restless wanderer on the earth" (Genesis 4: 8-12). Every day people are murdered in the world due to sin. This is horrible. Even Jesus Christ was murdered though not for his sins but ours. Apostle Paul said, "He was delivered over to death for our sins and was raised to life for our justification" (Roman 4:25). Apostle Peter confirmed this by saying, "He himself bore our sins" in his body on the cross, so that we might die to sins and live for righteousness; "by his wounds you have been healed"(1 Peter 2:24).

Murder can also happen in our thoughts when we hide bad feelings towards ourselves or others. Then we turn those bad feelings into action which result in murder. Even if those bad thoughts towards us or others did not turn into murder in the eyes of God it is murder. Jesus said, "But the things that proceed out of the mouth come from the heart, and those defile the man. For out of the heart come evil thoughts, murders, adulteries, fornications, thefts, false witness, and slanders. These are the things which defile the man; but to eat with unwashed hands does not defile the man" (Matthew 15: 18-20).

Before Adam and Eve sinned, there was no murder. Therefore, we can also say that murder is one of the acts of the bedroom of Adam and Even. Murder is the product of our depravity. It should not be allowed to happen in our midst. Since murder is a sin therefore the blood of Jesus can cleanse it away from our soul (1 John 1:9). This action, though how brutal it can be, can be forgiven through the blood of our Lord Jesus Christ.

Paul was a murderer, but God forgave him and even chose him to be his servant in the ministry (Acts 9: 3-19).

But this is not the license to commit murder. There is always going to a penalty to murder in a civil society which may lead to execution or prison time.

Lying

Lying is not telling the truth knowingly or unknowingly. There is no small lie or bigger lie all is lying. The bible says all lies come from the devil that is called the father of all lies. Confronting the Pharisees, Jesus said, "You belong to your father, the devil, and you want to carry out your father's desires. He was a murderer from the beginning, not holding to the truth, for there is no truth in him. When he lies, he speaks his native language, for he is a liar and the father of lies" (John 8:44).

Nobody is immune to lying the psalmist knew this when he said, "in my alarm I said, "Everyone is a liar" (Psalms 116:11). Apostle Paul echoed the same thought in his letter to the Romans when he wrote that 'Not at all! Let God be true, and every human being a liar. As it is written: "So that you may be proved right when you speak and prevail when you judge' (Romans 3:4).

BEDROOM OF ADAM AND EVE

Lying is sin, whether we lie once or more often. Lying is the product of the fallen nature of man, which is inherited from Adam and Eve. It is okay to say lying is the fruit of the bedroom of Adam and Eve. Human beings have fallen in love with the bedroom of Adam and Eve that lying becomes the nature act to them by the blood of Jesus comes to play in their lives.

Can a Christian lie? Yes, a Christian can lie, but he is not supposed to lie, knowingly or unknowingly. But if he does lie, he must confess his sin of lying and ask forgiveness through the blood of our Lord Jesus Christ. Conviction of the sin of lying is done by the power of the spirit of God. We cannot stop someone from lying, but the spirit of God through the blood of Jesus Christ can. God sees our heart the root seat of our depravity and sprinkles the blood of his son to make it pure from all sin (1 John 1:9).

Anger

Anger is a deep emotional feeling of madness in our hearts caused by unwelcome situation. Anger is the absence of peace in our lives. Anger is the nuclear war within our hearts.

God hates anger in all its forms or sharp. Moses did not enter the Promised Land because of his anger towards the people of God.

"And Moses and Aaron gathered the assembly before the rock. And he said to them, "Listen now, you rebel; shall we bring forth water for you out of this rock?" Then Moses lifted up his hand and struck the rock twice with his rod; and water came forth abundantly, and the congregation and their beasts drank. But the LORD said to Moses and Aaron, "Because you have not believed Me, to treat Me as holy in the sight of the sons of Israel, therefore you shall not bring this assembly into the land which I have given them."… (Numbers 20:10-12).

In the eyes of God anger is the same as murder;

You have heard that it was said to the people long ago, 'You shall not murder, and anyone who murders will be subject to judgment.' But I tell you that anyone who is angry with a brother or sister will be subject to judgment. Again, anyone who says to a brother or sister, 'Raca, is answerable to the court. And anyone who says, 'You fool!' will be in danger of the fire of hell.

"Therefore, if you are offering your gift at the altar and there remember that your brother or sister has something against you; leave your gift there in front of the altar. First go and be reconciled to them; then come and offer your gift.

"Settle matters quickly with your adversary who is taking you to court. Do it while you are still together on the way, or your adversary may hand you over to the judge, and the judge may hand you over to the officer, and you may be thrown into prison. Truly I tell you, you will not get out until you have paid the last penny" (Matthew 5: 21-26).

Anger in relationship to sin is the bedroom of Adam and Eve. Cain killed his brother because he was angry that God did not accept his offering but accepted his brother's offering.

Now Abel kept flocks, and Cain worked the soil. In the course of time Cain brought some of the fruits of the soil as an offering to the Lord. And Abel also brought an offering-fat portions from some of the firstborn of his flock. The Lord looked with favor on Abel and his offering, but on Cain and his offering he did not look with favor. So, Cain was very angry, and his face was downcast. Then the Lord said to Cain, "Why are you angry? Why is your face downcast? If you do what is right, will you not be accepted? But if you do not do what is right, sin is crouching at your door; it desires to have you, but you must rule over it."

Now Cain said to his brother Abel, "Let's go out to the field." While they were in the field, Cain attacked his brother Abel and killed him (Genesis 4:2-8).

Can a Christian get angry? Yes, he can but he is not supposed to do so. Another question can be asked like this; how far can a Christian remain angry on unrighteous act on himself or others? There is no right measurement of our anger for ourselves or others, therefore it is better to refrain from being angry at all costs lest we sin. There are passages in the bible where God got angry of his people due to their disobedience. There are also passages in the bible where the servant or people of God got angry because some individuals or group of people did not follow the righteousness of God. We can say that there is bad anger and good anger, but to be on the safe side, it is better to treat all anger as being bad and unwanted feelings in our midst.

Jesus is our best example when he went through all sorts of sufferings and even being nailed on the cross, yet he never got angry at the people that mistreated him and finally killed him.

Paul to the Philippians said, "But emptied Himself, taking the form of a bond-servant, and being made in the likeness of men. Being found in appearance as a man, He humbled Himself by becoming obedient to the point of death, even death on a cross. For this reason, also, God highly exalted Him, and bestowed on Him the name which is above every name…" (Philippians 2:7-9).

God understands our anger and has provided a solution in his Son Jesus Christ. The grace of God through faith in Jesus Christ brings peace to us when we feel angry. We need to trust in the finished work of our Lord Jesus Christ to continue experiencing joy and peace in times of bitterness in our lives. This is not easy, but in Christ all things are possible (Mathew 19:26; Mark 9:23).

Suicide

Suicide is taking the life of self. Suicide is said to have happen when one takes the life of himself or herself. Nature death is when someone dies from natural causes such as sickness or aging and many other factors but not by suicide.

Death is the separation between the soul and the body due to sin. When God said to Adam if you eat the fruit from the tree in the middle of the garden you will surely die he meant just that. Death came to be real in the family of Adam and Eve when Cain killed his brother Abel. It is said in the bible that while the body of Abel was lying on the ground where Cain hid it and at the same time the soul (blood) of Abel was speaking with God in heaven.

Now Cain said to his brother Abel, "Let's go out to the field." While they were in the field, Cain attacked his brother Abel and killed him.

Then the Lord said to Cain, "Where is your brother Abel?"

"I don't know," he replied. "Am I my brother's keeper?"

The Lord said, "What have you done? Listen! Your brother's blood cries out to me from the ground. Now you are under a curse and driven from the ground, which opened its mouth to receive your brother's blood from your hand. When you work the ground, it will no longer yield its crops for you. You will be a restless wanderer on the earth."

Cain said to the Lord, "My punishment is more than I can bear. Today you are driving me from the land, and I will be hidden from your presence; I will be a restless wanderer on the earth, and whoever finds me will kill me."

But the Lord said to him, "Not so; anyone who kills Cain will suffer vengeance seven times over." Then the Lord put a mark on Cain so that no one who found him would kill him. So Cain went out from the Lord's presence and lived in the land of Nod, east of Eden" (Genesis 4:8-16).

Abel did not commit suicide, his brother Cain killed him. We have people in the bible that committed suicide;

BEDROOM OF ADAM AND EVE

Abimelech - Judges 9:54

After having his skull crushed under a millstone that was dropped by a woman from the Tower of Shechem, Abimelech called for his armor bearer to kill him with a sword. He did not want it said that a woman had killed him.

Samson - Judges 16:29-31

By collapsing a building, Samson sacrificed his own life, but in the process destroyed thousands of enemy Philistines.

Saul and His Armor Bearer - 1 Samuel 31:3-6

After losing his sons and all of his troops in battle, and his sanity long before, King Saul, assisted by his armor bearer, ended his life. Then Saul's servant killed himself.

Ahithophel - 2 Samuel 17:23

Disgraced and rejected by Absolom, Ahithophel went home, put his affairs in order, and then hung himself.

Zimri - 1 Kings 16:18

Rather than being taken prisoner, Zimri set the king's palace on fire and died in the flames.

Judas - Matthew 27:5

After he betrayed Jesus, Judas Iscariot was overcome with remorse and hung himself.

Whether someone is taking his own life he is committing suicide. Life is sacred from God and must not be taken off by ourselves. Therefore, Suicide is a sin.

Can a Christian lose his salvation due to suicide? Or can a Christian go to hell because he died through suicide?

The Bible says, "we are saved by the grace of God through faith in Jesus Christ. It is not by our works so that none of us should boast of being saved." It is the blood of Jesus that saves us from all our sins and that includes the sin of suicide. But we cannot stand in the place of God and pass judgement on whether the person who committed suicide is in heaven or in hell. It is up to the divine mercy of God himself declare holy justice. But we must also know that all our bad actions in life have consequences here on earth but also towards God himself. But if we know someone is trying to commit suicide or have thoughts of committing suicide let us pray for him or if possible, talk to him about what our Lord Jesus did for him on the cross when he died a shameful death. The blood of Jesus is powerful to forgive this man or even stop the thing that triggered suicide thoughts (I John 1:8-9).

The fact remains that suicide is death. People commit because of sin. Therefore, it is right to say that suicide is the product of the bedroom of Adam and Eve.

We should approach with the spirit of comfort and pastoral care to the families of the person that committed suicide. We must refrain from passing judgmental statements to the person that committed suicide because we may not fully know and understand the trigger of that deadly self-inflicted action.

The Idol worship

An idol is a physical or non-physical thing worshipped as god. An idol can be both a noun and a verb. As a noun an idol is a thing and as a verb that thing demands action which often leads to idol worshipping. Therefore, anything that demands worship apart from the God of the Bible is an idol. God in biblical term is ONE but revealed up himself in three persons: God the Father, God the Son and God the Holy Spirit. Each person is truly God and demands our worship. Idol worship is an abomination to our God. Idol worship led to death in the Old Testament and leads to hell in the New Testament if not repented through the blood of Jesus Christ before death. The very first commandment of God talks about worshipping God alone and not idols; And God spoke all these words, saying,

"I am the Lord your God, who brought you out of the land of Egypt, out of the house of slavery.

"You shall have no other gods before me.

"You shall not make for yourself a carved image, or any likeness of anything that is in heaven above, or that is in the earth beneath, or that is in the water under the earth. You shall not bow down to them or serve them, for I the Lord your God am a jealous God, visiting the iniquity of the fathers on the children to the third and the fourth generation of those who hate me, but showing steadfast love to thousands of those who love me and keep my commandments (Exodus 20:1-6). One great example of the consequences of worshipping idols was the death of many Israelites who worshipped the calf Aaron made in the wilderness. The name of Aaron is mentioned here just because he was the leading man when Israel made the café image when Moses was in the mountain talking with God.

Here is the story of The Golden Calf:

"When the people saw, that Moses was so long in coming down from the mountain, they gathered around Aaron and said, "Come, make us gods who will go before us. As for this fellow Moses, who brought us up out of Egypt, we don't know what has happened to him."

Aaron answered them, "Take off the gold earrings that your wives, your sons and your daughters are wearing, and bring them to me." So, all the people took off their earrings and brought them to Aaron. He took what they handed him and made it into an idol cast in the shape of a calf, fashioning it with a tool. Then they said, "These are your gods, Israel, who brought you up out of Egypt."

When Aaron saw this, he built an altar in front of the calf and announced, "Tomorrow there will be a festival to the Lord." So, the next day the people rose early and sacrificed burnt offerings and presented fellowship offerings. Afterward they sat down to eat and drink and got up to indulge in revelry. Then the Lord said to Moses, "Go down, because your people, whom you brought up out of Egypt, have become corrupt. They have been quick to turn away from what I commanded them and have made themselves an idol cast in the shape of a calf. They have bowed down to it and sacrificed to it and have said, 'These are your gods, Israel, who brought you up out of Egypt.' "I have seen these people," the Lord said to Moses, "and they are a stiff-necked people. Now leave me alone so that my anger may burn against them and that I may destroy them. Then I will make you into a great nation."

But Moses sought the favor of the Lord his God. "Lord," he said, "why should your anger burn against your people, whom you brought out of Egypt with great power and a mighty hand? Why should the Egyptians say, 'It was with evil intent that he brought them out, to kill them in the mountains and to wipe them off the face of the earth'? Turn from your fierce anger; relent and do not bring disaster on your people. Remember your servants Abraham, Isaac and Israel, to whom you swore by your own self: 'I will make your descendants as numerous as the stars in the sky and I will give your descendants all this land I promised them, and it will be their inheritance forever.'" Then the Lord relented and did not bring on his people the disaster he had threatened.

Moses turned and went down the mountain with the two tablets of the covenant law in his hands. They were inscribed on both sides, front and back. The tablets were the work of God; the writing was the writing of God, engraved on the tablets.

When Joshua heard the noise of the people shouting, he said to Moses, "There is the sound of war in the camp."

Moses replied:

"It is not the sound of victory, it is not the sound of defeat; it is the sound of singing that I hear."

When Moses approached the camp, and saw the calf and the dancing, his anger burned and he threw the tablets out of his hands, breaking them to pieces at the foot of the mountain. And he took the calf the people had made and burned it in the fire; then he ground it to powder, scattered it on the water and made the Israelites drink it.

He said to Aaron, "What did these people do to you, that you led them into such great sin?"

"Do not be angry, my lord," Aaron answered. "You know how prone these people are to evil. They said to me, 'Make us gods who will go before us. As for this fellow Moses, who brought us up out of Egypt, we don't know what has happened to him.' So, I told them, 'Whoever has any gold jewelry, take it off.' Then they gave me the gold, and I threw it into the fire, and out came this calf!"

Moses saw that the people were running wild and that Aaron had let them get out of control and so become a laughingstock to their enemies. So, he stood at the entrance to the camp and said, "Whoever is for the Lord, come to me." And all the Levites rallied to him.

Then he said to them, "This is what the Lord, the God of Israel, says: 'Each man straps a sword to his side. Go back and forth through the camp from one end to the other, each killing his brother and friend and neighbor.'" The Levites did as Moses commanded, and that day about three thousand of the people died. Then Moses said, "You have been set apart to the Lord today, for you were against your own sons and brothers, and he has blessed you this day."

The next day Moses said to the people, "You have committed a great sin. But now I will go up to the Lord; perhaps I can make atonement for your sin."

So, Moses went back to the Lord and said, "Oh, what a great sin these people have committed! They have made themselves gods of gold. But now, please forgive their sin-but if not, then blot me out of the book you have written."

The Lord replied to Moses, "Whoever has sinned against me I will blot out of my book. Now go, lead the people to the place I spoke of, and my angel will go before you. However, when the time comes for me to punish, I will punish them for their sin."

And the Lord struck the people with a plague because of what they did with the calf Aaron had made (Exodus 32).

Another great example of death to idol worshippers in the Old Testament is that famous act Alijah did to the prophet of Baal;

Elijah Kills the Prophets of Baal

"During the third year without rain, the Lord spoke his word to Elijah: "Go and meet King Ahab, and I will soon send rain." So, Elijah went to meet Ahab.

By this time there was no food in Samaria. King Ahab sent for Obadiah, who was in charge of the king's palace. (Obadiah was a true follower of the Lord. When Jezebel was killing all the Lord's prophets, Obadiah hid a hundred of them in two caves, fifty in one cave and fifty in another. He also brought them food and water.) Ahab said to Obadiah, "Let's check every spring and valley in the land. Maybe we can find enough grass to keep our horses and mules alive and not have to kill our animals." So, each one chose a part of the country to search; Ahab went in one direction and Obadiah in another.

While Obadiah was on his way, Elijah met him. Obadiah recognized Elijah, so he bowed down to the ground and said, "Elijah? Is it really you, master?"

"Yes," Elijah answered. "Go tell your master that I am here."

Then Obadiah said, "What wrong have I done for you to hand me over to Ahab like this? He will put me to death. As surely as the Lord your God lives, the king has sent people to every country to search for you. If the ruler said you were not there, Ahab forced the ruler to swear you could not be found in his country. Now you want me to go to my master and tell him, 'Elijah is here'? The Spirit of the Lord may carry you to some other place after I leave. If I go tell King Ahab you are here, and he comes and doesn't find you, he will kill me! I have followed the Lord since I was a boy. Haven't you been told what I did? When Jezebel was killing the Lord's prophets, I hid a hundred of them, fifty in one cave and fifty in another. I brought them food and water. Now you want me to go and tell my master you are here? He will kill me!"

Elijah answered, "As surely as the Lord All-Powerful lives, whom I serve, I will be seen by Ahab today."

So, Obadiah went to Ahab and told him where Elijah was. Then Ahab went to meet Elijah.

When he saw Elijah, he asked, "Is it you-the biggest troublemaker in Israel?"

Elijah answered, "I have not made trouble in Israel. You and your father's family have made all this trouble by not obeying the Lord's commands. You have gone after the Baals. Now tell all Israel to meet me at Mount Carmel. Also, bring the four hundred fifty prophets of Baal and the four hundred prophets of Asherah, who eat at Jezebel's table."

So, Ahab called all the Israelites and those prophets to Mount Carmel. Elijah approached the people and said, "How long will you not decide between two choices? If the Lord is the true God, follow him, but if Baal is the true God, follow him!" But the people said nothing.

Elijah said, "I am the only prophet of the Lord here, but there are four hundred fifty prophets of Baal. Bring two bulls. Let the prophets of Baal choose one bull and kill it and cut it into pieces. Then let them put the meat on the wood, but they are not to set fire to it. I will prepare the other bull, putting the meat on the wood but not setting fire to it. You prophets of Baal, pray to your god, and I will pray to the Lord. The god who answers by setting fire to his wood is the true God." All the people agreed that this was a good idea.

Then Elijah said to the prophets of Baal, "There are many of you, so you go first. Choose a bull and prepare it. Pray to your god, but don't start the fire."

So, they took the bull that was given to them and prepared it. They prayed to Baal from morning until noon, shouting "Baal, answer us!" But there was no sound, and no one answered. They danced around the altar they had built.

At noon Elijah began to make fun of them. "Pray louder!" he said. "If Baal really is a god, maybe he is thinking, or busy, or traveling! Maybe he is sleeping so you will have to wake him!"

The prophets prayed louder, cutting themselves with swords and spears until their blood flowed, which was the way they worshiped. The afternoon passed, and the prophets continued to act like this until it was time for the evening sacrifice. But no voice was heard; Baal did not answer, and no one paid attention.

Then Elijah said to all the people, "Now come to me." So, they gathered around him, and Elijah rebuilt the altar of the Lord, which had been torn down. He took twelve stones, one stone for each of the twelve tribes, the number of Jacob's sons. (The Lord changed Jacob's name to Israel.) Elijah used these stones to rebuild the altar in honor of the Lord. Then he dug a ditch around the altar that was big enough to hold about thirteen quarts of seed. Elijah put the wood on the altar, cut the bull into pieces, and laid the pieces on the wood. Then he said, "Fill four jars with water, and pour it on the meat and on the wood." Then Elijah said, "Do it again," and they did it again. Then he said, "Do it a third time," and they did it the third time. So, the water ran off the altar and filled the ditch.

At the time for the evening sacrifice, the prophet Elijah went near the altar. "Lord, you are the God of Abraham, Isaac, and Israel," he prayed. "Prove that you are the God of Israel and that I am your servant. Show these people that you commanded me to do all these things. Lord, answer my prayer so these people will know that you, Lord, are God and that you will change their minds." Then fire from the Lord came down and burned the sacrifice, the wood, the stones, and the ground around the altar. It also dried up the water in the ditch. When all the people saw this, they fell down to the ground, crying, "The Lord is God! The Lord is God!"

Then Elijah said, "Capture the prophets of Baal! Don't let any of them run away!" The people captured all the prophets. Then Elijah led them down to the Kishon Valley, where he killed them.

In the Old Testament, the ultimate punishment of idol worship was death. Moses saw how the calf worshippers died and Alijah did the actual killing of those that worshipped Baal. But we do not live under the old written cord now but under grace. Even in our situation it is sin to worship idols.

Whenever there is no clear creator creature distinction idol worshipping takes place. Christians must maintain the fact that God is the creator and everything else in this world is creature. Creature can never be creator and creator will never be creature. Therefore, no one can form God of the Bible with human hands and neither can God be a creature.

New Testament writers taught and even preached against idol worship among the people of God. Jesus Christ warned the church in Pergamum about the dangers of idol worshipping;

"Nevertheless, I have a few things against you: There are some among you who hold to the teaching of Balaam, who taught Balak to entice the Israelites to sin so that they ate food sacrificed to idols and committed sexual immorality. Likewise, you also have those who hold to the teaching of the Nicolaitans. Repent therefore! Otherwise, I will soon come to you and will fight against them with the sword of my mouth" (Revelation 2:14-16).

To the church in Thyatira Jesus said;

"Nevertheless, I have this against you: You tolerate that woman Jezebel, who calls herself a prophet. By her teaching, she misleads my servants into sexual immorality and the eating of food sacrificed to idols. I have given her time to repent of her immorality, but she is unwilling. So, I will cast her on a bed of suffering, and I will make those who commit adultery with her suffer intensely, unless they repent of her ways. I will strike her children dead. Then all the churches will know that I am he who searches hearts and minds, and I will repay each of you according to your deeds" (Revelation 2: 20-23).

The disciples of Jesus Christ warned the church not to worship man made things as God,

"For in him we live and move and have our being, 'as some of your own poets have said, 'We are his offspring.' "Therefore, since we are God's offspring, we should not think that the divine being is like gold or silver or stone-an image made by human design and skill" (Acts 17: 28-29).

Paul preached against idol worship in the city of Athens. He wanted the people know that God alone was worth of worship.

"Paul then stood up in the meeting of the Areopagus and said: "People of Athens! I see that in every way you are very religious. For as I walked around and looked carefully at your objects of worship, I even found an altar with this inscription: to an unknown god. So, you are ignorant of the very thing you worship-and this is what I am going to proclaim to you

The God who made the world and everything in it is the Lord of heaven and earth and does not live in temples built by human hands. And he is not served by human hands, as if he needed anything. Rather, he himself gives everyone life and breath and everything else" (Acts 17:20-25).

Now while Paul waited for them in Athens, his spirit was provoked within him when he saw that the city was given over to idols...Then Paul stood in the midst of the Areopagus and said...'God, who made the world and everything in it, since He is Lord of heaven and earth, does not dwell in temples made with hands. Nor is He worshipped with men's hands, as though He needed anything' (Acts 17:16, 22, 24-25).

Professing to be wise, they became fools, and changed the glory of the incorruptible God into an image made like corruptible man--and birds and four footed animals and creeping things (Romans 1:22-23).

But now I have written to you not to keep company with anyone named a brother, who is...an idolater. The Bible is very clear that worshipping of Idols is not allowed among the people of God.

"Do not be yoked together with unbelievers. For what do righteousness and wickedness have in common? Or what fellowship can light have with darkness? What harmony is there between Christ and Belial? Or what does a believer have in common with an unbeliever? What agreement is there between the temple of God and idols? For we are the temple of the living God. As God has said:

"I will live with them

and walk among them,
and I will be their God,
and they will be my people."

Therefore,

"Come out from them
and be separate,
says the Lord.
Touch no unclean thing,
and I will receive you."

And,

"I will be a Father to you,
and you will be my sons and daughters,
says the Lord Almighty" (2 Corinthians 6: 14-18).

The last apostle to die was John and he also warned about worshipping idols;

Little children, keep yourselves from idols (I John 5:21).

But the rest of mankind, who were not killed by these plagues, did not repent of the works of their hands, that they should not worship demons, and idols of gold, silver, brass, stone, and wood, which can neither see nor hear nor walk (Revelation 9:20).

But ...idolaters...shall have their part in the lake which burns with fire and brimstone, which is the second death (Revelation 21:8).

But outside are...idolaters (Revelation 22:15).

Idol worship of any form is sin against God. Any idea or thought in our mind that we treasure more than our God is an idol and therefore needs to be repented now through the blood of Jesus Christ.

Witchcraft

Idol worship leads to witchcraft. Witchcraft is the practice or belief in secret knowledge or activities associated with the devil and its demons (magic and sorcery). Knowledge used in witchcraft is always from below and not from above. Witchcraft never leads to heaven but to the dark side (Hell). Witchcraft is sin. God hates witchcraft. This is what the bible says about witchcraft according to King James Version;

Leviticus 19:31 - Regard not them that have familiar spirits, neither seek after wizards, to be defiled by them: I [am] the LORD your God.

Exodus 22:18 - Thou shalt not suffer a witch to live.

Leviticus 20:27 - A man also or woman that hath a familiar spirit, or that is a wizard, shall surely be put to death: they shall stone them with stones: their blood [shall be] upon them.

Deuteronomy 18:9-12 - When thou art come into the land which the LORD thy God giveth thee, thou shalt not learn to do after the abominations of those nations.

Deuteronomy 18:10 - There shall not be found among you [any one] that maketh his son or his daughter to pass through the fire, [or] that useth divination, [or] an observer of times, or an enchanter, or a witch,

Leviticus 20:6 - And the soul that turneth after such as have familiar spirits, and after wizards, to go a whoring after them, I will even set my face against that soul, and will cut him off from among his people.

Galatians 5:19-21 - Now the works of the flesh are manifest, which are [these]; Adultery, fornication, uncleanness, lasciviousness,

Revelation 21:8 - But the fearful, and unbelieving, and the abominable, and murderers, and whoremongers, and sorcerers, and idolaters, and all liars, shall have their part in the lake which burneth with fire and brimstone: which is the second death.

Isaiah 8:19 - And when they shall say unto you, Seek unto them that have familiar spirits, and unto wizards that peep, and that mutter: should not a people seek unto their God? for the living to the dead?

Galatians 5:20-21 - Idolatry, witchcraft, hatred, variance, emulations, wrath, strife, seditions, heresies,

2 Chronicles 33:6 - And he caused his children to pass through the fire in the valley of the son of Hinnom: also he observed times, and used enchantments, and used witchcraft, and dealt with a familiar spirit, and with wizards: he wrought much evil in the sight of the LORD, to provoke him to anger.

2 Kings 21:6 - And he made his son pass through the fire, and observed times, and used enchantments, and dealt with familiar spirits and wizards: he wrought much wickedness in the sight of the LORD, to provoke [him] to anger.

Revelation 22:15 - For without [are] dogs, and sorcerers, and whoremongers, and murderers, and idolaters, and whosoever loveth and maketh a lie.

1 Samuel 15:23 - For rebellion [is as] the sin of witchcraft, and stubbornness [is as] iniquity and idolatry. Because thou hast rejected the word of the LORD, he hath also rejected thee from [being] king.

Acts 19:19 - Many of them also which used curious arts brought their books together, and burned them before all [men]: and they counted the price of them, and found [it] fifty thousand [pieces] of silver.

1 Chronicles 10:13-14 - So Saul died for his transgression which he committed against the LORD, [even] against the word of the LORD, which he kept not, and also for asking [counsel] of

[one that had] a familiar spirit, to enquire [of it];

Isaiah 19:3 - And the spirit of Egypt shall fail in the midst thereof; and I will destroy the counsel thereof: and they shall seek to the idols, and to the charmers, and to them that have familiar spirits, and to the wizards.

Jesus died for this sin of witchcraft too (Acts 13:38-39). Therefore, witchcraft can be forgiven through the blood of Jesus Christ if confessed under the conviction of the power of the Holy Spirit but if not it can lead to hell;

" The acts of the flesh are obvious: sexual immorality, impurity and debauchery; idolatry and witchcraft; hatred, discord, jealousy, fits of rage, selfish ambition, dissensions, factions and envy; drunkenness, orgies, and the like. I warn you, as I did before, that those who live like this will not inherit the kingdom of God" (Galatian 5:19-21).

Abortion

General definition

It is the deliberate termination of a human pregnancy, most often performed during the first 28 weeks of pregnancy.

The expulsion of a fetus from the uterus by natural causes before it is able to survive independently.

Biological definition

It is the arrest of the development of an organ, typically a seed or fruit. An object or undertaking regarded by the speaker as unpleasant or badly made or carried out.

Medical Definition of abortion

The termination of a pregnancy after, accompanied by, resulting in, or closely followed by the death of the embryo or fetus: *a*: spontaneous expulsion of a human fetus during the first 12 weeks of gestation-compare miscarriage *b*: induced expulsion of a human fetus *c*: expulsion of a fetus of a domestic animal often due to infection at any time before completion of pregnancy.

arrest of development of an organ so that it remains imperfect or is absorbed

the arrest of a disease in its earliest stage <abortion of a cold> http://www.merriam-webster.com/medical/abortion

I got these two definitions of abortion online and they mean just that. Yes, there are times when the baby in the womb of the mother has some incurable disease and therefore death or abortion is the final solution for the survivor of the mother. Sometimes the mother is incapable of holding on the baby in the womb due to illness or accident as the result abortion is carried out.

Abortion is not a Republican or a Democratic issue but a depravity issue. We look at this issue from a deprived state of human beings.

I do not think God intention on that fetus was to be aborted before birth regardless of circumstances surrounding it. Therefore, whenever we see or hear the word abortion the first thing that should come to our mind is the word sin. Whether it is done with good intentions or not, abortion is plain evil because it deliberately takes away the life of unborn defenseless baby. It is plain murder.

We are now under the grace and not under the law but we can still learn from the law especially what it said to people that caused harm to unborn babies;

BEDROOM OF ADAM AND EVE

"If people are fighting and hit a pregnant woman and she gives birth prematurely (abort) but there is no serious injury, the offender must be fined whatever the woman's husband demands and the court allows. But if there is serious injury, you are to take life for life, eye for eye, tooth for tooth, hand for hand, foot for foot, burn for burn, wound for wound, bruise for bruise" (Exodus 21:22-25).

Though there are not many passages in the bible that teach on the topic of abortion, God still speaks against the killing of innocent children and babies. In Psalm 106, "God said of his people; "They mingled with the nations and adopted their customs. They worshiped their idols which became a snare to them. They sacrificed their sons and their daughter to demons. They shed innocent blood, the blood of their sons and daughters whom they sacrificed to the idols of Canaan and the land was desecrated by their blood."

God hates the practice of abortion just as he hates all acts of sins known and unknown. But he has provided the remedy for sin; Jesus Christ the savior of the world. "For God so loved the world that he gave his one and only Son, that whoever believes in him shall not perish but have eternal life (John 3:16). Whoever is an infinite pronoun describing an infinite number. This number includes all who will believe in Jesus Christ and all who are believing in Jesus Christ and all who have believed in Jesus Christ have life everlasting regardless of the nature of sin committed which includes abortion. But this is not the license to practice abortion.

Sexual Harassment

Unwelcome sexual advances, requests for sexual favors, and other verbal or physical conduct of a sexual nature that tends to create a hostile or offensive work environment. This is a general workplace definition of sexual harassment. It is a zero-tolerance policy in all workplaces across USA.

To be precise sexual harassment must be defined as a continue unwelcome advances, requests for sexual favors, and other verbal or physical conduct of a sexual nature by any human being everywhere at any time here on earth. Therefore, sexual harassment must be a zero-tolerance policy in all workplaces, homes, towns, cities and villages in the world.

No one is to be subjected to sexual harassment though no one is immured from sexual harassment. The workplace will not define the root cause of sexual harassment but the word of God does. The root cause of sexual harassment is the bedroom of Adam and Eve. It is the deprived condition of our humanity.

Behind rape, adultery, and fornication is sexual harassment. Though the bible explicitly does not mention the name sexual harassment implicitly it does.

Joseph refused to have sexual relationship with a wife of Potiphar who constantly harassed him to have sex with her;

"Meanwhile, Joseph had been delivered to Egypt and turned over to Potiphar, one of Pharaoh's court officials and the Commander-in-Chief of the imperial guards. An Egyptian, he bought Joseph from the Ishmaelites, who had brought him down there.

But the LORD was with Joseph. He became a very prosperous man while in the house of his Egyptian master, 3 who could see that the LORD was with Joseph, because the LORD made everything prosper that Joseph did. 4 That's how Joseph pleased Potiphar as he served him. Eventually, Potiphar appointed Joseph as overseer of his entire household. Moreover, he entrusted everything that he owned into his care. From the time, he appointed Joseph to be overseer over his entire household and everything that he owned, the LORD blessed the household of the Egyptian because of Joseph. The LORD's blessing rested on Joseph, whether in Potiphar's household or in

Potiphar's fields. Everything that he owned, he entrusted into Joseph's care. He never concerned himself about anything, except for the food he ate.

Potiphar's Wife Accuses Joseph of sexual harassment though it was her who continuously harassed Joseph for sex.

Now Joseph was well built and good looking. That's why, sometime later, Joseph's master's wife looked straight at Joseph and propositioned him: "Come on! Let's have a little sex!"

But he refused, telling his master's wife, "Look! My master doesn't have to worry about anything in the house with me in charge, and he has entrusted everything into my care. No one has more authority in this house than I do. He has withheld nothing from me, except you, and that's because you're his wife. So how can I commit such a horrible evil? How can I sin against God?"

She kept on talking to him like this day after day, but he wouldn't listen to her. Not only would he refuse to have sex with her, he refused even to stay around her. One day, though, he went into the house to do his work. None of the household servants were inside, so she grabbed Joseph by his outer garment and demanded "Let's have some sex!"

Instead, Joseph ran outside, leaving his outer garment still in her hand. When she realized that he had left his outer garment right there in her hand, she ran outside and yelled for her household servants. "Look!" she cried out. "My husband brought in a Hebrew man to humiliate us. He came in here to have sex with me, but I screamed out loud! When he heard, me starting to scream, he left his outer garment with me and fled outside." She kept his outer garment by her side until Joseph's master came home, and then this is what she told him: "That Hebrew slave whom you brought to us came in here to rape me. But when I started to scream, he left his outer garment with me and ran outside."

Finally, Joseph is locked in prison for refusing to sin against God

When Joseph's master heard his wife's claim to the effect that "This is how your servant treated me," he flew into a rage, arrested Joseph, and locked him up in the same prison where the king's prisoners were confined. So, Joseph remained there in prison (Genesis 39:1-20).

Sexual harassment feeds on continue sexual thoughts in the minds towards someone other than the spouse. That is why there is a continue need for our minds to be renewed by the word of God (Romans 12:2).

Listen to this bible story again. A brother loved his sister and raped her after long periods of sexual harassments;

'In the course of time, Amnon son of David fell in love with Tamar, the beautiful sister of Absalom son of David. Amnon became so obsessed with his sister Tamar that he made himself ill. She was a virgin, and it seemed impossible for him to do anything to her.

Now Amnon had an adviser named Jonadab son of Shimeah, David's brother. Jonadab was a very shrewd man. He asked Amnon, "Why do you, the king's son, look so haggard morning after morning? Won't you tell me?"

Amnon said to him, "I'm in love with Tamar, my brother Absalom's sister."

"Go to bed and pretend to be ill," Jonadab said. "When your father comes to see you, say to him, 'I would like my sister Tamar to come and give me something to eat. Let her prepare the food in my sight so I may watch her and then eat it from her hand.'"

So Amnon lay down and pretended to be ill. When the king came to see him, Amnon said to him, "I would like my sister Tamar to come and make some special bread in my sight, so I may eat from her hand."

BEDROOM OF ADAM AND EVE

David sent word to Tamar at the palace: "Go to the house of your brother Amnon and prepare some food for him." So, Tamar went to the house of her brother Amnon, who was lying down. She took some dough, kneaded it, made the bread in his sight and baked it. Then she took the pan and served him the bread, but he refused to eat.

"Send everyone out of here," Amnon said. So, everyone left him. Then Amnon said to Tamar, "Bring the food here into my bedroom so I may eat from your hand." And Tamar took the bread she had prepared and brought it to her brother Amnon in his bedroom. But when she took it to him to eat, he grabbed her and said, "Come to bed with me, my sister."

"No, my brother!" she said to him. "Don't force me! Such a thing should not be done in Israel! Don't do this wicked thing. What about me? Where could I get rid of my disgrace? And what about you? You would be like one of the wicked fools in Israel. Please speak to the king; he will not keep me from being married to you." But he refused to listen to her, and since he was stronger than she, he raped her.

Then Amnon hated her with intense hatred. In fact, he hated her more than he had loved her. Amnon said to her, "Get up and get out!"

"No!" she said to him. "Sending me away would be a greater wrong than what you have already done to me."

But he refused to listen to her. He called his personal servant and said, "Get this woman out of my sight and bolt the door after her." So, his servant put her out and bolted the door after her. She was wearing an ornate robe, for this was the kind of garment the virgin daughters of the king wore. Tamar put ashes on her head and tore the ornate robe she was wearing. She put her hands on her head and went away, weeping aloud as she went.

Her brother Absalom said to her, "Has that Amnon, your brother, been with you? Be quiet for now, my sister; he is your brother. Don't take this thing to heart." And Tamar lived in her brother Absalom's house, a desolate woman.

When King David heard all this, he was furious. And Absalom never said a word to Amnon, either good or bad; he hated Amnon because he had disgraced his sister Tamar" (2 Samuel 13:1-22).

At the end of this event Absalom hated his brother Amnon for raping their sister Tamar that he killed him (2 Samuel 13:23-39).

Sexual harassment can happen by anyone to anyone. It can happen intentionally or unintentionally. It happens amongst us because of sin. But through the blood of our Lord Jesus sexual harassment can and will be stopped. It is wise not to entertain sexual thoughts in our minds that may lead to sexual acts with people other than our spouse. If we do, we have Jesus besides and in us through his spirit and he will be able to cleanse us from all unrighteousness;

John the apostle of Jesus Christ said, "If we confess our sins, he is faithful and just and will forgive us our sins and purify us from all unrighteousness" (1John 1:9).

Paul urged us to feed our minds with the word of God daily. "Do not conform to the pattern of this world, but be transformed by the renewing of your mind. Then you will be able to test and approve what God's will is--his good, pleasing and perfect will (Romans 12:2).

Adultery

Adultery is when a married man has sexual relationship with a married woman who is not his wife and when a married woman has sexual relationship with a married man who is not her husband. Sex between a husband and a wife was meant to be enjoyed in a marriage relationship. But affair in the marriage relationship disowners' marriage vows therefore turns into adultery which is one of the products of the bedroom of Adam and Eve.

Adultery is a fountain of many issues in a family which may lead to unhappiness, depression, divorce and even murder in case of King David.

David and Bathsheba;

In the spring, at the time when kings go off to war, David sent Joabout with the king's men and the whole Israelite army. They destroyed the Ammonites and besieged Rabbah. But David remained in Jerusalem.

One evening David got up from his bed and walked around on the roof of the palace. From the roof, he saw a woman bathing. The woman was very beautiful, and David sent someone to find out about her. The man said, "She is Bathsheba, the daughter of Eliam and the wife of Uriah the Hittite." Then David sent messengers to get her. She came to him, and he slept with her. (Now she was purifying herself from her monthly uncleanness.) Then she went back home. The woman conceived and sent word to David, saying, "I am pregnant."

So, David sent this word to Joab: "Send me Uriah the Hittite." And Joab sent him to David. When Uriah came to him, David asked him how Joab was, how the soldiers were and how the war was going. Then David said to Uriah, "Go down to your house and wash your feet." So Uriah left the palace, and a gift from the king was sent after him. But Uriah slept at the entrance to the palace with all his master's servants and did not go down to his house.

David was told, "Uriah did not go home." So, he asked Uriah, "Haven't you just come from a military campaign? Why didn't you go home?"

Uriah said to David, "The ark and Israel and Judah are staying in tents, and my commander Joab and my lord's men are camped in the open country. How could I go to my house to eat and drink and make love to my wife? As surely as you live, I will not do such a thing!"

Then David said to him, "Stay here one more day, and tomorrow I will send you back." So, Uriah remained in Jerusalem that day and the next. At David's invitation, he ate and drank with him, and David made him drunk. But in the evening Uriah went out to sleep on his mat among his master's servants; he did not go home.

In the morning, David wrote a letter to Joab and sent it with Uriah. In it he wrote, "Put Uriah out in front where the fighting is fiercest. Then withdraw from him so he will be struck down and die."

So, while Joab had the city under siege, he put Uriah at a place where he knew the strongest defenders were. When the men of the city came out and fought against Joab, some of the men in David's army fell; moreover, Uriah the Hittite died.

Joab sent David a full account of the battle. He instructed the messenger: "When you have finished giving the king this account of the battle, the king's anger may flare up, and he may ask you, 'Why did you get so close to the city to fight? Didn't you know they would shoot arrows from the wall? Who killed Abimelech son of Jerub-Besheth? Didn't a woman drop an upper millstone on him from the wall, so that he died in Thebez? Why did you get so close to the wall?' If he asks you this, then say to him, 'moreover, your servant Uriah the Hittite is dead.'"

The messenger set out, and when he arrived he told David everything Joab had sent him to say. The messenger said to David, "The men overpowered us and came out against us in the open, but we drove them back to the entrance of the city gate. Then the archers shot arrows at your servants from the wall, and some of the king's men died. Moreover, your servant Uriah the Hittite is dead."

BEDROOM OF ADAM AND EVE

David told the messenger, "Say this to Joab: 'Don't let this upset you; the sword devours one as well as another. Press the attack against the city and destroy it.' Say this to encourage Joab."

When Uriah's wife heard that her husband was dead, she mourned for him. After the time of mourning was over, David had her brought to his house, and she became his wife and bore him a son. But the thing David had done displeased the Lord"' (2 Samuel 11).

Adultery can also be committed in our mind as Jesus said it "but the things that proceed out of the mouth come from the heart, and those defile the man. For out of the heart come evil thoughts, murders, adulteries, fornications, thefts, false witness, and slanders. These are the things which defile the man; but to eat with unwashed hands does not defile the man" (Matthew 15:18-20). Jesus said it again, "You have heard that it was said, 'YOU SHALL NOT COMMIT ADULTERY'; but I say to you that everyone who looks at a woman with lust for her has already committed adultery with her in his heart.... (Mathew 5: 27).

Adultery is sin therefore it must not be entertained in our marriage relationship. If it does happen we have the blood of Jesus Christ that forgives us all from all unrighteousness (1John 1:8-9). This again is not a license to living in adulterous condition knowingly or unknowingly.

Sexual relationship with your spouse is not adultery. See what the bible says about lawful sex among married couple in the article a Christian teen expert December 31:2015 about sex by Kelli Mahoney towards the end of this chapter.

Fornication

Fornication is a sexual intercourse performed between unmarried male and unmarried female. Sex intercourse was meant to be done in a marriage relationship and not outside marriage.

The word of God teaches all people to flee from all forms of sexual immorality.

"Flee from sexual immorality. All other sins a person commits are outside the body, but whoever sins sexually, sins against their own body. Do you not know that your bodies are temples of the Holy Spirit, who is in you, whom you have received from God? You are not your own; you were bought at a price. Therefore, honor God with your bodies" (1 Corinthians 6:18-20).

Elsewhere in the New Testament, it is written again about sexual immorality saying;

"Now for the matters you wrote about: "It is good for a man not to have sexual relations with a woman." But since sexual immorality is occurring, each man should have sexual relations with his own wife, and each woman with her own husband. The husband should fulfill his marital duty to his wife, and likewise the wife to her husband. The wife does not have authority over her own body but yields it to her husband. In the same way, the husband does not have authority over his own body but yields it to his wife. Do not deprive each other except perhaps by mutual consent and for a time, so that you may devote yourselves to prayer. Then come together again so that Satan will not tempt you because of your lack of self-control. I say this as a concession, not as a command. I wish that all of you were as I am. But each of you has your own gift from God; one has this gift, another has that. Now to the unmarried and the widows I say: It is good for them to stay unmarried, as I do. But if they cannot control themselves, they should marry, for it is better to marry than to burn with passion" (1 Corinthians 7:1-9).

In both passages, Apostle Paul warned the church of Corinth not to indulge in sexual immorality because the body of a believer is the home of the Holy Spirit. God dwells in us in Christ through the Spirit. Therefore, we must glorify God together with the body and the Spirit in us. When we have sexual intercourse with someone other than our spouse we are committing sexual immorality.

Sexual intercourse in marriage relationship is the duty of both spouses which the word of God says ought to be fulfilled. The husband should fulfill his marital duty to his wife, and likewise the wife to her husband (1 Corinthians 7:3). It is not wrong to have sex with the spouse since both of you are doing what is intended to be done rightly as married couple.

Can a Christian practice fornication? The answer is yes but he is not supposed to do so since his body is the temple of the Holy Spirit. Apostle Paul heard that there were Christians in the Corinthians church doing fornication with one another even with their mothers which was worse than what was practiced among pagans. He was very quick to warn them of deadly consequences of their actions.

"It is actually reported that there is sexual immorality among you, and of a kind that even pagans do not tolerate: A man is sleeping with his father's wife. And you are proud! Shouldn't you rather have gone into mourning and have put out of your fellowship the man who has been doing this? For my part, even though I am not physically present, I am with you in spirit. As one who is present with you in this way, I have already passed judgment in the name of our Lord Jesus on the one who has been doing this. So, when you are assembled and I am with you in spirit, and the power of our Lord Jesus is present, hand this man over to Satan for the destruction of the flesh, so that his spirit may be saved on the day of the Lord" (1 Corinthians 5:1-5).

Sexual immorality is sin and will lead into hell if not confessed and forgiven by the blood of Jesus before death (Galatian 5:19-21). Apostle John while in spirit saw those who committed sins {including sexual immorality} and died before accepting Jesus Christ that there will be thrown into the lake of fire. These people will experience second death.

"But the cowardly, the unbelieving, the vile, the murderers, the sexually immoral, those who practice magic arts, the idolaters and all liars-they will be consigned to the fiery lake of burning sulfur. This is the second death" (Revelation 21:8). Fornication is also the product of the bedroom of Adam and Eve. It is rooted in total depravity.

Divorce

Divorce is a permanent separation by court of a lawful married relationship between a wife and a husband. In Christian circles the end of marriage is the death of one or both spouses and not by the court. Divorce is a separation of a marriage by lawful authority between a man and his wife or between a wife and her husband. But the marriage is said to be there until one of the couples dies.

"For example, by law a married woman is bound to her husband if he is alive, but if her husband dies, she is released from the law of marriage.

References for Romans 7:2

So then, if she marries another man while her husband is still alive, she is called an adulteress. But if her husband dies, she is released from that law and is not an adulteress even though she marries another man" (Romans 7: 2-3).

Though Paul is talking about the law, and not divorce, his example shades light to what happens in marriage when one spouse dies. Paul suggests that there is no longer marriage. The remaining spouse is free to get married. Death and only death brings the ultimate end to marriage. Adultery and any other unfaithfulness in marriage can be reconcilable and forgiven through the blood of Jesus except death of the spouse or both.

God intended rightful marriage relationship between a man and a woman for life.

"The Lord God said, "It is not good for the man to be alone. I will make a helper suitable for him."

Now the Lord God had formed out of the ground all the wild animals and all the birds in the sky. He brought them to the man to see what he would name them; and whatever the man called each living creature, that was its name. So, the man gave names to all the livestock, the birds in the sky and all the wild animals.

But for Adam no suitable helper was found. So, the Lord God caused the man to fall into a deep sleep; and while he was sleeping, he took one of the man's ribs and then closed up the place with flesh. Then the Lord God made a woman from the rib he had taken out of the man, and he brought her to the man.

The man said,

"This is now bone of my bones and flesh of my flesh; she shall be called 'woman,' for she was taken out of man."

That is why a man leaves his father and mother and is united to his wife, and they become one flesh.

Adam and his wife were both naked, and they felt no shame" (Genesis 2: 18-24).

God initiated marriage and then ordained it. Therefore, what God has ordained, no man can separate.

"Haven't you read," he replied, "that at the beginning the Creator 'made them male and female,' and said, 'For this reason a man will leave his father and mother and be united to his wife, and the two will become one flesh' So they are no longer two, but one flesh. Therefore, what God has joined together, let no one separate" (Matthew 19:4-6).

There is a soul mate bond in marriage between a wife and a husband which cannot be broken.

Marriage is spiritual and must not be taken lightly. Relationship in marriage between a wife and a husband is like the relationship of Christ and his church;

"Husbands, love your wives, just as Christ loved the church and gave himself up for her to make her holy, cleansing her by the washing with water through the word, and to present her to himself as a radiant church, without stain or wrinkle or any other blemish, but holy and blameless. In this same way, husbands ought to love their wives as their own bodies. He who loves his wife loves himself. After all, no one ever hated their own body, but they feed and care for their body, just as Christ does the church- for we are members of his body. "For this reason, a man will leave his father and mother and be united to his wife, and the two will become one flesh." This is a profound mystery-but I am talking about Christ and the church. However, each one of you also must love his wife as he loves himself, and the wife must respect her husband (Eph. 5: 25-33).

Why is there divorce among married couple? It is because of the hardness of human heart due to depravity. Marriage was meant to be a lifelong bond between a wife and a husband till death.

Because of the heart, sinful issues, divorce certificate is granted to end marriage relationship though the bond between the two remains. In case of the 'if clause' in the passage below, refers to putting away the unfaithful spouse and causing separation to occur, but not ending the bond of marriage that was ordained by God.

"If a man marries a woman who becomes displeasing to him because he finds something indecent about her, and he writes her a certificate of divorce, gives it to her and sends her from his house, and if after she leaves his house she becomes the wife of another man, and her second husband dislikes her and writes her a certificate of divorce, gives it to her and sends her from his house, or if he dies, then her first husband, who divorced her, is not allowed to marry her again after she has been defiled. That would be detestable in the eyes of the Lord. Do not bring sin upon the land the Lord your God is giving you as an inheritance (Deuteronomy 24: 1-4).

Our Lord Jesus Christ explained that 'if clause' was given by Moses to the 'innocent party' because of the hardness of our hearts and therefore it is not a license to divorce.

"It was also said, whoever puts away his wife; let him give her a bill of divorce. But I say to you, whoever puts away his wife, apart from a matter of fornication, causes her to commit adultery. And whoever shall marry the one put away commits adultery" (Matthew 5:31-32). "And I say to you, whoever shall put away his wife, if not for fornication, and shall marry another, commits adultery. And the one who marries her put away commits adultery" (Matthew 19:9). "And He said to them, whoever may dismiss his wife and marries another, commits adultery against her. And if a woman puts away her husband and marries another, she commits adultery" (Mark 10:11-12). "Everyone putting away his wife, and marrying another, commits adultery. And everyone marrying her who has been put away from a husband commits adultery" (Luke 16:18).

The purpose of the word of God is to show the righteousness of God and not righteousness of man. In the sight of God divorce is sin, though how messy, painful, and horrible it may be. The initial intent of God was for a man to get married and live a life of harmony together for life. This perfect marriage harmony got destroyed when Adam and Eve sinned against God. Therefore, it is right to say divorce is the fruit of all people everywhere for living in the bedroom of Adam and Eve. The 'If clauses,' or 'exceptional clauses,' that we see in the Bible, are not the final solution to the end of marriage, though they help us get divorced certificates due to our deprived nature.

There is no marriage in heaven, therefore there will be no divorce in heaven (Matthew 22:30).

Hormosexualism

Hormosexualism is a life style that does not follow traditional or normal way of creation order. It is a life style that God himself does not accept. Hormosexualism is one of the acts of our fallen nature. In the beginning, God created man and woman to be wife and husband in order to multiply and fill the earth. God blessed Adam and Eve when they were made. The word of God says, "He created them male and female and blessed them. And he named them "Mankind" when they were created" (Genesis 5:2).

Man, and woman have the liberty to enjoy sexual relationship as married couple. That is a biblical normal of looking at marriage. Man, and woman may get married and not man with another man or woman with another woman. God ordained marriage between man and woman when he made a woman out of the rib of Adam and brought her to Adam. It was easy for God to duplicate Adam, but instead he made a woman suitable for Adam to marry.

"So, the LORD God caused a deep sleep to fall upon the man, and he slept; then He took one of his ribs and closed up the flesh at that place. The LORD God fashioned into a woman the rib which He had taken from the man, and brought her to the man.

The man said,

'This is now bone of my bones,

And flesh of my flesh;
She shall be called Woman, because she was taken out of Man.'

For this reason, a man shall leave his father and his mother, and be joined to his wife; and they shall become one flesh. And the man and his wife were both naked and were not ashamed" (Genesis 2: 21-25).

BEDROOM OF ADAM AND EVE

The word of God calls the lifestyle of Hormosexualism sin. The God punished some people who were practicing homosexual lifestyle in the Old Testament. In fact, God destroyed two entire nations of Sodom and Gomorrah because of the sin of Hormosexualism.

"The two angels arrived at Sodom in the evening, and Lot was sitting in the gateway of the city. When he saw them, he got up to meet them and bowed down with his face to the ground. "My lords," he said, "please turn aside to your servant's house. You can wash your feet and spend the night and then go on your way early in the morning."

"No," they answered, "we will spend the night in the square."

But he insisted so strongly that they did go with him and entered his house. He prepared a meal for them, baking bread without yeast, and they ate. Before they had gone to bed, all the men from every part of the city of Sodom-both young and old-surrounded the house. They called to Lot, "Where are the men who came to you tonight? Bring them out to us so that we can have sex with them."

Lot went outside to meet them and shut the door behind him and said, "No, my friends. Don't do this wicked thing. Look, I have two daughters who have never slept with a man. Let me bring them out to you, and you can do what you like with them. But don't do anything to these men, for they have come under the protection of my roof."

"Get out of our way," they replied. "This fellow came here as a foreigner, and now he wants to play the judge! We'll treat you worse than them." They kept bringing pressure on Lot and moved forward to break down the door.

But the men inside reached out and pulled Lot back into the house and shut the door. Then they struck the men who were at the door of the house, young and old, with blindness so that they could not find the door.

The two men said to Lot, "Do you have anyone else here-sons-in-law, sons or daughters, or anyone else in the city who belongs to you? Get them out of here, because we are going to destroy this place. The outcry to the Lord against its people is so great that he has sent us to destroy it."

So, Lot went out and spoke to his sons-in-law, who were pledged to marry his daughters. He said, "Hurry and get out of this place, because the Lord is about to destroy the city!" But his sons-in-law thought he was joking.

With the coming of dawn, the angels urged Lot, saying, "Hurry! Take your wife and your two daughters who are here, or you will be swept away when the city is punished."

When he hesitated, the men grasped his hand and the hands of his wife and of his two daughters and led them safely out of the city, for the Lord was merciful to them. As soon as they had brought them out, one of them said, "Flee for your lives! Don't look back, and don't stop anywhere in the plain! Flee to the mountains or you will be swept away!"

But Lot said to them, "No, my lords, please! Your servant has found favor in your eyes, and you have shown great kindness to me in sparing my life. But I can't flee to the mountains; this disaster will overtake me, and I'll die. Look, here is a town near enough to run to, and it is small. Let me flee to it-it is very small, isn't it? Then my life will be spared."

He said to him, "Very well, I will grant this request too; I will not overthrow the town you speak of. But flee there quickly, because I cannot do anything until you reach it." (That is why the town was called Zoar.

By the time, Lot reached Zoar, the sun had risen over the land. Then the Lord rained down burning sulfur on Sodom and Gomorrah-from the Lord out of the heavens. Thus, he overthrew those cities and the entire plain, destroying all those living in the cities-and the vegetation in the land.

But Lot's wife looked back, and she became a pillar of salt.

Early the next morning Abraham got up and returned to the place where he had stood before the Lord. He looked down toward Sodom and Gomorrah, toward all the land of the plain, and he saw dense smoke rising from the land, like smoke from a furnace.

So, when God destroyed the cities of the plain, he remembered Abraham, and he brought Lot out of the catastrophe that overthrew the cities where Lot had lived" (Genesis 19:1-19).

Can homosexual life style be cured or forgiven after believing in the Christ Jesus? Yes, and here is what the word of God says in the New Testament;

"Or do you not know that the unrighteous will not inherit the kingdom of God? Do not be deceived; neither fornicators, nor idolaters, nor adulterers, nor effeminate, nor homosexuals, nor thieves, nor the covetous, nor drunkards, nor revilers, nor swindlers, will inherit the kingdom of God. Such were some of you; and listen to the conjunction word 'but' in the following three sentences; but you were washed, but you were sanctified, but you were justified in the name of the Lord Jesus Christ and in the Spirit of our God" (I Corinthians 6: 9-11).

Hormosexualism is a sin like many other sins mentioned in the bible that can be forgiven by the blood of Jesus Christ. The word of God says, "Such were some of you" but no longer now because the blood of Jesus Christ has washed you when you believed. Nothing is impossible with God (Luke 1:27).

Therefore, it is right to say Hormosexualism is one of the products of the bedroom of Adam and Eve. Jesus came to get us out of the bedroom of Adam and Eve but due to disobedience our nature has totally been immersed in depravity that we are unable to come to the knowledge of God without his spirit helping us.

Masturbation

Sexual harassment is done with other people but masturbation is done by oneself. This too is sin. It is a product of the garden of Adam and Eve. Masturbation is sin because it centered on self-glorification and not God glorification. Masturbation is playing with one's body especially private parts in order to arouse false gratification sexually.

Goal of masturbation is self-temporary happiness motivated by unclean minds. If many people are doing it does not make it to be right before our Lord. The word of God says, "Do not conform to the pattern of this world, but be transformed by the renewing of your mind. Then you will be able to test and approve what God's will is--his good, pleasing and perfect will (Rom.12:2).

Pure happiness and joy lies in the word of God and not in personal centered activity;

Psalm 119:35-37 - "Direct me in the path of your commands, for there I find delight. Turn my heart toward your statues and not toward selfish gain. Turn my eyes away from worthless things; preserve my life per your word."

Psalm 119: 10-12- "With all my heart, I have sought you; Do not let me wander from your commandments. Your word I have treasured in my heart that I may not sin against you. Blessed are You, O LORD; teach me your statutes."

Do not twist the word of God to support self-centered gratification. Onan was instructed to sleep with his deceased brother's wife but instead he chose to masturbate. This is not a support verse for masturbation.

Genesis 38:8-10 - "Then Judah said to Onan, 'Lie with your brother's wife and fulfill your duty to her as a brother-in-law to produce offspring for your brother.' But Onan knew that the off-

BEDROOM OF ADAM AND EVE

spring would not be his; so, whenever he lay with his brother's wife he spilled his semen on the ground to keep from producing offspring for his brother. What he did was wicked in the Lord's sight; so, he put him to death also."

Masturbation in any form, whether done by a man or a woman, is a product of the garden of Adam and Eve. It is rooted in human depravity caused by the original sin of Adam and Eve. It is the act of coveting your own body which is at best idolatry. The word of God says;

"Neither... will idolaters...inherit the kingdom of God" (I Corinthians 6:9-10).

And do not become idolaters as were some of them...Therefore, my beloved, flee from idolatry (I Corinthians10:7,14). And what agreement has the temple of God have with idols? (II Cor. 6:16).

Now the works of the flesh are evident...idolatry (Galatians 5:19, 20).

For this you know that no... Idolater has any inheritance in the kingdom of Christ and God (Ephesians 5:5).

Therefore, put to death...covetousness, which is idolatry (Colossians 3:5).

...you turned to God from idols to serve the living and true God (I Thessalonians 1:9).

This sinful act can be forgiven through the blood of our Lord Jesus Christ (1 John1:9). (I Corinthians 5:11).

CHAPTER SIX. QUESTIONS TO ANSWER

Why do we do acts of sins?

How can you treat addiction?

Is depression sinful?

What is suicide?

What is masturbation and why is it sinful?

How can you explain hormosexualism according to Genesis 19:1-19? and Genesis 38:8-10?

What is divorce? Explain Roman 7:2-3

What is fornication and what does 1 Corinthian 6: 18-20 mean to you?

What does the bible say about adultery?

What is Sexual harassment?

What is rape?

What does the bible say about abortion?

Is witchcraft a sin? What does the word of God say about it?

Why is the word of God against any form of idol worshipping?

Is lying a sin?

Define murder?

What is anger?

Can a Christin sin?

Can a Christian live in sin?

How much sin does it take to sin?

Are you a sinner?

Who has the power to forgive sin?

Is your sin forgiven or forgivable?

BEDROOM OF ADAM AND EVE

CHAPTER 7

WHAT DOES THE BIBLE SAY ABOUT SEX?

See what the bible says about lawful sex among married couple in the article a Christian teen expert December 31:2015 about sex by Kelli Mahoney in this chapter. The article also discusses pre-marital sex among teens. I have paraphrased and even added materials to the Kelli article on sex. Kelly starts discussion with a question;

Question: What the Bible Says About...Sex

Let's talk about sex…yes, the "S" word. You may think, with all the warnings about not having sex before marriage that sex is bad, but the Bible says something quite contrary. Sex is biblical, if looked at from a Godly perspective. So, what does the Bible have to say about sex?

Answer:

Sex is a Good Thing

"What? Sex is a good thing? Well, God created sex. He created man and woman to create babies. The Bible says that sex is a way for a husband and wife to express their love for one another. God did create sex to be a beautiful and enjoyable expression of love. Kelli Mahoney: Christian Teens Expert

Genesis 1: 27-28 - "So God created man in his own image, in the image of God he created him; male and female he created them. God blessed them and said to them, "Be fruitful and increase in number;" How could they have been fruitful without sleeping together?

It is said that Adam knew his wife and bore a son. The verb knew meant sexual relationship. Adam had sex with his wife and resulted into a baby. This is lawful sex that lies in the limit of marriage bond. "And Adam knew Eve his wife; and she conceived, and bare Cain, and said, I have gotten a man from the LORD" (Genesis 4:1 KJV) and in the New International Version Bible the same verse says, "Adam made love to his wife Eve, and she became pregnant and gave birth to Cain. She said, "With the help of the LORD I have brought forth a man."

Early own the word of God says, "For this reason a man will leave his father and mother and be united to his wife, and they will become one flesh" (Genesis 2:24).

Proverbs 5:18-19 - "May your fountain be blessed, and may you rejoice in the wife of your youth. A loving doe, a graceful deer - may her breasts satisfy you always, may you ever be captivated by her love."

King of Israel once said, "How beautiful you are and how pleasing, O love, with your delights!" (Song of Songs 7:6).

Apostle Paul wrote, "The body is not meant for sexual immorality, but for the Lord, and the Lord for the body" (1 Corinthians 6:13) So, Sex is Good, but Premarital Sex is Not?

Right. There is a lot of talk going on around you about sex. Sex is in just about every magazine, newspaper, television show, and movie. It is the point of a lot of music. Our world has gotten lax about sex, making it seem like premarital sex is okay because it feels good, but the Bible does not agree. God calls us all to control our passions and wait for marriage.

The word of God is quite clear when it says, "But since there is so much immorality, each man should have his own wife, and each woman her own husband. The husband should fulfill his marital duty to his wife, and likewise the wife to her husband" (1 Corinthians 7:2-3).

It is not right for a married couple to deny each other sex for selfish reasons. In doing so may lead into fights, affairs, and even divorce.

Hebrew writer said, "Marriage should be honored by all, and the marriage bed kept pure, for God will judge the adulterer and all the sexually immoral" (Hebrews 13:4).

Paul admonished the church saying, "It is God's will that you should be sanctified: that you should avoid sexual immorality; that each of you should learn to control his own body in a way that is holy and honorable" (1 Thessalonians 4:3-4).

What if I've Already Had Unlawful Sex?

Everyone falls to sin in some area or another. If your area happens to be sex, there is still hope. While you cannot become a virgin again, you can obtain God's forgiveness. You just have to ask for it and try not to sin that way again. What truly angers God is willful sin, when you know you are sinning and keep on participating in that sin. While giving up sex may be difficult, God calls us to remain sexually pure until marriage.

Can I be forgiven of sexual sin? Yes, you can. The bible speaks of forgiveness of all sins through the blood of Jesus Christ.

"Therefore, my brothers, I want you to know that through Jesus the forgiveness of sins is proclaimed to you. Through him everyone who believes is justified from everything you could not be justified from by the law of Moses" (Acts 13:38-39).

What if I do not want to stop sleeping around? I do like affairs or pre-marital sex.

Here are some of the verses in the Bible that warn us of this reckless and wicked behavior;

"There is a way that appears to be right, but in the end it leads to death" NIV (Proverbs 16:25).

"There is a way that seemeth right unto a man, but the end thereof are the ways of death" KJV (Proverbs 16:25).

If it seems or feels right to us, it does not mean that it is always right or okay with God. God made us and put us here on earth and only God has the final say on our lives. But if we continue living in sin after continuously being warned by God himself in his law then we bear consequences to our deeds.

Apostle Paul had this to say to some of the Christians who continued practicing sexual immoralities despite being warned by the Spirit of God "Therefore God gave them over in the sinful desires of their hearts to sexual impurity for the degrading of their bodies with one another" (Romans 1:24).

But It's So Tempting!

As a Christian you fight off temptation every day. Being tempted is not the sin, but giving into the temptation is. So how do you fight off the temptation? The desire to have sex can be very strong, especially if you have already had sex. It is only by relying on God for strength that you can truly fight off the temptation to have sex.

"No temptation has seized you except what is common to man. And God is faithful; he will not let you be tempted beyond what you can bear. But when you are tempted, he will also provide a way out so that you can stand up under it" (1 Corinthians 10:13). End of paraphrase of Kelli article.

Every person likes doing right thing all the time. It is called ethics. Doing the right thing at workplace, school place, church place or home place is practicing good ethics. In fact, all the companies I have worked for have company ethics. But God has his own ethics stipulated in the Bible. Right ethics on sex is to listen and do to what the word of God says on sex in the Bible.

God created man and woman to enjoy sex in a marriage relationship. Therefore, any sexual acts outside marriage are bad ethics toward God. The answer for bad sex ethics is forgiveness through the blood of Jesus Christ (1 John 1:8-9).

Bad sex ethics includes orgies, rape, fornication, adultery, sexual harassment and even masturbation. All these acts can be forgiven through the blood of Jesus Christ (Acts 13:38-39). But if not forgiven through his blood bad sex ethics would lead to hell;

"The acts of the flesh are obvious: sexual immorality, impurity and debauchery; idolatry and witchcraft; hatred, discord, jealousy, fits of rage, selfish ambition, dissensions, factions and envy; drunkenness, orgies, and the like. I warn you, as I did before, that those who live like this will not inherit the kingdom of God" (Galatian 5:19-21).

CHAPTER SEVEN. QUESTIONS TO ANSWER

What does the bible say about sex?

What do you think about sex?

How do you deal with sex?

Explain 1 Thes. 4: 3-4?

Explain Song of Songs 7:6

Is sex sinful?

Was sex made by God?

Can Jesus, forgive me all my sinful sexual deeds?

Why is sex outside marriage bad?

Can sinful sexual acts lead to hell? Explain Galatian 5:19-21?

Did Adam commit a sex act when he sinned against God?

What is the solution to our bad sexual relationships?

CHAPTER 8

OMISSION AND UNKNOWN SINS

What does the Bible say about sins of omission?

People sometimes speak of sins of commission and sins of omission. Sins of commission are those sinful actions that are proactively done. Lying or stealing are examples of sins of commission. A sin of omission is a sin that takes place because of not doing something that is right. Examples could include not praying, not standing up for what is right, or not sharing Christ with others. James 4:17 is often used as a key verse regarding sins of omission: "So whoever knows the right thing to do and fails to do it, for him it is sin." This overarching theme provides the basis for the concept of a sin of omission.

In Luke 10:30-37 Jesus gives a clear example of a sin of omission in the account of the Good Samaritan. Two different men came upon an injured man who had been robbed and was lying alongside the road. Both men passed by without helping. A third man stopped and helped, proving himself as the one who did the right thing. The two men who did not help could be considered as those committing a sin of omission.

Matthew 25 offers another example regarding the sin of omission. Verses 44-45 note, "Then they also will answer, saying, 'Lord, when did we see you hungry or thirsty or a stranger or naked or sick or in prison, and did not minister to you?' Then he will answer them, saying, 'Truly, I say to you, as you did not do it to one of the least of these, you did not do it to me.'" Here Jesus clearly indicates that our lack of action can be considered sinful.

First John 3:17-18 offers yet another example: "But if anyone has the world's goods and sees his brother in need, yet closes his heart against him, how does God's love abide in him? Little children, let us not love in word or talk but indeed and in truth." John commanded those who follow Jesus to live in ways that show this love to others.

Matthew 5:16 offers an important reason why Christians are to act in ways that help others and not commit sins of omission: "In the same way, let your light shine before others, so that they may see your good works and give glory to your Father who is in heaven." Such actions bring glory to God and point others to God who may not yet know Him. Galatians 6:9 adds, "And let us not grow weary of doing good, for in due season we will reap, if we do not give up."

The apostle Paul was very clear that we are not to be conformed to the world, but rather transform the world through godly living: "Do not be conformed to this world, but be transformed by the renewal of your mind, that by testing you may discern what is the will of God, what is good and acceptable and perfect" (Romans 12:2). This attitude and corresponding actions are vital in both avoiding sins of commission and sins of omission (from Got Questions Ministries on line).

What the bible says about the consequences of committing unknown sin;

"The LORD commanded Moses to tell the people of Israel that anyone who sinned and broke

BEDROOM OF ADAM AND EVE

any of the LORD's commands without intending to, would have to observe the following rules.

"If it is the High Priest who sins and so brings guilt on the people, he shall present a young bull without any defects and sacrifice it to the LORD for his sin. He shall bring the bull to the entrance of the Tent, put his hand on its head, and kill it there in the LORD's presence. Then the High Priest shall take some of the bull's blood and carry it into the Tent. He shall dip his finger in the blood and sprinkle it in front of the sacred curtain seven times. Then he shall put some of the blood on the projections at the corners of the incense altar in the Tent. He shall pour out the rest of the blood at the base of the altar used for burning sacrifices, which is at the entrance of the Tent. From this bull, he shall take all the fat, the fat on the internal organs, the kidneys and the fat on them, and the best part of the liver. The priest shall take this fat and burn it on the altar used for the burnt offerings, just as he does with the fat from the animal killed for the fellowship offering. But he shall take its skin, all its flesh, its head, its legs, and its internal organs, including the intestines, carry it all outside the camp to the ritually clean place where the ashes are poured out, and there he shall burn it on a wood fire.

If it is the whole community of Israel that sins and becomes guilty of breaking one of the LORD's commands without intending to, then as soon as the sin becomes known, the community shall bring a young bull as a sin offering. They shall bring it to the Tent of the LORD's presence; The leaders of the community shall put their hands on its head, and it shall be killed there. The High Priest shall take some of the bull's blood into the Tent, dip his finger in it, and sprinkle it in front of the curtain seven times. He shall put some of the blood on the projections at the corners of the incense altar inside the Tent and pour out the rest of it at the base of the altar used for burning sacrifices, which is at the entrance of the Tent. Then he shall take all its fat and burn it on the altar. He shall do the same thing with this bull as he does with the bull for the sin offering, and in this way, he shall make the sacrifice for the people's sin, and they will be forgiven. Then he shall take the bull outside the camp and burn it, just as he burns the bull offered for his own sin. This is an offering to take away the sin of the community. If it is a ruler who sins and becomes guilty of breaking one of the LORD's commands without intending to, then as soon as the sin is called to his attention, he shall bring as his offering a male goat without any defects. He shall put his hand on its head and kill it on the north side of the altar, where the animals for the burnt offerings are killed. This is an offering to take away sin. The priest shall dip his finger in the blood of the animal, put it on the projections at the corners of the altar, and pour out the rest of it at the base of the altar. Then he shall burn all of its fat on the altar, just as he burns the fat of the animals killed for the fellowship offerings. In this way, the priest shall offer the sacrifice for the sin of the ruler, and he will be forgiven.

If any of you people sin and become guilty of breaking one of the LORD's commands without intending to, then as soon as the sin is called to your attention, you shall bring as your offering a female goat without any defects. You shall put your hand on its head and kill it on the north side of the altar, where the animals for the burnt offerings are killed. The priest shall dip his finger in the blood of the animal, put it on the projections at the corners of the altar, and pour out the rest of it at the base of the altar. Then he shall remove all its fat, just as the fat is removed from the animals killed for the fellowship offerings, and he shall burn it on the altar as an odor pleasing to the LORD. In this way, the priest shall offer the sacrifice for the man's sin, and he will be forgiven.

If you bring a sheep as a sin offering, it must be a female without any defects. You shall put your hand on its head and kill it on the north side of the altar, where the animals for the burnt

offerings are killed. The priest shall dip his finger in the blood of the animal, put it on the projections at the corners of the altar, and pour out the rest of it at the base of the altar. Then he shall remove all its fat, just as the fat is removed from the sheep killed for the fellowship offerings, and he shall burn it on the altar along with the food offerings given to the LORD. In this way, the priest shall offer the sacrifice for your sin, and you will be forgiven" (Levit. 4:3-35).

The writer of Psalms also confirmed that God sees and forgives our hidden sins;

The heavens declare the glory of God; the skies proclaim the work of his hands.

Day after day they pour forth speech; night after night they reveal knowledge.

They have no speech; they use no words; no sound is heard from them.

Yet their voice goes out into all the earth, their words to the ends of the world.

In the heavens, God has pitched a tent for the sun.

It is like a bridegroom coming out of his chamber, like a champion rejoicing to run his course.

It rises at one end of the heavens and makes its circuit to the other; nothing is deprived of its warmth.

The law of the Lord is perfect, refreshing the soul.

The statutes of the Lord are trustworthy, making wise the simple.

The precepts of the Lord are right, giving joy to the heart.

The commands of the Lord are radiant, giving light to the eyes.

The fear of the Lord is pure, enduring forever.

The decrees of the Lord are firm, and all of them are righteous.

They are more precious than gold, than much pure gold; they are sweeter than honey, than honey from the honeycomb.

By them your servant is warned; in keeping them there is great reward.

But who can discern their own errors?

Forgive my hidden faults.

Keep your servant also from willful sins; may they not rule over me.

Then I will be blameless, innocent of great transgression.

May these words of my mouth and this meditation of my heart be pleasing in your sight,

Lord, my Rock and my Redeemer (Psalms 19).

The Psalmists mentioned hidden faults in the prayer. What are hidden faults? These were hidden faults that he could not know. These were the unknown sins which God needed to forgive him. In other words, the Psalmists knew he had committed many unknown sins in his life and God could forgive them all.

The apostle John known as the beloved apostle of Jesus Christ wrote about the power of the blood of Jesus in forgiving us all our sins including those unknown.

"This is the message we have heard from him and declare to you: God is light; in him there is no darkness at all. If we claim to have fellowship with him and yet walk in the darkness, we lie and do not live out the truth. But if we walk in the light, as he is in the light, we have fellowship with one another, and the blood of Jesus, his Son, purifies us from all sin. If we claim to be without sin, we deceive ourselves and the truth is not in us. If we confess our sins, he is faithful and just and will forgive us our sins and purify us from all unrighteousness. If we claim we have not sinned, we make him out to be a liar and his word is not in us" (1 John 1:5-10).

BEDROOM OF ADAM AND EVE

John says that if we confess our sins implying the sins we commit in our daily life; Jesus Christ is able to forgive them all. John continued saying in doing that Jesus Christ is also able to purify us from all unrighteousness. The all here means all unknown sins that we have committed or will commit in life. The blood of Jesus Christ will clean us from all of them completely.

Every human being commits omission sins or unknown sins. God understands this and thus why he has provided the blood of his son Jesus Christ to cleanse his own people from all unrighteousness. In fact, the law requires that nearly everything be cleansed with blood, and without the shedding of blood there is no forgiveness (Hebrews 9:22).

CHAPTER EIGHT. QUESTIONS TO ANSWER

What is omission sin?

What does the Bible say about omission sins?

What is unknown sin?

What does the word of God say about unknown sins?

CHAPTER 9

ORIGINAL SIN VS THE IMAGE OF GOD

Image of God in a broader sense

Man, was made by the transcended God. Genesis 1:1 says, "In the beginning God". This statement means that before God made all that he made He was there. God has no beginning and no ending. God is the great I AM. God IS the cause of all things that are in existence.

God made the body of man first and it was lifeless until he made the spirit and breathed in it. Therefore, it is right to say that the body without the spirit is dead though the same God makes both. God can bring the dead rotten body unit again with the departed spirit. The story of Lazarus in the bible is a great example.

"Then Jesus, deeply moved again, came to the tomb. It was a cave, and a stone lay against it.

Jesus said, "Take away the stone." Martha, the sister of the dead man, said to him, "Lord, by this time there will be an odor, for he has been dead four days." Jesus said to her, "Did I not tell you that if you believed you would see the glory of God?" So, they took away the stone. And Jesus lifted his eyes and said, "Father, I thank you that you have heard me. I knew that you always hear me, but I said this because the people standing around, that they may believe that you sent me." When he had said these things, he cried out with a loud voice, "Lazarus, come out."

The man who had died came out, his hands and feet bound with linen strips, and his face wrapped with a cloth. Jesus said to them, "Unbind him, and let him go" (John 11: 38-44).

God made man due to his own divine counsel and purpose. God wanted man ultimately to know him as his creator, love him with all his heart, live with him in the blessed eternal life and finally praising and glorifying him.

Second reason God made man on earth was to fill this planet with his posterities, subdue the earth and have dominion over the earth.

What does the bible mean when it says man is the image of God? Does it suggest that the body of man is the image of God, or just the spirit of man, or both the body and the spirit?

The bible is quite clear when it speaks of a single human being with body and spirit as the image of God. Then God said, "Let us make mankind in our image, in our likeness, so that they may rule over the fish in the sea and the birds in the sky, over the livestock and all the wild animals, and over all the creatures that move along the ground" (Genesis 1:26).

God called mankind the image of God though he did not explain the nature or meaning of the phrase the image of God. The Bible is silent on this though God revealed what mankind was going to do in relationship to the edworld. Mankind was going to rule over all creatures.

God also said that mankind was going to have a likeness as God. This means that the mankind as the image of God would also have the likeness of God.

BEDROOM OF ADAM AND EVE

Even after the fall mankind was and still is the image of God; "Whoever sheds human blood, by humans shall their blood be shed; for in the image of God has God made mankind" (Genesis 9:6).

Two facts I have learnt from the word image of God; Man, is not God though made in the image of God. Man, is subservient to God alone and not to creation. God gave mankind dominion over creation and not worship or idolize it.

Mankind as image of God means man or woman both physically and spiritually is the image of God regardless of religious stand in the world. Each person as an individual is the image of God. There is no individual, tribe or race above one another. God calls us his images with equal status. There is no room for racism or tribalism since we are all made equal in the eyes of God.

Therefore, every mankind in the world has the capacity to reason and use intellect. Mankind has moral and understandings of things. These items in mankind distinguish him from animals and therefore enforce the fact that he is special being in the eyes of the creator. Mankind is the image of the highest being called the transcended God because God so called him himself.

In the New Testament, the phrase the image of God is attributed to Jesus Christ too. The Apostle Paul declared Jesus superior over all creation." He is the image of the invisible God, the firstborn of all creation. For by Him all things were created, both in the heavens and on earth, visible and invisible, whether thrones or dominions or rulers or authorities-- all things have been created through Him and for Him...." (Colossians 1: 15-16).

The Bible says if we have seen Jesus then we have seen the father also; "Jesus answered: "Don't you know me, Philip, even after I have been among you such a long time? Anyone who has seen me has seen the Father. How can you say, 'Show us the Father' (John14; 9)? Elsewhere it is said that Jesus is God and has direct link with his father in heaven, "No one has ever seen God, but the one and only Son, who is himself God and is in closest relationship with the Father, has made him known" (John 1:18).

For mankind to experience true and perfect image of God as originally intended by God the creator, he must be a believer or saint of our Lord and savior Jesus Christ. "For those God foreknew he also predestined to be conformed to the image of his Son, that he might be the firstborn among many brothers and sisters" (Romans 8: 29).

Therefore, we can say that before the fall mankind (Adam and Eve) lived full and perfect life as image of God. Adam and his wife Eve could use their perfect reason, perfect intellect and perfect knowledge to glorify God. They had perfect morals between one another before the fall.

But after the fall, the life of mankind as the image of God in broader sense was distorted but not destroyed. Mankind continued to be unique than animals. He continued to reflect the morals, intellect, reason, and knowledge given by God though not in good standing with God.

Image of God in a narrow sense

The life of mankind as the image of God is restored by being in Jesus Christ alone. The original sin did not destroy mankind as the image of God in the broader understanding though distorted it but destroyed the upright standing with God the creator. This is a narrow understanding of the image of God. After the fall mankind no longer enjoyed the fellowship with God except with Christ though God still calls him his image.

Mankind as the image of God means mankind not in parts. This mankind can be a redeemed image of God or un redeemed image of God. Either way God sees mankind as the image of God all the time. The image of God that knows Jesus Christ will live in glorification with him in heaven for ever. While the image of God that does not know Jesus, Christ will spend eternity in hell.

CHAPTER NINE. QUESTIONS TO ANSWER

What is the image of God?

What is the image of God in a broader sense?

What is the image of God in the narrow sense?

Explain Genesis 9:6?

What did the original sin do to the image of God?

What does it mean by saying that man is subservient to God alone and not to create?

How did man and woman live before the fall?

Who is the image of God in the New Testament?

BEDROOM OF ADAM AND EVE

CHAPTER 10

JESUS TOOK CARE OF ORIGINAL SIN AND ALL ITS FRUITS?

Jesus became truly man

The writings in the Old Testament pointed to the coming of Jesus Christ in flesh as the Messiah; Prophet Isaiah wrote, "Therefore the Lord himself will give you a sign: The virgin will be with child and will give birth to a son, and will call him Immanuel" (Isaiah 7:14). Again, Isaiah said, "For to us a child is born, to us a son is given, and the government will be on his shoulders. And he will be called Wonderful Counselor, Mighty God, Everlasting Father, Prince of Peace" (Isaiah 9:6). While one of the Minor Prophets Micah also prophesied the birth of Jesus saying, "But you, Bethlehem Ephrathah, though you are small among the clans of Judah, out of you will come for me one who will be ruler over Israel, whose origins are from of old, from ancient times" (Micah 5:2). In the New Testament prophesies about the birth of Jesus Christ were fulfilled when Jesus was born. First the Angel Gabriel told Mary and Joseph that there were going to have a son and would call him Jesus, "She will give birth to a son, and you are to give him the name Jesus, because he will save his people from their sins." All this took place to fulfill what the Lord had said through the prophet: "The virgin will conceive and give birth to a son, and they will call him Immanuel" (which means "God with us") (Matthew 1:21-23).The time Jesus was born Mary wrapped him in a cloth and laid him in a manger since there was no good room for them to put Jesus in; "And she gave birth to her firstborn son and wrapped him in swaddling clothes and laid him in a manger, because there was no place for them in the inn" (Luke 2:7).

After Jesus was born the shepherds confirmed the birth of Jesus Christ; Luke wrote; "When the angels went away from them into heaven, the shepherds said to one another, "Let us go over to Bethlehem and see this thing that has happened, which the Lord has made known to us." And they went with haste and found Mary and Joseph, and the baby lying in a manger. And when they saw it, they made known the saying that had been told them concerning this child. And all who heard it wondered at what the shepherds told them. But Mary treasured up all these things, pondering them in her heart. And the shepherds returned, glorifying and praising God for all they had heard and seen, as it had been told them" (Luke 2:15-20).

Jesus grew up like one of us with body and spirit here on earth. People saw him including his parents who nurtured him physically and spiritually as he grew up in wisdom. John called the beloved disciple of Jesus Christ said, "The true light, which gives light to everyone, was coming into the world. He was in the world, and the world was made through him, yet the world did not know him. He came to his own, and his own people did not receive him. But to all who did receive him, who believed in his name, he gave the right to become children of God, who were born, not of blood or of the will of the flesh or of the will of man, but of God. And the Word became flesh and dwelt among us, and we have seen his glory, glory as of the only Son from the Father, full of grace and truth" (John 1:9-14).

John again said "For God so loved the world, that he gave his only Son, that whoever believes in him should not perish but have eternal life (John 3:16). The apostle Paul wrote to the Galatians about the birth of Jesus Christ, "But when the fullness of time had come, God sent forth his Son, born of woman, born under the law" (Galatians 4:4). Jesus Christ was born human therefore he was truly human like all of us. He felt hungry and thirsty. He walked, slept and even got tired. He suffered and died like human beings. He was buried in the grave.

Jesus Christ died.

The question we need to answer is this, why did he became man? We know that God the Father, God the Son, and God the Holy Spirit is ONE God who revealed himself into those three persons, not three gods. Christians worship ONE God who revealed himself into three persons. Before Jesus incarnated in the world he existed as God the son internally with no beginning and no ending. The three persons had everlasting ontological relationship among themselves forever. Why then did Christ come to be born as human and lived among us leaving heavenly glory of his father? This is the answer; Christ was born to die. We deduce from scripture that Christ was both fully man and fully God. As God, he never sinned while living here on earth though he was tempted in all points. "He committed no sin, and no deceit was found in his mouth" (1 Peter 2: 22).

The writer of Hebrews wrote; "For we do not have a high priest who is unable to empathize with our weaknesses, but we have one who has been tempted in every way, just as we are--yet he did not sin" (Hebrews 4:15). The apostle Paul said, "God made him who had no sin to be sin for us, so that in him we might become the righteousness of God (2 Corinthians 5:21). The disciple John wrote, "But you know that he appeared so that he might take away our sins. And in him is no sin" (1 John 3:5).

Jesus Christ was born so that he would die to bring life to all his people that believe. Jesus became human to destroy the original sin brought by Adam and Eve by dying on the cross. He had to be human to suffer for us and ultimately die for us believers. Prophet Isaiah described Jesus as Messiah in this way, "He was despised and rejected by mankind, a man of suffering, and familiar with pain. Like one from whom people hide their faces he was despised, and we held him in low esteem. Surely, he took up our pain and bore our suffering, yet we considered him punished by God, stricken by him, and afflicted but he was pierced for our transgressions, he was crushed for our iniquities; the punishment that brought us peace was on him, and by his wounds we are healed. We all, like sheep, have gone astray, each of us has turned to our own way; and the LORD has laid on him the iniquity of us all. He was oppressed and afflicted, yet he did not open his mouth; he was led like a lamb to the slaughter, and as a sheep before its shearers is silent, so he did not open his mouth" (Isaiah 53: 3-7).

Adam brought original sin to mankind that alienated mankind from enjoying true fellowship with God. Jesus came into this world as human to die for our sins and bring life everlasting to those that believed in him.

Double imputation in Christ

God worked divine miraculous act through Jesus Christ's death on the cross. The death of Jesus Christ brought justification through faith to all saints of God. Jesus death brought double imputation to all believers in him. Apostle Paul wrote that, "God made him who had no sin to be sin for us, so that in him we might become the righteousness of God (2 Corinthians 5:21).

The first part of the sentence suggests that our sin or sins are imputed on Christ. Jesus Christ took our sins away therefore we are now justified before God the father. Paul said right when he said, "Therefore, there is now no condemnation for those who are in Christ Jesus, because through Christ Jesus the law of the Spirit who gives life has set you free from the law of sin and death" (Romans 8:1-2). Jesus Christ took our guilty away which was imputed on us due to the fall of Adam and Eve. We now received justification by God the Father through faith in Jesus Christ alone. The second part of 2 Corinthians 5:21 where Paul says, "so that in him we might become the righteousness of God" suggests that all Christians are clothed with the righteousness of Christ when God through Jesus Christ justify them. Christ's righteousness is imputed on his believers.

Our sins are imputed on Jesus Christ and his righteousness is imputed on us. This double imputation, is done by God through Jesus Christ for our benefit.

Jesus Christ took out the original sin in us that Adam and Eve brought by his act of double imputation. After justification, we enter the process of sanctification. Justification removes our guilty before God and sanctification continues to remove the pollution in us brought by the original sin. Sanctification is the ongoing inner transformation process in the lives of all believers through the blood of Jesus Christ and the spirit of God. This process never ends until we die.

CHAPTER TEN. QUESTIONS TO ANSWER

How did Jesus take care of original sin?

Why did Jesus Christ become human?

What does this statement mean to you JESUS CHRIST DIED?

What is double imputation?

Did Jesus die for your sins?

Did Jesus die for all?

Explain Isaiah 53?

CHAPTER 11

RESULTS OF CHRIST FINISHED WORK

Reconciliation

Reconciliation is an act of causing two hostile groups or persons become friendly again. When Adam and Eve sinned against God the relationship between them and God was broken. But when Jesus Christ died on the cross he took away our sin and brought that lost relationship back. Reconciliation is the result of Christ's finished work on the cross. The Bible has many texts that speak about reconciliation in Jesus Christ; "Be kind to one another, tenderhearted, forgiving one another, as God in Christ forgave you" (Ephesians 4:32).

"If your brother sins against you, go and tell him his fault, between you and him alone. If he listens to you, you have gained your brother. But if he does not listen, take one or two others along with you, that every charge may be established by the evidence of two or three witnesses. If he refuses to listen to them, tell it to the church. And if he refuses to listen even to the church, let him be to you as a Gentile and a tax collector" (Matthew 18:15-17).

All this is from God, who through Christ reconciled us to himself and gave us the ministry of reconciliation; that is, in Christ God was reconciling the world to himself, not counting their trespasses against them, and entrusting to us the message of reconciliation. Therefore, we are ambassadors for Christ, God making his appeal through us. We implore you on behalf of Christ, be reconciled to God. For our sake, he made him to be sin who knew no sin, so that in him we might become the righteousness of God" (2Corinthians 5:18-21).

"So, if you are offering your gift at the altar and there remember that your brother has something against you, leave your gift there before the altar and go. First be reconciled to your brother, and then come and offer your gift. Come to terms quickly with your accuser while you are going with him to court, lest your accuser hand you over to the judge, and the judge to the guard, and you be put in prison. Truly, I say to you, you will never get out until you have paid the last penny" (Matthew 5: 23-26).

"For if while we were enemies we were reconciled to God by the death of his Son, much more, now that we are reconciled, shall we be saved by his life" (Romans 5: 10). And Paul also wrote, "And through him to reconcile to himself all things, whether on earth or in heaven, making peace by the blood of his cross" (Colossians 1:20).

Eternal Life

The most known verse in the Bible is John 3:16 which says, "For God so loved the world that he gave his one and only Son, that whoever believes in him shall not perish but have eternal life." The phrase 'Eternal life' has two meanings. The Greek word used in this verse is 'Aionios' and 'Zoe'. Zoe means life while 'Aion' which is the root word of Aionios means 'age' and in plural 'Aionios' means 'ages'. This means that when we entrust our life in the finished work of Jesus

BEDROOM OF ADAM AND EVE

Christ on the cross we have eternal life not only in one age but in all ages. Jesus Christ who lives in us will be with us throughout all ages now and forever. Believers in Jesus Christ have eternal life right now in this age. Thus, what the Bible says. We should not doubt our salvation when we become children of God through Jesus Christ our Lord. "This is eternal life, that they may know You, the only true God, and Jesus Christ whom You have sent" (John 17: 3). "Many of those who sleep in the dust of the ground will awake, these to everlasting life, but the others to disgrace and everlasting contempt. Those who have insight will shine brightly like the brightness of the expanse of heaven, and those who lead the many to righteousness, like the stars forever and ever" (Daniel 12:2-3). "For this reason I endure all things for the sake of those who are chosen, so that they also may obtain the salvation which is in Christ Jesus and with it eternal glory" (2Timothy 2:10)."These will go away into eternal punishment, but the righteous into eternal life" (Matthew 25:46)."For God so loved the world that He gave His only begotten Son, that whoever believes in Him shall not perish, but have eternal life" (John 3:16).Jesus said, "The thief comes only to steal and kill and destroy; I came that they may have life, and have it abundantly" (John 10:10). But whoever drinks of the water that I will give him shall never thirst; but the water that I will give him will become in him a well of water springing up to eternal life" (John 4:4). "And everyone who has left houses or brothers or sisters or father or mother or children or farms for my name's sake, will receive many times as much, and will inherit eternal life" (Matthew 19:29).

So, Jesus said to the twelve, "You do not want to go away also, do you?" Simon Peter answered Him, "Lord, to whom we shall go? You have words of eternal life. "We have believed and have come to know that you are the Holy One of God" (John 6:67-69). "I have been crucified with Christ; and it is no longer I who live, but Christ lives in me; and the life which I now live in the flesh I live by faith in the Son of God, who loved me and gave Himself up for me" (Galatians 2:20). "Therefore, we have been buried with Him through baptism into death, so that as Christ was raised from the dead through the glory of the Father, so we too might walk in newness of life" (Romans 6:4).

"If Christ is in you, though the body is dead because of sin, yet the spirit is alive because of righteousness. But if the Spirit of Him who raised Jesus from the dead dwells in you, He who raised Christ Jesus from the dead will also give life to your mortal bodies through His Spirit who dwells in you" (Romans 8:10-11).

"Jesus said to him, "I am the way, and the truth, and the life; no one comes to the Father but through me" (John 1:4).

"What was from the beginning, what we have heard, what we have seen with our eyes, what we have looked at and touched with our hands, concerning the Word of Life-- and the life was manifested, and we have seen and testify and proclaim to you the eternal life, which was with the Father and was manifested to us— "(1 John 1:1-2).

"And we know that the Son of God has come, and has given us understanding so that we may know Him who is true; and we are in Him who is true, in His Son Jesus Christ This is the true God and eternal life" (1 John 5:20).

No Second death

All people will die one day due to sin that came in the world through Adam and Eve but not all people will experience second death once they die. Believers in Jesus Christ will never experience second death once they leave this planet earth. First death is physical but temporally since all humans will be resurrected from the dead at the end of all things. But the second death though physical too will be permanent. Second dead is separation from the goodness of God for ever. Ungodly people will rise to face judgement then continue being in a state without the blessings of God-this is second death. Four passages in the bible talk about second death;

"Whoever has ears, let them hear what the Spirit says to the churches? The one who is victorious will not be hurt at all by the second death" (Revelation 2:11).

John the apostle wrote, "Blessed and holy are those who share in the first resurrection, the second death has no power over them, but they will be priests of God and of Christ and will reign with him for a thousand years" (Revelation 20:6). "Then death and Hades were thrown into the lake of fire. The lake of fire is the second death" (Revelation 20:14). This is Hell and its more than oblivion. "But the cowardly, the unbelieving, the vile, the murderers, the sexually immoral, those who practice magic arts, the idolaters and all liars—they will be consigned to the fiery lake of burning sulfur. This is the second death" (Revelation 21:8). Second death is HELL bound to ungodly.

Heaven for us

Some people think heaven is not real. But the truth is clear from the words of God in the bible that there is a place called heaven and it is real. There is a place where God and his heaven hosts live. This heavenly world is called spiritual world. It cannot be seen with our own naked eyes but through spiritual eyes. Heaven is the place where believers in Jesus Christ will spent the rest of their times. It is a permanent home of us saints of the highest God.

We enter heaven when we believe in Jesus Christ though not yet in totality until when Jesus Christ himself comes back again. Jesus will take us with him in his kingdom forever. We will be reunited with God in heaven for ever. The bible teaches that there is heaven;

"See that you do not despise one of these little ones. For I tell you that their angels in heaven always see the face of my Father in heaven.

"What do you think? If a man owns a hundred sheep, and one of them wanders away, will he not leave the ninety-nine on the hills and go to look for the one that wandered off?

And if he finds it, truly I tell you, he is happier about that one sheep than about the ninety-nine that did not wander off. In the same way, your Father in heaven is not willing that any of these little ones should perish" (Matthew 18:10-14).

"He will swallow up death forever. The Sovereign LORD will wipe away the tears from all faces; he will remove his people's disgrace from all the earth. The LORD has spoken.

In that day, they will say, "Surely this is our God; we trusted in him, and he saved us. This is the LORD; we trusted in him; let us rejoice and be glad in his salvation." The hand of the LORD will rest on this mountain; but Moab will be trampled in their land as straw is trampled down in the manure. They will stretch out their hands in it, as swimmers stretch out their hands to swim. God will bring down their pride despite the cleverness of their hands. He will bring down your high fortified walls and lay them low; he will bring them down to the ground, to the very dust" (Isaiah 25:8-12).

Our golden rule says, "So in everything, do to others what you would have them do to you, for this sum up the Law and the Prophets. "Enter through the narrow gate. For wide is the gate and broad is the road that leads to destruction, and many enter through it. But small is the gate and narrow the road that leads to life, and only a few find it. "Watch out for false prophets. They come to you in sheep's clothing, but inwardly they are ferocious wolves" (Matthew 7: 12-15).

The Fulfillment of the Law

"Do not think that I have come to abolish the Law or the Prophets; I have not come to abolish them but to fulfill them. For truly I tell you, until heaven and earth disappear, not the smallest letter, not the least stroke of a pen, will by any means disappear from the Law until everything is accomplished. Therefore, anyone who sets aside one of the least of these commands and teaches others accordingly will be called least in the kingdom of heaven, but whoever practices and teaches these commands will be called great in the kingdom of heaven. For I tell you that unless your righteousness surpasses that of the Pharisees and the teachers of the law, you will certainly not enter the kingdom of heaven" (Matthew 5: 17-20).

"People will come from east and west and north and south, and will take their places at the feast in the kingdom of God. Indeed, there are those who are last who will be first, and first who will be last" (Luke 13: 29-30). "My Father's house has many rooms; if that were not so, would I have told you that I am going there to prepare a place for you? And if I go and prepare a place for you, I will come back and take you to be with me that you also may be where I am. You know the way to the place where I am going."

Jesus the Way to the Father

Thomas said to him, "Lord, we don't know where you are going, so how can we know the way?" Jesus answered, "I am the way and the truth and the life. No one comes to the Father except through me" (John 14: 2-6). Jesus Christ is the only way to the Father. When we believe in Jesus Christ we have everlasting life now even though we are not dead. "Now this is eternal life: that they know you, the only true God, and Jesus Christ, whom you have sent." John 17:3 John wrote, "And this is that testimony; God has given us eternal life, and this life is in His Son. Whoever has the Son has life; whoever does not have the Son of God does not have life." 1 John 5:12

Living as Those Made Alive in Christ

"Since, then, you have been raised with Christ, set your hearts on things above, where Christ is, seated at the right hand of God. Set your minds on things above, not on earthly things. For you died, and your life is now hidden with Christ in God. When Christ, who is your life, appears, then you also will appear with him in glory. Put to death, therefore, whatever belongs to your earthly nature: sexual immorality, impurity, lust, evil desires and greed, which is idolatry. Because of these, the wrath of God is coming. You used to walk in these ways, in the life you once lived" (Colossians 3: 1-7).

"Then one of the elders asked me, "These in white robes—who are they, and where did they come from?"

I answered, "Sir, you know."

And he said, "These are they who have come out of the great tribulation; they have washed their robes and made them white in the blood of the Lamb. Therefore,

"they are before the throne of God

and serve him day and night in his temple;

and he who sits on the throne

will shelter them with his presence.

'Never again will they hunger;

never again will they thirst.

The sun will not beat down on them,'

nor any scorching heat.

For the Lamb at the center of the throne

will be their shepherd;

'he will lead them to springs of living water.'

'And God will wipe away every tear from their eyes" (Revelation 7: 13-17).

John the apostles also said, "He will wipe every tear from their eyes. There will be no more death' or mourning or crying or pain, for the old order of things has passed away."

He who was seated on the throne said, "I am making everything new! "Then he said, "Write this down, for these words are trustworthy and true."

He said to me: "It is done. I am the Alpha and the Omega, the Beginning and the End. To the thirsty I will give water without cost from the spring of the water of life. 7 Those who are victorious will inherit all this, and I will be their God and they will be my children. But the cowardly, the unbelieving, the vile, the murderers, the sexually immoral, those who practice magic arts, the idolaters and all liars—they will be consigned to the fiery lake of burning sulfur. This is the second death" (Revelation 21:4-8). Prophet Ezekiel said, "No longer will the people of Israel have malicious neighbors who are painful briers and sharp thorns. Then they will know that I am the Sovereign Lord.

This is what the Sovereign Lord says: When I gather the people of Israel from the nations where they have been scattered, I will be proved holy through them in the sight of the nations. Then they will live in their own land, which I gave to my servant Jacob. They will live there in safety and will build houses and plant vineyards; they will live in safety when I inflict punishment on all their neighbors who maligned them. Then they will know that I am the Lord their God" (Ezekiel 28:24-26).

"Then the angel showed me the river of the water of life, as clear as crystal, flowing from the throne of God and of the Lamb down the middle of the great street of the city. On each side of the river stood the tree of life, bearing twelve crops of fruit, yielding its fruit every month. And the leaves of the tree are for the healing of the nations. No longer will there be any curse. The throne of God and of the Lamb will be in the city, and his servants will serve him. They will see his face, and his name will be on their foreheads. There will be no more night. They will not need the light of a lamp or the light of the sun, for the Lord God will give them light. And they will reign for ever and ever.

The angel said to me, "These words are trustworthy and true. The Lord, the God who inspires the prophets, sent his angel to show his servants the things that must soon take place."

"Look, I am coming soon! Blessed is the one who keeps the words of the prophecy written in this scroll" (Revelation 22: 1-7).

Our true home is heaven

1 Kings 8:30 "And listen to the plea of your servant and of your people Israel, when they pray toward this place. And listen in heaven your dwelling place, and when you hear, forgive."

1 Corinthians 2:7-9 "But we impart a secret and hidden wisdom of God, which God decreed before the ages for our glory. None of the rulers of this age understood this, for if they had, they would not have crucified the Lord of glory. But, as it is written, "What no eye has seen, nor ear heard, nor the heart of man imagined, what God has prepared for those who love him"

2 Corinthians 5:8 "Yes, we are of good courage, and we would rather be away from the body and

at home with the Lord."

Philippians 1:21-23 "For to me to live is Christ, and to die is gain. If I am to live in the flesh, that means fruitful labor for me. Yet which I shall choose I cannot tell. I am hard pressed between the two. My desire is to depart and be with Christ, for that is far better."

Philippians 3:20-21 "But our citizenship is in heaven, and from it we await a Savior, the Lord Jesus Christ, who will transform our lowly body to be like his glorious body, by the power that enables him even to subject all things to himself." John 14:4 Said, "Jesus Is the Only Way to Heaven." This is what he said in the gospel of John, "I am the way and the truth and the life. No one comes to the Father except through me."

Matthew 18:10 Jesus taught that, "See that you do not despise one of these little ones, for I tell you that their angels in heaven always see the face of my Father in heaven." Jesus also said the kingdom of God (Heaven) has come. Jesus meant that in him we have already experienced heaven on earth though not yet not in fullness (Matthew 3:2). Jesus taught the Pharisees that, "You are in error because you do not know the Scriptures or the power of God. At the resurrection people, will neither marry nor be given in marriage; they will be like the angels in heaven. But about the resurrection of the dead—have you not read what God said to you, 'I am the God of Abraham, the God of Isaac, and the God of Jacob? He is not the God of the dead but of the living. When the crowds heard this, they were astonished at his teaching" (Mat.22:29-33).

CHAPTER ELEVEN. QUESTIONS TO ANSWER

What are the results of Christ finished work?

Define reconciliation?

What is eternal life? John 3:3-5?

What is the second death? Will Christ people experience the second death?

What is the final home for believers in Jesus Christ?

Who is the only way to heaven?

Who fulfilled the requirements of the law?

What is it like living with Jesus forever?

CHAPTER 12

THE TEACHINGS OF REFORMED THEOLOGY.

Bedroom of Adam and Eve explains total depravity of human beings cause of the original sin. This fact has been explained already in the first few chapters of the book. Now I would like to concentrate on the core teachings of the Christian faith in the people who live in the bedroom of Jesus Christ. I am blessed to state that the content in this chapter and the chapters after wards were taken from my PhD thesis.

One of the goals of this book is to provide a platform for those that desire to teach reformed teachings in prisons across the globe. Therefore, I will try to bring the best of the teachings of the reformed theology.

When John Calvin continued teaching and formulating proper mainline reformed teaching, critics came along. Jacob Arminius and his followers became the main critic of the reformed faith. Calvin answered these critics by formulating what is now called The Five Points of Calvinism. This is not the whole package of reformed teaching, though it captures the essence of the reformed tradition. John Calvin believed in the total inability of man to receive salvation by himself. Man, is totally depraved, but Arminius camp did not believe it. This is what Calvin says, per House (1992, p. 99)

Because of the fall, man is unable of himself to savingly believe the gospel. The sinner is dead, blind and deaf to the things of God; his heart is sinful and desperately corrupt. His will is not free, it is in bondage to his evil nature, therefore he will not ---indeed he cannot---choose good over evil in the spiritual realm. Consequently, it takes much more than the Spirit's assistance to bring a sinner to Christ-it takes regeneration by which the spirit makes the sinner alive and gives him a new nature but is itself a part of God's gift of salvation. Salvation is God's gift to the sinner, not the sinner's gift."

Point number two was about unconditional election. Arminius camp taught that "God's choice of certain individuals to salvation before the foundation of the world was based on his foreseeing that they would respond to his call. He selected only those whom he knew would of themselves freely believe the gospel. Election therefore was determined by or conditioned on what a person would do. At this point, Calvin taught that

God's choice of certain individuals to salvation before the foundation of the world rested solely in his own sovereign will. His choice of particular sinners was not based on any foreseeing response or obedience on their part, such as faith and repentance, etc. On the central, God gives faith and repentance to each individual whom he selected. These acts are the result, not cause, of God's choice. Election therefore was not determined by or conditioned on any virtuous quality or act foreseen in man. Those whom God sovereignly elected, he brings through the power of the Spirit to a willing acceptance of Christ. Thus, God's choice of the sinner, not the sinner's choice of Christ, is the ultimate cause of salvation" House (1992, p. 99).

Arminius had a big shot at the teachings of Calvin here on the third point. I got my second masters of theology at Cincinnati Christian University, which based its theology on the teachings of Jacob Arminius. I know what they teach. They are big on this third point that if I did not study at Calvin Seminary before studying in Ohio I would not tell the difference between Arminius and reformed teachings. This is what Arminius believes about limited atonement

Christ's redeeming work made it possible for everyone to be saved, but not actually secure the salvation of everyone. Although Christ died for all people and for every person, only those who believe in him are saved. His death enabled God to pardon sinners on the condition that they believe, but it did not actually put away anyone's sins. Christ's redemption becomes effective only if a person chooses to accept it" (House 1992, p. 100). Calvin, on the other hand rose from the occasion and shot Arminius camp right on their core belief by saying,

Christ's redeeming work was intended to save the elect only and actually secured salvation for them. In addition to putting away the sins of his people, Christ's redemption secured everything necessary for their salvation, including faith, which unites them to him. The gift of faith is infallibly applied by the Spirit to all for whom Christ died, therefore guaranteeing their salvation." (House 1992, p. 100)

It is very easy for today's Christians that believe in the reformed teaching to look at this back and forth debate as being nothing else but cheap church theological politics. Remember in those days, even blood was shed just to protect and defend church theological beliefs. Worse still was that both camp based their arguments from the scriptures.

Four teachings of Calvin had to do with irresistible grace. Arminius camp believed man could resist the inner work of the Spirit of God in his life due to free will. This included that men and women were or can resist the grace of God. This is what they taught:

The Spirit calls inwardly all those who are called outwardly by the gospel invitation; he does all that he can to bring every sinner to salvation. But since man is free, he can successfully resist the Spirit's call. The Spirit cannot regenerate the sinner until he believes; faith (which is man's contribution) precedes and makes possible the new birth. Thus, man's free will limits the Spirit in the application of Christ's saving work. The Holy Spirit can draw to Christ only those who allow him to have his way with them. Until the sinner responds, the Spirit cannot give life; God's grace, therefore, is not invincible; it can be, and often is, resisted and thwarted by men." (House 1992, p. 100)

Reformers spearheaded by John Calvin answered back stating

In addition to the outward general call to salvation, which is made to everyone who hears the gospel, the Holy Spirit extends to the elect a special inward call that inevitably brings them to salvation. The external call (which is made to all without distinction) can be, and often is, rejected, whereas the internal (which is made only to the elect) cannot be rejected; it always results in conversation. By means of this special call the spirit irresistibly draws sinners to Christ. He is not limited in His work of applying salvation to man's will nor is he dependent on man's cooperation for success. The spirit graciously causes the elect sinner to cooperate, to believe, to repent, to come freely and willingly to Christ. God's grace, therefore, is invincible; it never fails to result in the salvation of those to whom it is extended." (House 1992, p. 100)

Can a Christian fall from the grace of God in Christ Jesus? Is it possible for a Christian to lose salvation? Arminius camp believes that a Christian can lose salvation once he or she became born again. Those who believe and are truly saved can lose their salvation by failing to keep up their faith. John Calvin camp on the other hand strongly holds to the belief that Christians born of the Spirit of God cannot lose their salvation.

Calvin says, "All who are chosen by God, redeemed by Christ, and given faith by the Spirit are eternally saved. They are kept in faith by the power of almighty God and thus persevere to the end." Though per House (1992, p. 100) some Arminian Christians agree on this fifth point of Calvinism.

Reformed teaching is very broad and is more than just Five Points of Calvinism stated above. There are many theologians in the reformed camp that have written systematic theological books describing the core teachings of reformed faith. All of them agree that reformed faith is centered on the sovereignty of God in this world and in the world to come.

Now let me research or expose the main teachings of reformed theology per Rev. M.J Bosma in his book *Exposition of Reformed Doctrine*. This is clearly a popular explanation of the most essential teachings of the reformed churches. The history of this man has already been told in the previous chapters.

Two Sources of Knowledge of God

Reformed churches teach that there are two sources where humans can get the knowledge of God and these are the knowledge of God from nature and the knowledge of God from Holy Scripture. Just by looking at what God has done in both creation and providence we can know something about God. This knowledge is sometimes called general revelation or general grace which does not lead us to true salvation. But also through the Scriptures we can know God and this knowledge can lead us to true salvation. This is part of special revelation or special grace. As we read his word the Holy Spirit starts his inner work in our hearts to regenerate our souls and spirits to the image of Jesus Christ. We can be born again. Bosma (1937, Ch. 1) Says, "Yes, we have a twofold revelation of God, one given in nature, and the other in Scripture, sometimes known as a general and special revelation." Furthermore, Berkhof (1933, p. 37) in his book Manual Christian Doctrine clearly defined the differences between special and general revelation. This is supported by Rev. Bosma also:

General revelation is rooted in creation and in general relations of God to man, is addressed to man considered simply as the creature and image-bearer of God, and aims at the realization of the end for which man was created and which can be attained only where man knows God and enjoys communion with Him. Special revelation on the other hand is rooted in the redemptive work of God, is addressed to man as a sinner and adapted to moral and spiritual needs of fallen man, and aims at leading the sinner back to God through the specific knowledge of God's redemptive love revealed in Jesus Christ." (Bosma 1927, p. 25)

We should be careful here because both revelations come from God and man cannot comprehend all of them perfectly in his nature mind without the help of God himself. Special relation leads to salvation while general revelation does not. Furthermore, in relation to special revelation, reformers believe that all 66 books of the bible are scriptures from God. The whole Bible contains the Infallible, Inspired, authoritative and divine word of God. Therefore, the whole bible is sufficient and necessary for our salvation. Scriptures can only be understood by faith through the power of the Holy Spirit. Therefore, per Calvin the word of God and the Spirit of God are inseparable. Both come from God and both are won in function as far as our redemptive work is concerned.

BEDROOM OF ADAM AND EVE
CHAPTER TWELVE. QUESTIONS TO ANSWER

What are the teachings of reformed faith?

Define two sources of knowledge of God?

Who was Bosma?

Who was John Calvin?

Can you lose your salvation?

CHAPTER 13

THE DOCTRINE OF GOD AND HIS CREATION

What does reformed teaching say about the doctrine of God and the doctrine of creation? The answer is quite clear in the first book of the bible first four words, "In the beginning God". This means in the beginning there was God and all that follows came due to the sovereign power of God Almighty. God made the world from nothing, all that is in it, seen and unseen. He did not use matter to form the world, but his own word. He formed it due to his own sovereign love for his own Glory. All that God created was good. Jacob (1817, p. 136) said, "Elohim saw all that he had made, and behold it was good."

No one forced God to what he did. He was not in competition either with the other gods in order to prove that he was the true by making the creation. Rather, God made creation due to his eternal love for his deeply divine glory. Therefore, we can say it was not necessary for God to create man and the world. God existed internally and independently forever before he even thought of creation. Also, we should not think that God created the world out of the accident either because scripture shows us that He made it all good for his own purpose in his divine decree.

Though the word Trinity is never mentioned in the whole Bible, six days after creating the world, we hear God the Father saying "Let us create man in our own image" Gen. 1:26. He divinely decreed this alone in his sovereign power. Here we hear internal relationships in function within the Godhead. God the father, God the Son, and God the Holy Spirit existed from eternity to eternity as three persons and not three gods. Neither of them is made, nor created. Neither of them has the beginning nor the end. All three are equal and made by one same divine essence. There is One God, but revealed himself in three persons. Each person is fully God.

Reformed theology teaches that God Created the world out of nothing, therefore the world is not an extension of the being of God. The world is not God because God exists independent of creation. Reformed theology teaches that God in his covenant relationship with man and the world maintains the creator/creature distinction and creator/creature relationship as well. Triune God is always distinct and independent of creation, though maintains a closer relationship with it through his Son Jesus Christ. Only the God of the covenant is transcendent and personal at the same time (Gore, p. 73).

Nature of God

God is ONE and this is what the bible teaches. Rev Bosma (1927, p. 17) says, "Bible declares there is only one God, and that he is an absolute unit, incapable of division." Moses declared this everlasting statement about God to the people of Israel in the wilderness, "Hear, O Israel: Jehovah our God is one Jehovah." Det. 6:4. These words are echoed by men and women that believed in Jesus Christ, especially Brother Mark and James "Thou believe that God is one; thou does well" James 2:19; Mark 10:19.

BEDROOM OF ADAM AND EVE
God is ONE Spirit

God is Spirit." John 4:24. God is one spirit that made all things as we read from the bible. The bible is not there to describe or define the being of God, it is the witness of the redemptive work of God to man through Jesus Christ alone. Rev. Bosma (1927, p. 55) says, "God is essentially spirit, so that all qualities which belong to the perfect idea of spirit are necessarily in Him; that he is a self-conscious and self-determining being. The fact He is a pure spirit necessity excludes the notion of the early Gnostics and medieval Mystics, that he has some sort of an ethereal or refined body. It also rules out the idea that he is visible and can be discerned by the bodily senses."

Essence of God

What is God made up of? Now we know that God is one and that he is the Spirit that made all things, therefore it is right to say that his essence is spiritual. Bosma (1927, p. 18) wrote, "God is a personal spiritual being of infinite perfection, existing in three persons. This is not intended as an adequate definition of God; which no one can give." Reformed theology teaches one God who revealed himself in three persons not three gods. Each of the three persons is fully God made up of the same essence. The three persons co-exist eternally through eternity, though different in function. Though each divine person has different function, they work together in all things, therefore it is right to believe that God the Father created all things, God the Son died for us and the entire world in order to provide redemption. And God the Holy Spirit applied the work of our Lord Jesus Christ in the lives of believers.

One God in Three Persons

Now we can say as we believe that God is one personal spiritual being but revealed himself in three persons. The word Trinity is never mentioned in the Bible, but is an attempt by man to try to explain how God of the bible has revealed his work in history. Christians that teach this doctrine to accept it through faith since they know their limitations their senses have in relationship to the nature of the triune God. The doctrine of the Trinity as it is called is a mystery to man though true. Here is what Grudem (1994, Ch. 14, p. 226) says:

The doctrine of the trinity is one of the most important doctrines of the Christian faith. To study the bible's teachings on the Trinity gives us great insight into the question that is at the center of all our seeking after God: What is God like himself? Here we learn that in himself, in his very being, God exists in the persons of Father, son, and Holy Spirit, yet he is one God." Grudem went on to say that, "The word Trinity is never found in the bible, though the idea represented by the word is taught in many places. The word trinity means tri-unity or three in oneness. It is used to summarize the teaching of scripture that God is three persons, yet one God."

Therefore, all reformed churches rightly agree with Benjamin Warfield (1988, p. 147) who says, "There is but one God. The Father, Son and Holy Spirit is God. Father, Son and Holy Spirit each is a distinct person."

WESTMINSTER SHORTER CATECHISM confirms this teaching also in these three questions and answers;

Q. 4. What is God?
A. God is a Spirit, infinite, eternal, and unchangeable, in his being, wisdom, power, holiness, justice, goodness, and truth.

Q. 5. Are there more Gods than one?
A. There is but one only, the living and true God.

Q. 6. How many persons are there in the Godhead?
A. There are three persons in the Godhead: The Father, the Son, and the Holy Ghost; and these three are one God, the same in substance, equal in power and glory.

Attributes of God

Since God is one spirit being he has special attributes that only applies to him. These attributes reveal further the nature and works of God. These attributes are called incommunicable attributes, but those attributes God chooses to share with us are called communicable attributes. Bosma (1927, p. 20) (---------) says:

In other words, all God's attributes are perfect gift to us all as they are the perfections of his being revealed to us. God is infinitely perfect; in most harmonious unity, all perfections are in God; his being is infinite perfection. We can hardly say that there are different perfections of God, as though God were a composition of various parts, for in him is an absolute unity. But God's Being is made known to us bearing various relations to his creatures, he manifests himself to us as unlimited in his presence, in power, in knowledge, etc. God cannot reveal the fullness of his being with us, but in various ways and at various times he manifests to us as we need to know him. Thus, he manifests himself to us as eternal, the unchangeable, the almighty supreme being."

Rev. Bosma (1927, p. 21) listed these five incommunicable attributes, God's independence, simplicity, eternity, omnipresence, and immutability while Grudem (1994, pp. 160ff) listed these attributes as applied to God alone, Independence (aseity), unchangeableness, eternity, Omnipresence, unity. Again Bosma (1927, p. 21) says, "God's independence signifies that God is self-existent, and self-sufficient. God depends on no one else for his existence, though the whole universe depends on him." I Acts 17:25 says, "Neither is he served by man's hands, as though he needed anything, seeing he himself gives to all life, and breath, and all things.

Bosma (1927, p. 21) says, "Because God is independent he is also sovereign, that is, to him belong the right to govern and dispose of all his creatures per his own good pleasure." On the attribute of simplicity Bosma says, "God's simplicity means that with him is no composition of various parts, but that's all-in God is a unity. He is a Spirit of infinity perfection" Bosma (1927, p. 22).

In regard to eternity God is unlimited in the duration of his existence; he is without beginning, without continuance, and without end. God exists above time. We exist in time, we are temporal. The past, the future is unchangeable present with God as the present (Bosma 1927, p. 22). In conclusion, God has both communicable and incommunicable attributes as seen in the whole bible.

God's Names

Many times, the name means something especially in the old African culture. My name is Edward Kavimba Lungu and I got this name through my grandfather. Read more of my bibliography by Lungu (2010, p. 25) <u>The African Way: Success and struggles of the life of Lungu.</u> Though I did not know what it meant when it was given to me, but when I was growing up it meant a lot to me. I felt I was the perfect representation of Edward my grandfather. I was very careful what I did every day in the village, especially when my grandfather was nearby me. When I did bad things, my grandfather used to get sad and mad, but when I did good things in the village he became proud and happy.

In the bible, the names of God reveal further the nature and works of God. As a reformed Christian person, I do believe this. Names of God are very important because they reveal something of God's perfection to us.

BEDROOM OF ADAM AND EVE

God can only be known as far as he has chosen to reveal himself to us… These names are not merely words to distinguish God from others, as our names are, but they to a certain extent declare who God is. Because the fullness of his perfection is so great, and the relations to his creatures are so varied, God has given us several names of himself. These names together, however, do not sufficiently express who God is. The infinite cannot be revealed by finite term (Bosma, 1927, p. 18).

Works of God

Reformed teaches that God works per his decrees as seen in his creation and providence. No one forced God to decree what he decreed. Thus, why he said in his word saying, "I am God and there is none like me; declaring the end from the beginning and from ancient times things that are not yet done, saying: My counsel shall stand, and I will do all my pleasure." Isaiah 46: 9, 10. Paul in the letter of Ephesian church said this about God's decree, "Having been foreordained per the purpose of him who works all things after the counsel of his will" Psalms, 139:16, 17.

God solely decreed by his good pleasure in what he decreed and his decrees are perfect, timely, eternal, unshakeable, and unchangeable. This includes the location of a man in this world, "He made of one every nation of men to dwell on the face of the earth, having determined their appointed seasons, and the bounds of their habitation." Ephesus 1:11.

We should be careful here to state that the decree of God was merely one of his creation and not on the providence. He made all things and decreed all things, but also provide life and stability for all things. God is not in hiding after making and decree. He is fully aware what is going on and fully involved in executing his action. The Psalmist said

I lift up my eyes to the mountains? Where does my help come from? My help comes from the Lord, the Maker of heaven and earth. He will not let your foot slip. He who watches over you will not slumber; indeed, he who watches over Israel will neither slumber nor sleep. The Lord watches over you the Lord is your shade at your right hand; the sun will not harm you by day, nor the moon by night. The Lord will keep you from all harm. He will watch over your life; The Lord will watch over your coming and going both now and forevermore." Psalms: 121. Nothing happens by chance in this world

Predestination

If the reformed doctrine includes believing and teaching about the decree of God, then the full teaching of predestination is fully taught as well. This doctrine like any other Christian teaching must be understood in the realm of faith in Jesus Christ by the power of the Holy Spirit. Bosma (1927, 50) taught, "It is the eternal counsel of God, whereby he has determined the eternal destiny of all mankind and includes two parts: the sovereign election of some to eternal life through Jesus Christ, and the righteous reprobation of the rest for their sins. Predestination therefore is a general term that includes two parts: election and reprobation."

This doctrine has been the cause of major controversy in the Christian community from the time of the Apostle Paul to present. Two camps in the Christian world have emerged in trying to understand the doctrine of predestination; The Arminian camp and the Calvinistic camp.

The Arminian camp spearheaded by their leader "Jacob Arminius, a Dutch professor (1560-1609) teach that God has eternally predestinated certain persons to eternal life, whom he foresaw would repent, and believe and persevere to life and salvation. The ground for election is, therefore, a foreseen repentance and faith. This view of election accompanies the theory of a universal atonement-that is, that Christ has offered a sufficient sacrifice for all mankind, but it becomes efficient only for such as have faith and believe in him.

Per this view (Bosma, 1927, p. 51), the reason some are saved and others not, is that some, by the act of their free will, believe, and others do not. The man himself, and not the sovereign place of God determines his eternal future." Per this view again man and his effort through free will leads to salvation and not God through his sovereign hand in Jesus Christ. On the hand, Calvin camp headed by John Calvin, per Bosma (1927, p. 51) says:

The French Reformed (1564) teaches that God has per the sovereign good pleasure of his will elected some of humanity to eternal life and has most righteously reprobated the rest to eternal condemnation. Therefore, ground of election is based not on the foreseeing faith of the person elected, but the sovereign good pleasure of God. In reply to the question why some are saved and others are not, the Calvinist answers, because God has, to the honor and glory of his name, chosen some to eternal life and ordained the means of their salvation, while he has left others in the misery which sin has brought upon them.

The doctrine of election must always be viewed in Christ alone. God does all the work of redemption in and through his son Jesus Christ alone. God chooses his elect in Christ alone and not without Christ. The doctrine of election is biblical; it is divine revelation (Stott 1982, p. 20).

Without the doctrine of predestination, which is deeply rooted in the doctrine of the sovereign of God, there is no doctrine of perseverance of the saints. The unshakeable ground here is the sovereignty of God and all others fall suit. We enter the kingdom of God by the grace of God through faith in Jesus Christ and stay in the kingdom of God by the same grace of God in Jesus Christ alone. None is by our effort even staying a Christian. It is hard and impossible to fully live a Christian life on our own effort and works without God's grace.

There are several verses in the Holy Bible that affirm the teaching of predestination, such as Ephesian 1: 4, 5: "Even as he chose us in him before the foundation of the world, that we should be holy and without blemish before him in love; having foreordained us unto adoption as sons through Jesus Christ unto himself, per the good pleasure of his will"

II Tim. 1:9: "Who saved us, and called us with a holy calling, not per our works, but per his own purpose and grace, which was given us in Christ Jesus before times eternal."

Rom. 9: 11-13 "And we know that to them that love God all things work together for good, even to them that are called per his purpose, for whom he foresaw knew, he also foreordained to be conformed to the image of his Son… and whom he foreordained, them he also called.'

Rom. 9:11-13: "For the children being not yet born, neither having done anything good or bad, that the purpose of God per election might stand, not of works, but of him that calleth, it was said unto her, the elder should serve the younger. Even as it is written, Jacob I loved, but Esau I hated." And my best verse for this is 15 where it is said: "For he said to Moses, I will have mercy on whom I have mercy, and I will have compassion on whom I have compassion." Vs 16: So then it is not of him that willeth, nor of him that runneth, but of God that hath mercy."

In conclusion God is Triune. God is one, but revealed up himself in three persons; Father, Son and the Holy Spirit. Each person is fully God distinct in function, but One in essence. Trinity is never mentioned in the bible, but it is believed to be right doctrine of the bible. Names and works of a triune God reveal more of the nature and character of our God who has both communicable and incommunicable attributes.

God is sovereign, which means he is all powerful, all knowing, and is everywhere present at the same time. God is unchangeable, eternal, simplicity. God is transcendent and imminent at the same time (Geisler, 1980, p. 272). Due to his sovereignty, he decreed all things and events. God predestinated our election, created all things, and upholds all things. He has total provided of all things in his hand alone. What do we mean by the providence of God? To answer this question

BEDROOM OF ADAM AND EVE

Heidelberg Catechism says;

The Almighty and everywhere present power of God; whereby, as it were by his hand, he upholds and governs heaven, earth, and all creatures; so, that herbs and grass, rain and drought, fruitful and barren years, meant and drink, health and sickness, riches and poverty, yes, and all things come not by chance, but his fatherly hand. Heb. 1:3.

CHAPTER THIRTEEN. QUESTIONS TO ANSWER

What is the doctrine of God?

What is the doctrine of creation?

What is the nature of God?

Is God ONE Spirit?

What is the essence of God?

Define this statement ONE GOD IN THREE PERSONS

What is a shorter Westminster catechism?

What is the name of God?

What are the names of God?

What is predestination?

What are the works of God?

CHAPTER 14

DOCTRINE OF MAN

Reformed teaching on the doctrine of man is quite clear in the bible that God made man in his image and likeliness. Manmade pure with no sin or evil and God made him for his own glory.

Then God said, "Let us make mankind in our image; in our likeliness, so that they may rule over the fish in the sea and the birds in the sky; over the livestock and all the wild animals, and over all creatures that move along the ground." So, God created mankind in his own image' in the image of God he created them; male and female he created them. Gen.1:26-27 and in chapter 2:7 it is said again, "Then the Lord God formed a man from the dust of the ground and breathed into his nostrils the breath of life, and the man became a living being.

Man, was created last after all else was made both in heaven and on earth and even underneath the earth. Rev. Bosma said, "Man was created last, all other things were done before him, that they might be ready for his service when he was brought forth. Man, was intended to be the crown creation, the vicegerent of God on earth" (Bosma, 1927, p. 84). It is very clear in the bible that God used soil to form the body of man and His breath of life for a man to be a living creature distinct of all animals that were made before him. Therefore, we humans are special in the eyes of the maker and we are meant to be the direct reflection of God on earth.

When man was put in the Garden of Eden he lived directly by being obedient to God. Adam knew what God wanted him to do and what God did not want him to do. He was operating on what the reformers call the covenant of works. This was the agreement based on works between God and man. Rev. Bosma said, "The covenant of works was an agreement between God and Adam, wherein God promised eternal life to Adam and all his posterity, upon condition of perfect obedience to the probationary command not to eat of the tree of knowledge of good and evil, God threatening that Adam would die in case he broke this command. Hosea 6:7 (R.S): "But they, like Adam, have transgressed the covenant." Indeed, Adam stood in a covenant relationship with God.

Adam and Eve broke this covenant relationship with God when they failed to be obedient to Him. The man brought upon himself, family and all mankind's misery, suffering and death. This is what sin and evil bring with us on earth. Adam disobeyed God by breaking the covenant, "And the Lord God commanded the man, "You are free to eat from any tree in the garden; but you must not eat from the tree of the knowledge of good and evil, for when you eat from it you will surely die." Gen. 2:16. Rev Bosma (1927, p. 93) said, "A strong proof of the covenant relationship between Adam and us is that everything said in the sentence pronounced on Adam and Eve after the fall has come to us. We suffer as they did, because we were counting on them, we sinned in them."

The fall of man is taught in the reformed churches and all other Christian denominations. Adam did fall by eating the forbidden fruit from the tree in the middle of the garden just as God told him not to do so. The Devil did not deceive Adam, his wife EVE was. Adam knowingly decided to rebel against God. He chose to be a rebellious being in turn all his posterity became polluted and corrupted with sin. Canons of Dordrecht III: I say:

Man, was originally formed after the image of God. His understanding was adorned with a true saving knowledge of his Creator, and of spiritual things; his heart and will were upright; all his affections pure; and the whole man was holy: but revolting from God by the instigation of the devil, and abusing the freedom of his own will, he forfeited these excellent gifts; and on the centrally entailed on himself blindness of mind, horrible darkness, vanity and perverseness of judgment; and became wicked, rebellious, and obdurate in heart and will, and impure in his affections.

What does it mean when we say man fell before God? Does it mean that man ceased to be the image of God after a fall? These are deep theological questions to be answered thoroughly in this thesis. After the fall man still stood before his creator as a man made in the image of God in the broader sense. Man, did not become an animal or a tree, but still had the breath and five senses as a human being.

He now knew what was good and evil within him. He knew his creator God was good thus why he ran away from him in the garden because the man he was totally contaminated with sin. I can say at the same time when he felt he had the good mind and evil mind in him with no neutral ground. He could not be good all the time as he was before the fall and also, he could not be all bad since he still was the image of God though broken with disobedience.

In the narrow sense man as the image of God was totally deprived. He fell into a pit that he dug himself and the pit was too deep for him to come out of his own effort. All his children, including us humans today are born while in this pit called the origin sin. No human can get out of this pit by human effort or works. This is because all the works and effort we were also in this pit with this pit.

There are two things that come to all humans due to the original sin of Adam; guilt and pollution or corruption. The Psalmist puts it right when he said, "Behold, I was brought forth in iniquity; and in sin did my mother conceive me." Ps. 51:5. Bosma (1927, p. 101) echoed the bible message when he said, "Original sin, as guilt, is from the first charged against us by God; it is the sin of breaking the probationary command in Adam, our representative. We are not charged with all of Adam's sin, only his sin of eating of the forbidden tree." Wages of sin is death. This is the reason why we die young and old because of the original sin from Adam.

When Adam sinned all his posterity are imputed with sin pollution or corruption. All human beings have inherited the pollution of sin and are just as guilty and polluted with sin as their first man was. According to Bosma (1927, p. 101) Hearts of human being are deeply saturated with sin.

Original sin, as pollution or corruption, is the internal depravity of heart, which we all inherit with the origin of our being from our ancestors. We are born without holy character, the godly nature of the heart, which Adam originally had, but instead our nature is unholy, the natural tendency of our lives is contrary to God. The nature of a human being, even of an infant, is either good or evil, there never were nor will be any neutral hearts, that are neither good nor evil, without any positive tendency and choice for good or evil. Everyone has a character or nature of the heart, if this nature is godly, the whole tendency of life will be godly, but if the heart is unholy the choice and direction of life is ungodly.

Though we have inherited the original sin from Adam and that we have guilt and pollution imputed to us from birth, we are still responsible for the acts of sins we do daily. Just as Adam was responsible for all the sins he did after the fall we too are responsible to God for acts of sins we do to ourselves, others and God. We are just as guilty as Adam was every time we disobey God because our hearts are sinful and evil. Bosma (1927, p. 105) taught what the bible said when he wrote, "From within, out of the heart of men, evil thoughts proceed, fornications, thefts, murderers, adulteries, covetings, wickedness, deceit, lasciviousness, an evil eye, railing, pride, foolishness; all these evil things proceed from within and defile the man. We commit actual sins by our thoughts, words and deeds."

The covenant of grace and not works brings total restoration of man. This is what man Adam and all his posterity needed to hear. The pitman dug was too deep that he needed help from outside of himself to lift him out of it. According to Bosma (1927, p. 110) Man needed to hear the message of Grace from God.

Following the discussion of the first man's fall into sin, of our own inherited and actual sin and its terrible consequences, comes the glad message of deliverance and salvation. All mankind is aware of misery, though all do not know its true nature, and all seek to rescue in some way. The heathen is ever sought in vain; only the grace of God can provide a way of escape from sin and its punishments. Deliverance must come from above. And deliverance has come from above. God has revealed an eternal counsel of redemption for the salvation of his people. Immediately after man sinned, God revealed his just anger against sin in the judgments he pronounced upon the transgressors, but he also revealed his grace in tempering judgment with mercy, and promising that he would establish enmity between the woman and her seed and the serpent and his seed, and that the seed of a woman would bruise the head of the serpent.

Man, broke the covenant of works when he disobeyed God and then God provided another covenant. Only this time, God himself sets the plan of saving man from the pit through his own grace. This time God keeps the covenant through his sovereign hand. The seed promised from a woman would not only widen the enmity between Adam posterity and the devil but also would provide redemption for all mankind that seek him. God promised, saying, "And I will put enmity between you and the woman, and between your offspring and hers; he will crush your head, and you will strike his heel." Gen. 3:15. I call this the mother of all the promises made by God.

CHAPTER FORTEEN. QUESTIONS TO ANSWER

What is the doctrine of man?

Who made man? Genesis 1: 26-27?

Was man made with or without sin? How did man fall?

Is man or woman spirit and flesh or spirit, flesh and soul?

What is a covenant of works?

What is a covenant of grace?

Why was man made by God?

CHAPTER 15

DOCRINE OF CHRIST

Jesus Christ is the promised seed in Gen.3:15 and the fulfillment of the covenant of grace. God in history worked out the plan of redemption from the time he promised to provide a seed from a woman till the birth of our Lord Jesus Christ. All other covenants God made with his people were based on the seed mentioned in Gen. 3:15. "When the man failed to obtain the blessing, offered in the covenant of works, it was necessary for God to establish another means, one by which man could be saved. The rest of scripture after the story of the fall in Genesis 3 is the story of God working out in history the amazing plan of redemption whereby sinful people could come into fellowship with himself" Grudem (1994, p. 516).

Though it is not easy to definitively state that the seed in the Old Testament referred to Jesus Christ, however, the bible has some hits that confirm this promise, especially during the time of Abraham. God promised a son, seed, that would inherit all things in spite his wife being old and barren.

After this, the word of the Lord came to Abram in a vision: Do not be afraid, Abram. I am your shield, your very great reward. Abram said, "Sovereign Lord, what can you give me since I remain childless and the one who will inherit my estate is Eliezer of Damascus?" You have given me no children; so, a servant in my house-hold will be my heir." The word of the Lord came to him: This man will not be your heir, but a son, seed, who is your own flesh and blood, will be your heir. He took him outside and said, look up at the sky and count them. Then he said to him, so shall your offspring be. Gen.15:1-5.

The apostle Paul in his letter to the Galatians clearly stated that the promised seed was Jesus Christ, "The promises were spoken to Abraham and to his seed. Scripture does not say, "and to seeds," meaning many people, but "and to your seed," meaning one person, who is Christ. What I mean is this: The law, introduced 430years later, does not set aside the covenant previously established by God and thus do away with the promise." Gal. 3:16-17. Again, in Galatians 4.4 Paul says, "But when the set time had fully come, God sent his son, born of a woman, born under the law, to redeem those under the law, that we might receive adoption to the son-ship." Luther (1998, p. 156) in his book <u>Galatians</u> said, "A certain man would come from Abraham's seed----that is, Christ---through whom the blessing would come afterwards upon all nations. Seeing therefore that it was Christ who would bless all nations, it was also he who would take the case away from them."

Who is Jesus Christ? What is His Nature?

We Christians believe in Jesus Christ alone for our salvation. Jesus Christ said to his disciples, "I am the way, the truth and the life. No one comes to the father except through me." John 14:6. Paul to the Philippian jailer said, "Believe in the Lord Jesus, you will be saved-you and your house-hold." Acts 16:29-31. Jesus Christ is our Lord and Savior. Still the question remains, who is this Jesus Christ? And what nature was he? To answer these questions, we need to read and understand the documents that our beloved Christians before us stated.

Reformed churches have documents that are part of the Christian tradition and are kept dearly in strengthening the faith. These documents are called creed and confessions and they are four to six, depending which reformed denomination one is in. Too sad that some of the churches do not even read or think these documents exist, and even when they do they pay no attention to even read or use them in their services or Bible studies. Some or not, many Christian churches have thrown out these great creeds and confessions and have replaced with nothing if not choir or contemporary music. No wonder many Christians today cannot define who Jesus Christ is, even though they believe him to be the savior of their lives.

In this thesis, I will not state historical context that triggered these creeds and confessions to be written, but rather write what they say about the nature of Jesus Christ. This is the right reformed teaching about the nature of Jesus Christ. Apostolic creed reveals who Jesus Christ was

I believe in God the father Almighty, maker of heaven and earth, and in Jesus Christ, His only Son, our Lord; Who was conceived by the Holy Ghost, born of the virgin Mary; suffered under Pontius Pilate, was crucified, dead and buried; He descended into hell, the third day rose from the dead; he ascended into heaven; and sitteth at the right hand of God the Father Almighty; from thence He shall come to judge the quick and the dead (Gore The *doctrine of Christ*, p. 121).

If Jesus Christ was born and suffered before dying and being buried, then he was fully human like us. He has been a man just like the rest of us. This is one of his two natures. The Nicene Creed (Western addition in brackets) states even more of the natures of Jesus. More Creeds of the church are found also in Christ. Creeds and the churches (1963) This Apostles creed are found in (Gore, the Doctrine of Christ p. 121).

I believe in one God the Father Almighty; Maker of heaven and earth, and of all things Visible and invisible. And in one Lord Jesus Christ, the only-begotten Son of God, begotten of the Father before all worlds (God of God, Light of Light), very God of very God, begotten, not made, being of one substance (consubstantiate) with the Father; by whom all things were made; who, for us men and for our salvation, came down from heaven, and was incarnate by the Holy Ghost of the virgin Mary, and was made man.

Jesus Christ was fully man and fully God with two natures perfectly inseparably in one man. Out of all the Christian creeds and confessions I have read and studied The Athanasian Creed summaries two names of Jesus Christ conclusively.

Furthermore, it is necessary to everlasting salvation; that he also believe faithfully the Incarnation of our Lord Jesus Christ. For the right Faith is, that we believe and confess; that our Lord Jesus Christ, the Son of God, is God and Man; God, of the Essence of the Father; begotten before the worlds; and Man, of the Essence of his Mother, born in the world. Perfect God; and perfect Man, of a reasonable soul and human flesh subsisting. Equal to the Father, as touching his Godhead; and inferior to the Father, as touching his Manhood. Who although he is God and Man; yet he is not two, but one Christ. One; not by conversion of the Godhead into flesh; but by assumption of the Manhood by God. One altogether; not by confusion of Essence; but by unity of Person. For as the reasonable soul and flesh is one man; so, God and Man is one Christ; Who suffered for our salvation; descended into hell; rose again the third day from the dead. He ascended into heaven; he sitteth on the right hand of the God the Father Almighty, from whence he will come to judge the living and the dead. At whose coming all men will rise again with their bodies; And shall give account for their own works. And they that have done good shall go into life everlasting; and they that have done evil, into everlasting fire. This is the catholic faith; which except a man believe truly and firmly, he cannot be saved (Gore (Doctrine of Christ, p. 122) also online

BEDROOM OF ADAM AND EVE

<http://en.wikipedia.org/wiki/Athanasian_Creed>.

Jesus Christ was the true mediator of the covenant of grace, though fully God and with the same essence as God the Father and God the Holy Spirit. He incarnated to become flesh. He was a messenger, advocate or intercessor and lastly a peacemaker between God the Father and the people in the world. Read Hodge. A. A (1928, pp 378-390) on the doctrine of Christ.

Jesus Christ truly and completely filled the three offices of Prophet, Priest and King. Reformed teachings teach that Jesus Christ served as a true Prophet, Priest and King and therefore all the prophets, priests and kings in the Old Testament pointed to Jesus Christ or were a type of Jesus Christ. Read what Bosma (1927, p. 146) says:

During the Old Testament dispensation, many of the prophets, priests and kings were anointed with holy oil. Whenever this was done, they were thus designated to their respective offices, and the oil was also a symbol of the gifts of the Holy Spirit fitting the appointed official for his history calling. See the history of Saul, David, Hazael, Elisha, Aaron and his sons. The prophets, priests and kings under Israel were types of Christ, and what the anointing means for them it also meant for Christ. He alone truly filled the three offices of Prophet, Priest and king.

I believe that even in the New Testament and also during our time Christ calls his servants to work as prophets, priests and kings, but always through him, in him and with him not without him. We serve in all these three offices when we are under the anointing of the Holy Spirit.

Amazingly Christians, even now begin to imitate Christ in each of these roles, though in a subordinate way. We have a prophetic role as we proclaim the gospel to the world and thereby bring God's saving word to people. In fact, whenever we speak truthfully about God to believers or to unbelievers, we are fulfilling a prophetic function using the word prophetic in a very broad sense). We are also priests because Peter calls us a royal priesthood (1Peter 2:9) ... We also share in part now in the kingly reign of Christ, since we have been raised to sit with him in the heavenly places (Eph.2:6). Read Grudem (1994, pp. 629-630).

The principles names of our mediator, Jesus and Christ reveal more of his nature and works. The name Jesus reveals the divine work commanded by his Father in heaven to do for us here on earth. Angel Gabriel said to Mary and Joseph: "Thou shalt call his name Jesus" which means he who saves his people from their sins. Matthew 1:21. Therefore, this name signifies the fact he is Him alone who saves and becomes the Lord of his people. While Christ is the official name of Jesus, which is referred in all three offices. Christ means Messiah or the anointed one. God anointed Christ with the Holy Ghost and ordained him to be our eternal prophet, priest and king. In him and with him we fulfill all three offices. There are many other names of our mediator in the bible which can further be discussed. According to Bosma (1927, p. 165)

After discussing the natures, offices, names of our mediator, Jesus Christ, we need to say some facts about his states. Christ has two states: a state of humiliation and the state of exaltation. State of humiliation reveals the incarnation of Jesus Christ becoming flesh. He was born fully human after being conceived in the womb of the Virgin Mary by the power of the Holy Ghost. In other words, he emptied up himself and became nothing. He became man and lived under the subjection to the law of the land yet never sinned. He was tempted in all things, yet never yielded to sin because he was fully God. He suffered under Pontius Pirate, crucified on the cross, died, buried and descended into hell. This means "that he suffered before his actual death the terrors of hell in his soul and thus was humbled into the very depths of death. This is Christ's full state of humiliation.

During the state of humiliation, Christ took upon himself all our guilty and sin and in relationship to the law, Christ satisfied all the requirements of the law when he died on the cross. Bosma (1927, p. 162) wrote:

In his incarnation, Christ took the exact place of his people, he assumed the position of guilt. He entered that relation to the law which his people occupy by nature. Therefore, Christ had to suffer the punishment which the law pronounces on the guilty. To undergo this punishment Christ was humiliated, that is, he emptied himself, taking the form of a servant, being made in the likeness of men… he humbled himself, becoming obedient even unto death, yea, the death of the cross. Philippians 2:7,8. This entering the position of guilt with its consequent suffering of punishment was Christ's state of humiliation.

After the state of humiliation Jesus Christ went into a state of Exaltation. Both these two states were done through the sovereign hand of God Almighty. Bosma (1927, p. 167) said:

We see Christ's state of exaltation in his resurrection, appearances to his followers, Ascension to his father in heaven, sitting at the right hand of the Father, Sending of the Holy Ghost to his people, interceding for us from heaven and his second coming at the end of all things. The work Christ was commanded to do here on earth by his father was now done and complete. He satisfied the requirements of the law, defeated Satan, death and sin by dying and rising from the dead. Therefore, Christian state of exaltation gives complete evidence "that he satisfied all the demands of the law, and could therefore now enter from under the wrath of God into his favor and pleasure.

Bosma went on to say that After Christ had satisfied the law in full he entered the relation of innocence toward the law, and being no longer counted guilty, he did not have to suffer any more, but was transferred to the fullest liberty and joy, he was lifted up to honor and glory, to the state of exaltation, in which he now is in heavenly glory. In the state of humiliation, Christ merited salvation for us; in the state of exaltation he applies salvation to us. Read more of what he wrote here (Bosma 1927, p. 162).

In conclusion about the doctrine of Christ reformed teaching teaches and confesses two natures of Jesus Christ: human nature and divine nature, three offices: Prophet, priest and king, two states: humiliation and exaltation, and two official names; Jesus and Christ though other people named Jesus too. Two states of Jesus Christ summarize the work he did here on earth from birth to death and from resurrection, ascension to the second coming,

BEDROOM OF ADAM AND EVE
CHAPTER FIFTEEN. QUESTIONS TO ANSWER

What is the doctrine of Christ?

Who is Jesus Christ?

What is the nature of Jesus Christ?

Define two natures of Jesus Christ?

Why did Jesus Christ never sin?

What three offices did Jesus fulfill?

What is the incarnation?

Was Jesus Christ present in the Old Testament?

What does the New Testament say about Jesus Christ?

Define two states of Jesus Christ?

CHAPTER 16

DOCTRINE OF SALVATION

It is impossible to have the doctrine of salvation without human beings here on earth. Jesus would not have come just to save the world without falling humans. Also, it is impossible to have the doctrine of salvation without triune God: God the Father, God the Son and God the Holy Spirit. Thus why Jesus Christ, the second person of the Godhead, came down from heaven became man in order to be our mediator. He was born, suffered, died, buried and rose from the dead, appeared to his believers, ascended into heaven, sited at the right hand side of God Almighty. Jesus Christ sent out the Holy Ghost to his believers. Jesus certainly is coming again.

Jesus Christ is the savior of the world who sacrificed his own body once for all for the sins of the world. The Hebrew author says, "Then he said, here I am, I have come to do your will. He sets aside the first to establish the second. And by that will, we have been made holy through the sacrifice of the body of Jesus Christ once for all." Hebrews 10: 9-10.

We have discussed that already in his humiliation, Christ secured salvation for us and in exaltation he applied salvation to us. Though the work of securing salvation does the work of applying still goes on until the second coming. How does Christ apply the blessings of salvation to us? What order should we follow? Firstly, we know a man can never apply the merits of Christ to himself without the help of the spirit of God. Bosma (1927, p. 170) says, "Man left to his own choice would never desire or be able to apply the merits of Christ to his salvation. Christ must and does apply his own merits. He does this through the Holy Spirit in a regularly ordained way or another." Again, what order is Bosma talking about here?

I remember during my young years just before I went to Justo Theological College, I memorized the following salvation plan words that we used to teach to one another in our youth fellowships; Regeneration, conversion, faith, justification, calling, and sanctification. This was the heart of a born-again movement in the reformed church in Zambia. We felt the duty of the Holy Spirit to make all members of the church be born again (regenerated) by the Holy Ghost. Sometimes we thought it was our work to make people born again rather than the work of the Holy Ghost. Thus the case when Christians think they can help the Holy Spirit instead of just relying on the operation of the divine work of God. In what order does Christ apply his merits to us? Or what does reformed church or theology say about this issue? Bosma (1927, p. 171) wrote:

We cannot, therefore, question the experience of the saints to know in what order Christ applies his blessings, but the study of the word of God reveals to us what plan God has established, and according to the established rule of God's word we must present the various parts of the scheme of salvation in their proper order. There is, however, on the part of those who have studied the Scriptures no unanimity of opinion as to the exact order in which the blessings of Christ are applied to us.

Per Rev Bosma there is no unanimity, meaning no uniformity or overwhelming support by Christian theologians that there is the exact order in which the blessings of Christ are applied to believers. However, he seemed to suggest that reformed theologians have some form of order when it comes in the exact order on this issue. Read what Bosma (1927, p. 1717) says on this issue "We will in our presentation follow the order that is very commonly followed by Reformed theologians. Per this plan the following are the blessings of Christ in the given order: Vocation, or Calling, regeneration, Conversion, Faith, Justification, and Sanctification."

What is the meaning of each of these common words which are widely used in the Christian circles? Since I am a reformed theologian writing a doctoral thesis on the reformed teachings in US Prisons, I will make a reformed stand on each of these words.

What is calling? In my Nsenga language calling means *kuyita* which simply means to call someone or something. For example, when villagers were about to eat food in their home, they had to call out for someone who was not around to come quickly to the house and be part of dinner or Lunch. In biblical sense calling has two stages; external and internal calling.

External calling is the declaration of the word of God, which includes the law and the gospel by the church of Christ to all mankind in the world. Christ commanded the church to go out into the world and declare that He was the only lord and savior of the world. This is the good news to the world. Matthew 28:19.

Internal call has two stages; creative and effectual calling. In creative calling God calls and creates things out of nothing. God calls things that were not as if they were. Bosma (1927, p. 176) wrote "God calls or speaks and by his speaking he creates. Thus, in the beginning he said, Let there be light, and there was light. The whole of creation was thus produced by the creative word of God… Creative calling is the first work of grace." God calls and speaks life into the dead. Romans 4:17; John 11:43-44; Acts 16:14.

How can that which has been called continue to be effected by the grace of the caller? Thus, what effectual calling reveals. Poor Lazarus was called out from death to life and now he still has to continue believing in the restoring power of the Lord Jesus Christ in his life through the Spirit. External calling does not bring continued restoration to a spiritual man, but internal calling does, especially effectual calling. Per Bosma (1927, p. 177):

By the effectual calling we mean that God calls the soul of man to turn from its state of alienation and enmity towards God into a new state of fellowship and obedience to God. The new life implanted by the creative calling is called into action to obey the revealed will of God by the effectual calling. The effectual calling accomplishes external calling when it is applied to the heart through the Holy Spirit. The effectual calling, therefore, mediate, that is, through outward means supernaturally applied. Effectual calling does not originate new life as a creative calling does, but it causes the new life to respond to the word of God.

Therefore, it is true to say that Christians are chosen in Christ from eternity and called effectually to Christ in time. Through faith, which itself is God's gracious gift, we receive Christ and all his benefits (Horton 2011, p. 99).

External calling is revealed when Christ commanded his disciples to go out and proclaim the good news to all nations; Creative calling is revealed when God the Father called out with his words and made the world; And effectual calling is revealed when Christ through his word and the spirit causes his people to obey him.

Regeneration

In theology, we have terms that mean the same, but used in different context. Creative calling may mean the same way as regeneration in different contexts. 1 Cor. 1:9 and 1 Thess. 2:12; Gal. 5:13. Regeneration is cleared mentioned by Jesus Christ in the discussion with Nicodemus in the gospel of John chapter 3: 1-8. Regeneration is defined "as the implanting of a new principle of life by the Holy Spirit in the heart of a sinner who is by nature dead in trespasses and sins." Bosma page 181. These are some of the biblical support texts for regeneration; John 3:3-5; Eph. 2:1, 5; 1John 3:14; James 1:18; John 1:13; John 5: 21; 1 Pet. 23; Titus 3:5; Deut. 30:6; Ezek. 36:26; Rom. 6:13; 11 Cor.5:17. In Christian circles regeneration means born again of the Spirit from above. Bosma (1927, p. 180) suggested that:

Because of this implanting of a new principle in the heart the nature of the heart is in principle changed, the old man or nature and disposition of the heart is mortified and dethroned; and we are also by regeneration made part of the spiritual body of Christ. Regeneration in the narrow sense, is produced by the creative calling of God… In the wider sense regeneration is the moral renewing of man by the Word and Spirit of God. In this wider sense faith, conversion and sanctification are included often under the term of regeneration.

Regeneration applies to all people infants and adults. Christ was very clear to Nicodemus when he said, "Unless you are born again, you cannot see the kingdom of God." If we believe that all hearts from conception till death are totally depraved and need the savior to save them, then we must believe God through his spirit cause's human hearts that believe (the elect) come to his son Jesus Christ. If we believe God creatively made the world out of nothing, then we must believe that God in Christ can cause an infant be in the kingdom of God by his creative calling. In other words, nothing is impossible with God. Regeneration, therefore, is the work of the spirit of God through Christ to make us his children. The inner man becomes regenerated forever.

Conversion

Langford Banda was the first pastor of Kamwala Reformed church in Zambia who experienced unique conversion in his life. One day he was driving his car and suddenly crashed and turned upside down many times. Fortunately, enough, he survived the crash with minor injuries. From that time, he thought God called him to the ministry. He dramatically changed his life and became a minister. Later, after serving the Lord Jesus Christ for some years he passed on to be with Him forever. Blessing Lungu has been brought up in a Christian home. She is a strong believer in the Lord Jesus Christ but never had a dramatic conversion like that of pastor Banda. Many Christians in the world are like Blessing Lungu but others like Banda as far as conversion experience is concerned. It is good to know about our conversion when it happened, but it is not necessary. What is important is to know that we have eternal life through Jesus Christ our Lord.

What really is conversion? It is the change from a sinful life to the life of service and obedience to God. Conversion is "turning about, and in a theological sense it means the act of turning or of being turned from a sinful course to a life of obedience and service. The words used in the original languages of scripture to designate conversion mean: to change the mind; to turn about, return; to repent" Bosma (1927, p. 185). A person that has experienced true conversion will have a change of mind and conduct. Thus, the heart of a regenerated man produces true conversion that affects all of his life. Therefore, true Christian conversion is the result of regeneration or effectual calling.

How many times does the conversion happen in a Christian life? It happens once. The actual conversion occurs once. After conversion, however, God's children are prone to wander away from God into sin, and they thereby lose conscious fellowship with God and the enjoyment of his presence and love. Then there must come again returning to God in confession of sin and invoking of his mercy through Jesus Christ. In fact, this will more or less be the continual and repeated experience of every Christian. Bosma (1927, p. 191).

How can I be assured of my conversion? I can be sure by feeling sorrowful of my sins, repent and then live a life of Jesus Christ. Let Jesus Christ be the center of my daily life. Live a life of service to him alone. Bosma (1927, p. 192) says, "A good way to pursue this end is to see if the fruits of conversion are found in our lives: sorrow for sin, trust in the merits of the savior, love to God, desire to do good works." Never base spiritual conversion on physical or feelings. Continue surrender to Jesus Christ and his kingdom will bring great assurance of my conversion.

Faith

What is faith? How can we know we have saving faith? Faith is believing in the truth, which means believing in what is true. Faith has two elements: 1) being convinced of the truth, being certain of reality, having evidence of unseen things, and 2) believing, hoping in, embracing, seizing the truth. Per Bosma (1927, p. 193) "faith in its first and most elementary sense is simply the reliance of one person on the truthfulness and integrity of another. When one believes the word of another, he has faith in him." There are three elements of faith? Someone who has faith must have these three elements; knowledge, consent, and trust or confidence. Knowledge is very important when it comes to believing in someone or something. We need to have a testimony or assurance of someone; something or else we will not be able to have faith in him, her or it. Once we have the knowledge then we need to be able to consent or accept and then build trust on it.

Reformed churches believe that true believers in Jesus Christ have saving faith, not temporary, historical, intellectual, or emotional faith. Temporary faith has no depth in it, especially when faced with storms and diversities of life. Read Mat.13:1-9 and Mat.8:23-27. Historical faith bases on the past events and narratives while intellectual and emotion, faith rest in human flesh which ultimately is vanity. Having saving faith in a broader sense is to believe with all the heart the whole counsel of the divine and inspired word of God. Great answer from the Catechism," True faith is not only a certain knowledge, whereby I hold to the truth all that God has revealed to us in his word, but also an assured confidence, which the Holy Spirit works by the gospel, in my heart; that not only to others, but to me also, remission of sin, everlasting righteousness, and salvation, are freely given by God, merely of grace, only for the sake of Christ's merits." Heidelberg Catechism Question 21

Saving faith or true faith is a gift from God that comes to believers through hearing the word of God. Therefore, these believers are called born again by the spirit of Jesus Christ. These Christians are now fully enlightened by the same spirit to understand the gospel and even appreciate life better. Believers in the Lord Jesus Christ have a better grasp of hope in this world and the world to come due to saving faith.

By this faith, a Christian believeth to be true whatsoever is revealed in the word, for the authority of God himself speaks therein; and acteth differently upon that which each particular passage, therefore, contains; yielding obedience to the commands, trembling at the threatening's, and embracing the promises of God for this life and that which is to come. But the principal acts of saving faith are, accepting, receiving, and resting upon Christ alone for justification, sanctification, eternal life, by virtue of the covenant of grace. Westminster confession of faith Chapter 14:11.

No one can or will ever come to true saving faith alone without the work of the Holy Spirit. Our sinful and rebellious nature constantly wages war against God and the things of God. By nature, we are incapable of touching the heart of God alone unless He does the initiative through divine grace in Christ alone. God creates faith in us to be able to believe in him. "For by grace you have been saved through faith; and that not of yourselves, it is the gift of God." Ephesian 2:8. There is no doubt in saving faith but maybe to a believer. For the Jesus said, "Verily, verily, I say unto you, He that hearth my word, and believeth him that sent me, hath eternal life, and cometh not into judgment, but has passed out of death into life." John 5:24

The Holy Spirit works this saving faith in us when we believe and live with Jesus Christ. We enter into the kingdom of God by the grace of God through faith in Jesus Christ and we stay in the kingdom of God by the grace of God through faith in Jesus Christ. Not by our works, that no one should boast. Bosma (1927, p. 202) taught that "Saving faith is the result of regeneration of the heart by the Holy Spirit, who dwells in those born again and turns them in hunger and thirst to Jesus Christ. Thus, the Spirit does through the agency of the word and according to the teaching and examples of the word. No one can or will of himself ever come to true faith, for are we all by nature dead through trespasses and sins, and true faith is the action of spiritual life in us."

Can true faith ever be lost? Now, it can never be lost because the covenant God who gives, it takes care of it with his sovereign hand. No one can snatch it from his hands not even the devil or its demons in hell. No snitchers here period. No, impossible, for God preserves it. Jesus confirmed this by saying, "And I give unto them eternal life; and they shall never perish, and no one shall snatch them out of my hand," John 10:28.

Why is it that some believers seem to be weak in faith and surely lack the certainty of salvation? The twofold answer here; First answer is that Christians behave badly so they found themselves at olds with God Almighty as they constantly grieve the person and work of the Holy Spirit. The word of God says, "And do not grieve the Holy Spirit of God, with whom you were sealed for the day of redemption. "Ephesian 4:30.

Secondly, Christians are very ignorant of the nature of true faith that they sorely base their belief in within themselves. Personal feelings and experiences take over faith matters and as the result the whole Christian walk in the Lord Jesus Christ becomes infertile. Christians who seem to have lack of salvation have incoherent views about God and His written word. The word of God says Christ Jesus came and died for our sins once and for all. Then he said, "Here I am, I have come to do your will. He sets aside the first to establish the second. And by that will, we have been made holy through the sacrifice of the body of Jesus Christ once for all." Hebrews 10: 9-10. Faith is the instrument by which we are linked to Christ and receive the grace of Justification (Sproul, 2004, p. 75).

Faith has the object which always is Jesus Christ and his kingdom. Faith is a leap into the kingdom of God. Faith is empty which means it is not associated with feelings, experience or emotions. Faith is therefore a gift of God and is not generated by human power. All humans are dead in their nature and actions and can only be made alive by the grace of God through faith in Jesus Christ alone. Paul in the letter of Ephesians wrote, "For it is by grace you have been saved, through faith-and this is not from yourselves, it is the gift of God-not by works, so that no one can boast." Eph. 2: 8-9. The power of the Holy Spirit does this.

Justification

What is justification? What is the nature, the ground, the means, and effect of justification? All human beings are in the court room with God. Judgment has already been passed and they have been found guilty of disobedience and rebellion against God. They have all sinned by breaking the law of God and therefore deserve suffering, death and a hello. This means they are not fit to be in the kingdom of God. But through divine mercy, justice came into the court room. Jesus comes into the scene and through total obedience to his father willingly and rightfully sets the records straight. Jesus becomes the only source of redemption through his sacrificial offering on the cross. He shed his pure blood for forgiveness of all human sins and guilt. Therefore, the position of man before God becomes right for the first time after the fall. Both Men and women called by his name are justified through faith in Jesus Christ alone. Per Bosma (1927, p. 205) this is the nature of justification;

BEDROOM OF ADAM AND EVE

It is first a judicial act of God, that is, an act of God as judge. The sinner appears before the tribunal of God, as guilty of breaking God's laws, and as eternally condemned by the justice of God because of his guilt. Now when God justifies the sinner the righteousness of Christ, that is, he credits or is put to the account of the sinner the merits of Jesus 'obedience, and on the ground of this obedience the sinner is pardoned and restored as a child of God forever. What does justification mean to Christians? I mean those men and women that have experienced saving faith in Jesus Christ? Justification for Christians means that "they are no longer subject to condemnation, the anger of God is removed, and his love is shown to their hearts. They now have peace with God, and joy in the Holy Spirit. They are also by the gratitude of their hearts moved to a holy life. Sanctification will follow justification" Bosma (1927, p. 213).

Those that are justified experience saving faith that produces good works since "faith, if it has not works, is dead in itself." James 2:17. If good works are neglected the believer loses the comfort and assurances of justification. The believer is delivered from the law as a condition to gain eternal life, but not as a rule of life. Rom.7:4.

A sinner is made right with God by the righteousness of Jesus Christ that is imputed to him. Justification, therefore "is that gracious act of God whereby he pardons the guilt of sin and adopts as his children and heirs unto eternal life, only for the righteous of Christ imputed to us, and received by faith alone" Bosma (1927, 204). The word of God says, "Being justified freely by his grace, through faith the redemption that is in Christ Jesus." Rom. 3:24 John writes, "But as many as received him, to them he gave the right (power) to become the sons of God, even to them that believe on his name." John 1:12.

A legal relationship or position of all believers in the Lord Jesus Christ has changed forever. They are now declared righteous before God by God himself. Christ has satisfied the right requirements of the law. God through Christ forgives all past, present, and future sins alone. Bosma said since all broke the law, therefore all are guilty, but all that believe through saving faith in Jesus Christ are declared right by the imputation of his sons 'righteousness. Bosma (1927, 205) said, "From this description it will be seen that justification does not change a person's inner heart or character, it changes his legal relation before God; it does not remove the pollution of sin, the internal corruption of the heart, as regeneration and sanctification do, but justification makes right the relation towards God's law, and in the law no longer condemns us, we shall not perish in sin."

The ground of justification is the righteousness of Jesus Christ and not our works which are not right or perfect. There is really nothing within us that God makes God justifies us. Justification does not depend on our faith and our works, but on the finished work of Jesus Christ. The word of God says, "If we are justified by works, Christ has died in vain." Gal. 2:21. Justification brings good works in our new life, though good works are not necessarily the sign of salvation. The word of God says, "For by grace have you been saved through faith; and that not of yourselves, it is the gift of God; not of works, that no man should glory. For we are his workmanship, created in Christ Jesus for good works, which God before prepared that we should walk in them." Eph. 2:8-10, also in Galatian 3:10, 11. Justification is the act of God. We are coming before God as if we have never sinned before. We are justified in Christ through faith alone (Sproul 2004, p. 75).

What is the means of justification? Faith in Jesus Christ alone is the means of our justification by God. The reformed teaching says that "Faith is not the ground or cause that merits justification, it is the means of appropriating Christ and his righteousness thus appropriated by faith we are justified. Justification is a gift of God's infinite grace; faith is our receiving of the gift. The more grace, faith is, therefore the more will there be enjoyment of justification" (Bosma, 1927, p. 210).

When does, justification occur? From the side of God, justification occurs in eternity through

Jesus Christ alone. Bosma says, "Many Reformed theologians, however, speak of justification from eternity by which they mean that God has from eternity looked down upon his people in Christ as justified, that is, as pardoned and his heirs… Later when he has given faith to his people he makes known minds that they are justified. This layer is then called justification from the subjective or human point of view." This is subject to discussion, but it is right reformed teaching (Bosma, 1927, p. 211).

Justification by God has done through, by, and in Christ alone. Justification by God is done in Christ Jesus alone, even If we believe in objective justification that says God declared us his people righteous before the foundation of the world or subjective justification that says we are justified from the time when God granted us faith to believe in Jesus Christ. Our churches, pastors, elders, chapels, chaplains, volunteers, and many other men and women God uses can never declare us right. All humans have sinned and fall short of the glory of God, but are freely justified through faith in Jesus Christ alone. This is a gift of God and above all it is a miracle of God to wash all our sins white as snow. Only God the Almighty can do this act of justification.

Sanctification follows justification.

Those justified by God live a life of sanctification in their walk with the Lord Jesus Christ. This too is the work of the grace of God through the spirit. Sanctification is the work of God's grace, whereby we are renewed in the whole man after the image of God, and are enabled increasingly to die unto sin, and to live unto righteousness. This is the message from shorter catechism. In the bible sanctification means to clean, to purify, and to separate or consecrate to God.

There are two sides to sanctification: When God justifies us, we now live lives fleeing or shunning sin and evil. Our old man is constantly killed or bitten by the renewing of our inner man through the spirit and the word of God. Secondly, when we're justified, we now live lives praising, pleasing, and glorifying God. We develop an inner desire to serve the Lord. We are committed to live holy lives because our Lord that called and justified us is holy. Bosma (1927, p. 215) said:

These two ideas it is necessary to put together that we may appreciate the meaning of sanctification. To cleanse from sin, turn from the common and the low, is one side of sanctification; to devote and consecrate to God is the other side. Mere turning from sin is not sanctification, there must go with it a whole-hearted devotion to God. A better understanding of sanctification may be gained by recalling what we said about conversion, that it is a turning from sin in hearty repentance, and turning to Christ in saving faith.

In sanctification, we continue turning away from sin and continue turning towards Christ in faith so that we may increase in holiness of life. This continued, turning is our sanctification.

At regeneration, the soul's new life began, a better, but not a sinless, life; a new nature was given to the soul, but the old nature was not destroyed and removed. A constant struggle will therefore result in the Christian; his life will be warfare. The old nature must be conquered by the new, and the new is to grow ever more in conformity to Jesus Christ. The soul was not only sick, but dead, God made it alive, now follows the putting off the old man, which is corrupt per the deceitful lusts, and the putting on of the new man, which after God is created in righteousness and true holiness. Ephesians 4:24.

Sanctification is possible only to those born again. It is their duty and not just a private matter. The word of God says, "Walk in the Spirit and you will not fulfill the lusts of the flesh." Therefore, sanctification is the work both of man and of God. God has given us the spirit the moment we were born again and this spirit helps us to walk after him. To advance in sanctification we must produce good works which come from our regenerated heart. The bible says, "For we are his workmanship, created in Christ Jesus for good works, which God afore prepared that we should walk in them." Eph.2:10. Also, it is said, "That you might walk worthy of the Lord unto all pleasing, being fruitful in every good work, and increasing in the knowledge of God. "Colossians 1:10.

Is it possible to have perfect and complete sanctification here on earth? No, it is not possible to have a complete and perfect sanctification here on earth, only when we are in heaven. No saints in the scripture were perfect in sanctification here on earth and no saint will ever be until after that promised home with Jesus Christ. The apostle Paul cried out and said, "Wretched man that I am." And to the Philippians, he wrote, "Not as though I had already attained, either were already perfect, but I follow after, if that I may apprehend that for which I also am apprehended of Christ Jesus." Phil. 3:12.

Can sanctification ever be entirely lost? No, because once justified by God, we are saints forever through his grace. Our bible teaches the perseverance of saints. This means that all true believers in the Lord Jesus Christ will be saved. We may have setbacks, problems and struggles in our Christian life, but never will we lose salvation in the Lord.

Why is this? The Bible says so in many passages. In a letter to the Romans, Paul wrote, "Therefore, there is now no condemnation for those who are in Christ Jesus, because through Christ Jesus the Law of the Spirit who gives life has set you free from the law of sin and death." Rom. 8:1-2. And Paul said, "I am persuaded that nothing shall separate me from the love of God, which is in Christ Jesus" Rom.8:38. John wrote, "I will give them eternal life, and they shall never perish; no one will snatch them out of my hand. My father who has given them to me, is greater than all; no one can snatch them out of my father's hand. I and my father are one." John 10:28-30. Our sanctification is rooted in the internal election of God in Christ Jesus. This is our security.

Prayer is part of our sanctification process. Prayer is central to our breathing as Christians. Prayer is our normal life as believers. It is offering up of our desires and wishes to God, per his will in Jesus Christ's name. In prayer, we also confess our sins and give glory and thanksgiving to God for all his mercies. Prayer is a communication with God. God talks to us and we listen and then we talk God listens. God's answer may be yes, no or wait. He always answers per his will. He knows what is best for us even before we ask him.

When we pray we constantly come into his presence through the help of the Holy Spirit. Paul wrote, "In the same way, the Spirit helps us in our weakness. We do not know what we ought to pray for, but the Spirit himself intercedes for us through wordless groans. And he who searches our hearts knows the mind of the Spirit, because the Spirit intercedes for God's people in accordance with the will of God." Rom. 8:26-27. Bosma (1927, 229) said, "The Spirit also helps our infirmities by preparing us to pray and guiding us in our own praying. He calls our attention to our needs, and leads us to repentance and faith, adoration, and praise. Christian life cannot exist without prayer."

E.M. Bounds in his little book called power through prayer wrote, "What the church needs today is not machinery or better, not new organizations or more and novel methods, but men whom the Holy Ghost can use-men of prayer, men mighty in prayer. The Holy Ghost does not flow through methods, but through men. He does not come on machinery, but on men. He does not anoint plans, but men-men of prayer" Bounds (1936, p. 12).

The secret of all successful praying is spending much time with the Lord in prayer. All men of God used by God spent lots of time talking with God. We need to breath to show that we are alive and we need to pray to remain alive and well in our sanctification process. Prayer less life kills the flow of the joy of our salvation. Prayer less preacher kills this joy and vision of the Lord in his life. Bounds (1936, p. 22) said, "Preaching that kills is prayer less preaching. Without prayer, the preacher creates death and not life."

In conclusion, reformed doctrine upholds the teaching of salvation which includes vocation or calling, regeneration, conversion, faith, justification, and sanctification. There is no sequence in the salvation process. Our salvation is rooted in God's election in Jesus Christ alone through the power of the Holy Spirit. Read also what Charles Hodge says in (Chapters 15-18).

CHAPTER SEXTEEN. QUESTIONS TO ANSWER

What is salvation?

What does ONCE FOR ALL means?

What is the order of salvation?

Define external and internal calling?

What is regeneration?

What is prayer?

What is conversion?

What is faith?

What is justification?

What is sanctification?

Are you regenerated by the Spirit of Christ? Romans 8:9.

What is the difference between born again and regeneration?

What is the difference between justification and sanctification?

BEDROOM OF ADAM AND EVE

CHAPTER 17

THE DOCTRINE THE CHURCH

What is reformed teaching on the church of God? In this section, we will discuss the meaning of the visible and invisible church. We will also discuss the attributes of the church, marks of the church, organization of the church, and offices of the church.

What is the church? Per Bosma (1927, p. 233) in the Testament the Greek word Ecclesia means "an assembly of citizens called together in some public place. In the Christian sense, Ecclesia means a company of believers who constitute together one body in a certain locality, or congregation." Ecclesia can also mean several believers in the Lord Jesus Christ everywhere and every time. Jesus Christ said these words to peter saying, "Upon this rock I will build my church." Matt. 16:18. The rock is Jesus Christ and not Peter nor the confession of Peter which says, "You are the Messiah, the Son of the living God." The rock of the church is Jesus Christ, whom Paul said, "And gave him to be head over all things to the church." Eph. 1:22. We can read these verses too about the church Eph. 3:10; Phil. 3:6; 1 Cor. 12:28; Acts 9:31.

What is the meaning of visible and invisible church? First, we must agree that the true church of Jesus Christ is one with Jesus as the head. This true spiritual church is invisible. One part is here on earth while the other part is in heaven with the Lord. The part that is here is called visible church. It is made up of believers in the Lord Jesus Christ. The part that is not here on earth is called invisible church. This part is made up of all believers in the Lord Jesus Christ that once lived here on earth but not anymore.

God calls all members of the church in Christ Jesus through the power of the Holy Spirit. Both visible and invisible church cannot exist without the Spirit of God. Bosma puts it right when he said, "The distinction between church visible and invisible is not that between two different churches, but, as we trust will be understood readily, between two sides of one and same church. The church visible is not an exact equivalent of the church invisible." Check Bosma (1927, 235). What are the attributes of the church? The attributes of the true spiritual church are holiness and oneness. The true church is holy and one at the same time. The head of this church is Jesus Christ. The word of God says, "But you are a chosen people, a loyal priesthood, a holy nation, God's special possession, that you may declare the praises of him who called you out of darkness into his wonderful light. Once you were not a people, but now you are a people of God; once you had not received mercy, but now you have received mercy." 1 Pet. 2: 9-10. The invisible church on earth has visible characteristic with it. It is not pure and holy, but always strived to be holy. The bible says, "As obedient children, do not conform to the evil desires you had when you lived in ignorance. But just as he who called you is holy, so be holy in all you do; for it is written be holy, because I am holy." 1 Pet. 1: 14-16.

The church of Christ is one and Christ himself is the head. This church is sometimes called catholic because it includes believers of every time and place. Bosma (1927, 236) says, "We Protestants, together with all Christians in every part of the world, from the Catholic Church, which is not bound by limits of place or nationality. All Christians are one in Christ, have one Spirit, one faith and one baptism."

The visible Christian church is made up of many different denominations, congregations and assemblies or churches. Differences within the visible Christian church are due to different languages, nationalities, organizations, teachings, and different understanding of the bible. Therefore, the visible church is not one united body.

What are the true marks of a Christian church? Reformed churches teach three marks of the visible church: True preaching of the word of God; proper administration of the sacraments; and proper exercise of Christian discipline. Bosma (1927, p. 237) says, "No portion of the church is entirely perfect, the aim of every part ought to be to become as perfect as possible. The nearer we come to the fulfillment of the above requirements, the purer will our church be."

The church of Jesus Christ our Lord has been given uncompromising task to preach good news to the whole world. If the church loses the zeal to preach the true living and inspired word to the world, it loses its saltiness. Once the church loses its saltiness and lightest in the world, it quickly looks like any other social organization. The bible says the church is unique and sacred in the world, "But you are a chosen people, a royal priesthood, a holy nation, God's special possession, that you may declare the praises of him who called you out of darkness into a wonderful light. "1 Pet. 2:9.

The message of the church comes from God to the world. "But you do not believe because you are not my sheep. My sheep listen to my voice; I know them, and they follow me." And elsewhere it is said, "If you hold to my teaching, you are really my disciples. Then you will know the truth, and the truth will set you free." John 8: 31-32; Acts 2:42; 1 Tim. 3:15; Gal. 1:8.

Reformed churches administer two sacraments which are believed to be instituted by God. These two sacraments are baptism and Holy Communion or Lords supper. The sacrament of baptism is done after believing in the Lord Jesus Christ or born in a covenant home. Sacrament of the Lord Supper is administered to believers who are baptized and examined in their hearts. I Cor. 11: 28. The last mark of the church is discipline. The church may discipline her members who need it after committing private or public sin, or spreading false teachings known as heresy. Members of the church have the responsibility of accountability to one another and to their leaders. They are not watchdogs looking for sinners or law breakers in the church.

The church officers are not expected to act as detectives to find out secret sins of the members, but open or known sins man not be tolerated, which would offend the church and be a scandal before the world… The church may not be able to say when or where a sin has been committed, but if it known that the members are living in sin, are by their connections with others violating the laws of God, the church must demand the forsaking of sin and then live in holiness of life (Bosma, 1927, p. 239).

Church discipline is done in the spirit of love. The discipline aims at bringing the individual back to the holy life in Christ than cutting members of the church away from the membership of the church. Discipline of the church must be done following scripture bases such as I Cor. 5:13, Mat. 18:15-18. Leaders as well as members of the church must constantly seek the leading of the Holy Spirit when exercising church discipline.

Reformed church has no high ranking in its church organization. There is no pope in the church, though some leaders and pastors may act like one. All members and leaders of the church are considered priests and saints before the Almighty God. But the church has different ranks in functions. The pastor teaches the flock while church elders and deacons run the administration. The pastor is called the teaching elder with the goal of bringing forth the gospel of Jesus Christ in the church and the world. The pastor is the mouthpiece of God to the world through the church.

BEDROOM OF ADAM AND EVE

The pastor does pastoral care to the church members. He must systematically visit his members at their home once a year, while the elders and the deacon make four times visits in their section. It is very important for the pastor and church leaders to know members of the church to promote the spirit of comradery. There is no elder or pastor without the flock to take care. In other words, pastors and elders are keepers of the people of God through the word. Church leaders must be called by God and installed by the local church. These people are full of wisdom, spirit, faith, love, integrity, and respect. Church leaders must carry their duties in an honest and professional manner. 1 Tim. 5:1-25; Titus 1: 5-9.

The reformed church organization operates from the bottom up. Local congregational leadership is made up of the pastor, elders, and deacons. These three form a church council or consistory. The consistory meets once a month for church business meeting.

Presbytery or class is made up of groups of local churches. The leadership of the class takes care of the business of all congregations under its jurisdiction. Class leaders must make systematic visitations of all its local churches once a year. Reformed church synod becomes the highest body of the church. The synod is made of elders and pastors of all its congregations. In conclusion, the reformed church has three church governments; Consistory or church council, classis or presbytery, and the synod. All three bodies do their duties per the church laws written in the book of orders or Buku Lamalamulo in Reformed Church in Zambia.

CHAPTER SEVENTEEN. QUESTIONS TO ANSWER

What is a Christian church?

Who is the head of a church?

Discuss the difference between visible and invisible church?

Discuss three governments of the reformed church?

What does the statement FROM BOTTOM UP means in this chapter?

What is church discipline?

Why no high rank in the reformed church?

Has the Christian Church replaced the nation of Israel?

CHAPTER 18

DOCTRINE OF THE MEANS OF GRACE

The doctrine of grace is not the means of grace and the means of grace is not the doctrine of grace. We already discussed the doctrine of grace and now we need to know the institutions used to administer the doctrine of grace. According to reformed teaching there are two means of grace: the word of God and Sacraments. The two are not on an equal level, though the two are tools God administers his miraculous benefits to our faith. These two strengthen our Christian faith when we take part in them. The sacraments cannot happen without the word of God through the word of God can be preached even without sacraments.

In reformed churches, everything else must be centered on the word of God. Whenever we preach the word we bring a live Jesus Christ in our lives and in the lives of listeners. Also, every time we participate in Holy Communion, we spiritually, come face to face with our lord Jesus Christ. We remember Jesus being dead, but alive forever. We grow in faith due to grace that flows in us through the word 11 Tim. 3:15-17 and sacraments 1 Cor. 11: 17-34, Mat. 28:16-20.

It is very important to read and obey the word of God and also is it great to take part in the sacraments; Baptism and Holy Commination. What do we understand by the means of grace? Means of grace are those institutions which God has ordained to be the ordinary channels of his grace; they are those instrumentalities through which the Holy Spirit operates upon the souls of men into their growth in grace. All grace is of God, has been obtained in the Church by Christ, and is applied by the Holy Spirit… These means are the word of God and the sacraments (Bosma, 1927, p. 248). This is a good definition of the sacraments found in our catechism. "The sacraments are holy signs and seals, appointed of God for this end, that by the use thereof, he may the more fully declare and seal unto us the promise of the gospel, viz: that he grants us freely, remission of sin and life eternal, for the sake of that one sacrifice of Christ, accomplished on the cross" (Bosma 1927, 252). Sacraments and the word of God points to finished work of Jesus Christ and his second coming.

Symbol, we use in baptism is water and in communion is bread and wine or juice. "These are outward visible sign used per Christ's own appointment. An outward spiritual grace thereby signified. Thus, the outward sign of baptism is water; of the Lord's Supper, bread and wine. The inward grace signified in baptism is the washing away of our sins, in the Lord's Supper the nourishing of our souls unto eternal life (Bosma, 1927, p. 253). Baptism can be administered through fully immersed in water or sprinkled with water on the forehead. The quantity of the water does not matter but the symbolism behind it thus what matters. Bosma (1927, p. 256) says, "The washing or sprinkling in baptism symbolizes the separation of the baptized person from a sinful life, and his entrance into a new life into the triune God, into a new relation to the Father, Son, and Holy Spirit, our covenant God."

Reformed doctrine upholds the teaching of infant baptism, though many reformed churches do not practice it these days. Infant baptism and adult baptism do not save us, but Christ alone through the grace of God. The word of God says before the foundation of the world I knew and called you. You are mine and you are in my hands and no one can remove you from my hands say the Lord. Isaiah 41; Eph. 1: 4; 1 Pet. 1:20.

Infants are baptized in the reformed churches not because they have faith to believe in Jesus Christ, but because they are born in the home of the covenant folks. It is heavily the responsibility of the believing parents to raise the baptized baby on the way of the Lord. It is also sorely the personal responsibility of the child to turn away from sins and accept Jesus Christ as he or she grows up in the statue and in the knowledge of the Lord Jesus Christ.

The infant is not aware what the parents are doing during infant baptism but God does. The parents who do not force God to bring faith on their child, but rather want to share covenanted blessings of baptisms to all households. There is no biblical support for infant baptism and neither is there clear biblical support against it. "No, there is no direct order for infant baptism, nor does the New Testament record one indisputable case of infant baptism. Our doctrine of the necessity of infant baptism is derived at inferentially; we gather our proofs from the prevailing view the Bible gives us of the relation wherein the children stand for the Lord and the church" Bosma (1927, p. 263).

Reading these passages below do not clearly shed light, whether the baptized household had kids or not. The Bible says all in the house were baptized. "One of those listening was a woman from the city of Thyatira named Lydia, a dealer in the purple cloth. She was a worshiper of God. The Lord opened her heart to respond to Paul's message. When she and the members of her household were baptized, she invited us to her home." Acts 16: 13-15. Elsewhere Paul said, "Yes, I also baptized the household of Stephanas; beyond that, I don't remember if I baptized anyone else."1 Cor. 1:16.

Water baptism is a symbol pointing to the finished work of our Lord and savior Jesus Christ. It is a command instituted by Jesus Christ and followed by his disciples and the early Christians. But true baptism is done in the heart with the sprinkling of the blood of Jesus Christ by the spirit of God.

CHAPTER EIGHTEEN. QUESTIONS TO ANSWER

What is the doctrine of the means of grace?

Explain how the word and sacraments are means of grace?

What are sacraments? Are they above the word of God?

How many sacraments does the reformed church practice?

What is the meaning of water baptism?

Does water baptism save?

Can you baptize a child?

Who must perform water baptism?

What is Holy Communion?

Who should participate in holy communion?

What are the symbols of baptism and communion?

What is the message of the church?

How can we grow in faith?

BEDROOM OF ADAM AND EVE

CHAPTER 19

THE DOCTRINE OF THE LAST THINGS

The doctrine of the last things is also called the second coming of Jesus Christ. What will happen during the second coming of Jesus Christ? In this section, we will discuss: the state of the soul after death; the second advent of Christ; Resurrection of the dead; final judgment and the eternal state of all creatures.

What happens when we die? Where does the soul go? First, the bible is very simplicity and specific about death. We die because our first parents disobeyed God and brought upon themselves sin, suffering and death. The word of God says, "And the Lord commanded the man. You are free to eat from any tree in the garden, but you must not eat from the tree of the knowledge of good and evil, for when you eat from it you will certainly die." And Paul to the Romans wrote, "For the wages of sin is death, but the gift of God is eternal life in Christ Jesus our Lord." Rom.6: 23.

Why do the justified die? They die because of sin, but they "death is necessary for them as a gateway to eternal life, the present constitution didn't fit for eternal glory. The sting of death is removed from them, and when this last enemy shall be destroyed, they shall be entirely freed from his grasp" (Bosma, 1927, p. 285).

Our souls are immortal and live forever, even when they are separated from the bodies in death. The word of God says, "And the dust returns to the ground it came from, and the spirit returns to God who gave it." Eccl. 12: 7. Jesus said, "Do not be afraid of those who kill the body but cannot kill the soul." Matt. 10: 28. Paul in II Cor. 5:8 and Phil. 1:22-24 defines death as a departing of the soul, and going to be with the Lord Jesus Christ.

When we die, our souls continue to have conscious existence. Our souls are independent of the bodies waiting for the resurrection, when they will reunite with immortal and spiritual bodies. The bible teaches that our souls after death will continue to have conscious existence and knowledge of their surroundings. These souls will be able to think and remember things. God is the God of the living and not of the dead. Our souls live forever with our God. 11 Cor. 5: 8; Luke 23: 43; Luke 20:38; Eph. 3: 25; Acts. 25; Rev.6: 9-11.

At the time of death our eternal resting places are assigned whether our souls will spend the rest of eternal life in heaven with the Lord Jesus Christ or in hell with the devil, demons and all fallen angels. There's no change of the state of our souls after death. No second chance after death. This means that at the time of death if we have Jesus Christ in our hearts we will be with Jesus Christ forever, but if we do not have Jesus Christ at the time of death we will not be with him forever. Jesus Christ is all that matters to secure eternal resting place in the kingdom of God.

Second Advert of Jesus Christ

We speak about the second advert because Jesus first came in the flesh, dead, rose from the dead and went back to his father in heaven. During the second advert Jesus Christ is coming back again to restore all things new. No one knows the time Jesus Christ is coming again. The word of God says, "But about that day or hour no one knows, neither the angels in heaven, nor the son, but only the father" Mark 14:32. The bible teaches that certain things will precede the second coming of Jesus Christ such as:

The spreading of the gospel to all nations Matt. 24:14

1. The return of the Jews to Christ. Isaiah 11:11-12; Ezek. 36: 34-35

2. The coming of many false prophets and false messiah. Mark 13:22

3. Signs in nature. Luke 21:25-27

4. The coming of the Ant-Christ. II Thess. 2:3

Nature of Christ return

Visible coming of Jesus Christ, Acts 1:11; 1Thes 4:16

Physical and Spiritual Acts 1: Rev. 1:7, Zech. 14:4, 1 Cor. 15

1. Visible and Bodily coming of Jesus Christ, Luke 21:27, Mt. 24: 23-27

2. Sudden and unexpected return 1 Thess. 5: 2-5, Matt. 24: 37-44

3. Glorious and triumphant return of Jesus Christ in Matt. 24: 30, 25: 31, Col. 3:4, 2 Thess. 1: 7-10, Rev. 11: 15-17; Rev. 19: 11-16; Dan. 2:44, 45; 7:13-14; Psalms 72: 8-11; 1 Corinthians 15:25.

What is meant by the premillennial advent of Christ? It means that Jesus Christ will suddenly and unexpectedly come and reign a thousand years in Jerusalem. This view is based on the literal explanation of Rev. 20: 2-7. I am not going to explain more on this view. You can read it in many systematic theology books, especially those written by professors from Dallas Theological Seminary.

Reformed Church does not take a literal interpretation on Rev. 20:2-7 but spiritual. It says, "Christ has in reverse for his church a period of universal expansion and preeminent spiritual prosperity, when the spirit and character of the noble army of martyrs shall be reproduced again in the great body of God's people in an unprecedented manner, and when these martyrs shall, in general triumph of their cause, and in the overthrow of that of their enemies, receive judgment over their foes and reign in the earth; while the party of Satan, the rest of the dead, shall not flourish again until the thousand years be ended, when it shall pre-Vail again a little season (Bosma 1927, p. 297 & Hodge 1928, pp. 566-572).

Reformed Church does not believe in pre- or post-millennial, but in Amillennial or no millennial at all. Normally when I am teaching on the second coming of the Lord Jesus Christ, I usually read this scripture where it says, "And if I come again and will take you to myself, so that where I am, there you may also be." Joh.14: 3; Col. 3: 4. What is important is to be where Jesus Christ will be whether a thousand years in the air or a thousand years in reign over Jerusalem here on earth. Both groups believe that Jesus Christ is coming again and when he comes he will be with his people forever. He will also come to judge those who did not believe in him. Rev 20: 11-15.

There is going to be a resurrection of the dead with new immortal and spiritual bodies when Jesus comes again. John 5: 28-29; 1 Thess. 4: 16; 1 Cor. 15:53. What will happen to those found alive when Jesus Christ comes? They will go through quick change to be like those raised from the dead. The word of God says, "Behold, I tell you a mystery; we all shall not sleep, but we shall be changed, in a moment, in the twinkling of an eye, at the last trump." 1 Cor. 15: 51, 52.

BEDROOM OF ADAM AND EVE

And elsewhere in the bible it says, "And the dead in Christ shall rise fist; then we that are alive, that are left, shall, together with them be caught up in the clouds, to meet the Lord in the air; and so, shall we ever be with the Lord" 1 Thess. 4: 16, 17. This will be the final brow to death and suffering, especially to us who believe in the Lord Jesus Christ. Death will be swallowed up in victory. No more death, sin, suffering and sorrow. Christ will wipe away all our sorrow and suffering. This is our great joy and comfort.

Final judgment will be after the resurrection and everyone is going to be judged per the revealed word of God. Christ himself will be the judge during the final judgment. He will sit on the judgment seat. Jesus said, "For the son of man shall come in the glory of his Father with his angels; and then shall he render unto every man per his deeds" Matt. 16:27; Acts 17: 31; Rom. 14: 9; Rev. 22:12; Acts 3: 21

Jesus Christ will use his angels to carry out the sentence of judgment. He said, "So shall be, it be at the end of the world; the angels shall come forth, and sever the wicked from among the righteous, and shall cast them into the furnace of fire." Matt. 13: 49. On his own people, Jesus said, "And he shall send forth his angels with a great sound of a trumpet, and they shall gather together his elect from the four winds, from one end of heaven to the other." Matt. 24:31

We the saints will reign with Christ forever. Bosma (1927, p. 302) says, "The saints are heirs with Christ, are in eternal union with him, and as they suffer with him, they shall also triumph and rule with him. All the saints will assent to Christ's judgment and glory therein." The word of God says, "Or know ye not that we shall judge the world?" 1 Cor. 6:2 and verse 3 says, "Know ye not that we shall judge angels?"

Judgment at the final judgment will affect both the people Matt. 25: 32, Rev. 20:12, 1 Cor. 15: 51, 52; 1 Thess. 4: 17 and evil angels "For if God spared not angels when they sinned, but cast them down to hell, and committed them to pits of darkness, to be reserved unto judgment." 11 Pet. 2:4.

There are two places where eternal life will be experienced: Heaven and Hell. Satan and all fallen evil angels will spend the rest of their lives in hell. Worse still all non-believers in the Lord Jesus Christ at the time of their death will spend their lives in Hell as well. This is a shame. Matt. 25: 41, 46; 1 Thess. 1:19; Matt. 24: 41; Rev.9: 12; 20: 14; 21:8; Mark 9:44.

All of us that believe in the Lord Jesus Christ before death will spend the rest of our everlasting lives in heaven with him. Heaven is where the glory of God is finally manifested, where the human nature of Christ is, and where saints and angels are. John 17: 24; Rev.5:6. In short, all people whose names are in the book of life will be in heaven with the Lord forever. Rev. 20: 12, 15. They will experience blessed eternal life or blessed salvation in the Lord. Matt. 19: 16; 28: 46; Rom. 5: 2; Heb. 5:9.

CHAPTER NINTEEN. QUESTIONS TO ANSWER;

What is the doctrine of the last things?

Name different names of the doctrine of the last things in the bible?

What is the state of a soul after death?

What is the resurrection of the dead?

What is a final judgment?

What will be the final, eternal state of all creation?

Why do righteous or justified die? Romans 6:23

Is your soul everlasting?

Where will your soul live forever and why?

CHAPTER 20

THE DOCTRINE OF THE HOLY SPIRIT

Reformed church teaching on the Holy Spirit is crucial to the entire work of the sovereignty God. God is the Spirit and all his work is done in, though, with, and by the Spirit. Who is the Holy Spirit? What are the nature and role of the Holy Spirit? What are the fruits and gifts of the Holy Spirit?

Who is the Holy Spirit? The Holy Spirit is the third person of the God head: God the Father, God the Son and God the Holy Spirit. In the chapter dealing with the doctrine of God, we said that God is one, but revealed himself into three persons and each person is truly God. All three persons are made up of one same essence. But each of the three persons has different function to do. God the Father created all things, God the Son provided salvation by dying for us on the cross, and God the Holy Spirit applied the work of salvation in the lives of believers. The Holy Spirit points to Jesus Christ. Holy Spirit does not bring glory to himself, but to Jesus Christ. The word of God says:

But when He, the Spirit of truth, comes, he will guide you into all the truth. He will not speak on his own; he will speak only what he hears, and he will tell you what is yet to come. He will glorify me, because it is from me that he will receive what he will make known to you. All that belongs to the Father is mine. That is why I said the Spirit will receive from me what he will make known to you. John 16:13-15. Therefore, it is true to say that the Holy Spirit is both God and a person.

1. The deity of the Holy Spirit.

A. Divine attributes ascribed to the Holy Spirit

1. Eternity, Heb. 9:14
2. Omnipresence, Ps. Ps. 139:7
3. Omniscience, 1 Cor. 2:10
4. Omnipotence, 1 Cor. 12:4-6

B. Divine works are ascribed to the Holy Spirit.

1. Creation, Gen 1:2
2. Regeneration, John 6:63; Titus 3:5
3. Sanctification, 1 Peter 1:2
4. Preserving, Eph. 1: 13, 4: 30
5. The giving of the gives to the church, 1 Cor. 12:3-11
6. Uniting the believers to Christ, 1 Cor. 12:13; Eph. 2:22

7. Adoption, Rom. 8: 15

8. Resurrection, Rom. 8: 10

C. Divine names are ascribed to him.

1. Spirit of God, Gen. 1:2

2. Spirit of Yahweh, Judges 3:10

3. Holy Spirit. Isa. 63: 10

4. Spirit of Christ, Rom. 8:9

5. Holy Spirit of God, Eph. 4:30

2. Personality of the Holy Spirit.

A. The use of personal pronouns proves the personality of the Spirit, John 15: 26, 16:13. The muscular personal pronoun HE is ascribed to the Spirit of God. The Holy Spirit is not it as if it is a force, wind, or a thing. He is He. He is a gentleman.

B. Personal actions and works ascribed to him prove this:

1. Searching, 1 Cor. 2:11

2. Judging, Acts 15: 28

3. Hearing, John 16: 13

4. Speaking, John 14: 26

5. Wishing, 1 Cor. 12:11

6. Teaching, John 14: 26

7. Interceding, Rom. 8:27

8. Witnessing, John 15: 26

C. In all this the Holy Spirit works together with the Father and the Son.

3. The work of the Holy Spirit.

The work of the Holy Spirit in relationship to our salvation is centered on the application of the work of Christ in our lives. The Holy Spirit at Pentecost applied the entire work of salvation in the lives of believers. The bible says;

When the day of Pentecost came, they were all together in one place. Suddenly a sound like the blowing of a violent wind came from heaven and filled the whole house where they were sitting. They saw what seemed to be tongues of fire that separated and came to rest on each of them. All of them were filled with the Holy Spirit and began to speak in other tongues as the Spirit enabled them. Acts 2:1-5.

The bible says all believers in the upper room including a female who were there got baptized in the Holy Ghost. What does it mean to be filled or baptized in the Holy Spirit? It means to be completely immersed in the Holy Ghost not in the water. Water baptism is not Holy Spirit baptism. Jesus Christ was both baptized in the water by John and then baptized in the Holy Ghost by his Father in heaven on the same day. "When all the people were being baptized, Jesus was baptized too. And as he was praying, heaven was opened, and the Holy Spirit descended on him

BEDROOM OF ADAM AND EVE

in bodily form like a dove." Luke 3: 21-22.

Jesus did not receive the Holy Spirit for regeneration, but for mission. We need the Holy Spirit, both for regeneration and for mission. To be baptized by the Holy Spirit is to have the Holy Spirit in us. When do we first have the Holy Spirit? We have him at the time of regeneration or born again. That means all believers in the Lord Jesus have the Spirit of Christ. The bible says, "You, however, are not in the realm of the flesh, but in the realm of the Spirit, if indeed the Spirit of God lives in you. And if anyone does not have the Spirit of Christ, they do not belong to Christ." Rom. 8: 9. Membership and traditions of the church do not make us Christian, but sometimes help us be better Christians.

How does the Holy Spirit make us Christians? He opens our rebellious hearts so that we can see Jesus and his kingdom. He convicts us of our sins, makes us repent and then help us to accept Jesus Christ in our hearts. We start saying this prayer to Jesus Christ

Lord Jesus, I am a sinner, because I was born a sinner and my sin against you and your laws all the time. I need you to forgive me all my sins through your blood that was shed on the cross. Yes, Jesus, come into my heart, in my life today. Holy Spirit, fill me today so that I walk with Jesus all my life. Thanks Father for Jesus Christ and the Holy Spirit. Thanks, you Jesus and through your name I pray. Amen.

It is not just by praying this prayer that we become believers, but by faith in Jesus Christ that what he said he would do for us will be done. Prayer does not change him, but we change in his image and into his will when we pray. Then if you desire the baptism of the Holy Spirit in your life pray this prayer;

Lord Jesus, thank you for being in my heart, thank you for forgiving all my sins. Lord Jesus, baptize me with the Holy Spirit for your mission. Holy Spirit, fill me up so that I walk and work for the kingdom of God. I pray in your name Jesus Christ. Amen.

What if nothing happens? You do not look for feeling, but faith walk. God answers in his own time, according to his will and purpose. Continue with the prayer with fasting and meditations on the word of God. Remember people's hands will not anoint you, Christ will.

Baptism of the Holy Ghost means the application of the work of Jesus Christ in our lives permanently. In the Old Testament, the Spirit of God would leave the men and women of God if they constantly disobey God. Psalms 51:11, Judges 16. Baptism of the Holy Spirit happens at regeneration, during inner conversion and internal calling of the Spirit of God. All that are regenerated by Christ through His Spirit have the fruits of the Spirit embedded in their lives. "But the fruit of the Spirit is love, joy, peace, forbearance, kindness, goodness, faithfulness, gentleness and self-control. Against such things there is no law." Galatians 5: 22

Jesus Christ talked about the Holy Spirit as another helper, "But the advocate, the Holy Spirit, whom the father will send in my name, will teach you all things and will remind you of everything I have said to you." John 14:26. The Holy Spirit does not do stuff for us, but helps us do mission work per the will of God the Father through Jesus Christ his Son.

Second baptism of the Holy Spirit does not lead us into heaven, but makes us faithful witnesses of the work of Jesus Christ here on earth. First baptism is when we are born again and second baptism is when we are baptized in the Holy Ghost for the mission of spreading the gospel to all nations. Jesus told his disciples to go to all nations and make his disciples. Matt. 28: 16-20. But in Acts Chapter one he said, "Do not leave Jerusalem, but wait for the gift my Father promised, which you have heard me speak about. For John baptized with water, but in a few days, you will be baptized with the Holy Spirit." Acts 1:4-5. The disciples did not know what Jesus was talking about; to them being with him was all that matters. Jesus was enough for all their needs. They thought he would be with them forever. They thought Jesus would now defeat all their enemies and be the king of earthly Israel forever. It was cool for them to have arisen king who could go through walls with no doors and even travel in space with no plan? Jesus to them was more than a superman.

But hear what he said to his disciples in trying to redirect them to the mission he came to do and that now he was handing that mission to them, "It is not for you to know the times or dates the Father has set by his own authority. But you will receive power when the Holy Spirit comes on you; and you will be my witnesses in Jerusalem, and in all Judea and Samaria, and to the ends of the earth. After he said this, he was taken up before their very eyes, and a cloud hid him from their sight." Acts1:7, 9. Pay attention to the last words, people say when they leave you. It is very important for me to have second baptism to do the mission of God. I cannot be a faithful witness to my Lord and Savior without the anointing of the Holy Ghost in me for the ministry. In other words, there is no mission without the Holy Spirit baptism. It does not matter whether we have the first baptism or the second baptism. All we need is the baptism of the Holy Spirit in our lives to do the works of God the father. Without the Holy Spirit, we cannot be the children of God. Without the Holy Spirit, we cannot walk as children of Jesus Christ either. Christians need the continual filling of the Holy Spirit (Green, 1975, p. 152).

Therefore, in the reformed teaching to be baptized in the Holy Spirit as far as the mission is concerned is to be filled with the Holy Spirit. And to be filled with the Holy Spirit means to be led by the Spirit of God. When the Holy Spirit baptized Jesus Christ, the Holy Spirit led him. "Jesus, full of the Holy Spirit, left the Jordan and was led by the Spirit into the wilderness." Luke 4: 1. Where does the Holy Spirit lead us after he baptizes us? The Holy Spirit leads us in the wilderness of his choice. He will guide us in the wilderness for his purpose. When the Holy Spirit baptized the disciples of Jesus Christ, the Spirit led them to preach the gospel about Jesus Christ.

Then Peter stood up with the Eleven, raised his voice and addressed the crowd: "Fellow Jews and all of you who live in Jerusalem, let me explain this to you; Listen carefully to what I say, these people are not drunk, as you suppose. It's only nine in the morning! No, this is what was spoken by the prophet Joel; in the last days, God says, I will pour out my Spirit on all people. Your son and your daughters will prophesy; your young men will dream dreams. Even on my servants, both men and women, and I poured out my Spirit in those days, and they will prophesy." Acts2:14-18.

We are all at the mercy of God in Christ because it is dangerous and treacherous to be in the ministry without the second baptism of the Holy Ghost on us. It is like playing the Judas way trying to follow and work with Jesus with wrong motives. Mission or ministry should never be driven by money, fame, title or power. It is more joyful and fulfilling to be under the anointing of the Holy Spirit in a local church them being miserable elsewhere, making money in the name of Jesus without the anointing of the Holy Ghost.

When do I know, I have the anointing of the Holy Ghost? When the anointing or the baptism of the Holy Spirit happens in your life you will know it. Do not waste time trying to figure out or let dozens of people lay hands on you to have the baptism of the Spirit. The Bible is clear God the father and the Son sends the Holy Spirit on us for specific missions. Jesus told his disciples to wait and I know as they waited they were praying and fasting. We can also do the same way as we wait for God to act in our ministry per his will. Ask him to anoint you.

What signs should I have to show I am baptized with the Holy Spirit for the ministry? Again, when the Holy Spirit anoints us for the ministry we will know with sings or no signs. But during the era of the disciples of Jesus and the early Christian church signs and wonders were associated with the baptism of the Holy Ghost. The bible says, "The apostles performed many signs and wonders among the people... Thus, people brought the sick into the streets and laid them on beds and mats so that at least Peter's shadow might fall on some of them as he passed by. Crowds gathered also from the towns around Jerusalem, bringing their sick and those tormented by impure spirits, and all of them were healed." Acts 5: 12, 15, 16.

What about the gifts of the Holy Spirit, do they accompany me when I am baptized in the Holy Spirit? Yes, but we do not need to seek after them. Listen again to what he said, "But you will receive power when the Holy Spirit comes upon you; and you will be my witness." Acts 1:8. He wants us to be his witnesses. This is the main reason he pours his own Spirit on us. He gives us gifts for his mission and not for personal or denomination gain. All the gifts of the Holy Spirits are welcome and accepted if they come in one package. The package should be the Holy Spirit. They are gifts and that means we do not need to work for them. They come to us once we have the anointing of the Holy Ghost on us. I do not think the disciples of Jesus Christ at Pentecost decided to speak in tongues or cast out demons after they were filled with the Spirit of Christ. All gifts of the Holy Ghost come at us when we have his mercy of the anointing for his purpose. Isaiah 11: 2-3, Acts 2:38, Acts 8; 1 Cor. 12-14. The gift of the Holy Spirit relates to the saving work of Christ in the heart of the lost. The gifts of the Holy Spirit are given for the service of a believer in the world (Baxter, 1983, p6). These gifts of the Holy Spirit given to us? They are given for the use in his own church and not for personal glorification. We know the Holy Spirit is given to us to give glory to Christ and therefore all the gifts of the Holy Spirit must glorify the Lord Jesus as well and not us.

Can the gifts of the Holy Spirit cease at some time? I will give the answer that no other theologian has done. No the gifts of the Holy Spirit will never cease since they belong to God. God can never cease to be God and neither can his power that comes through his Spirit cease. We cease because we are human, but his love, faith and righteousness will never cease. He can withdraw his gifts of the Spirit from us, but He cannot withdraw eternal life from us after we are born again. But if we continually live in sin his gifts will seem to cease to flow in our lives. Our pipes are dusty, rusty and broken which hinder the flow of his joy in us. This does not mean his gifts are gone from our era.

What is the right definition of the gifts of the Holy Spirit? There are the capabilities God gives through the Spirit to Christians in his service. Walvood said, "Spiritual gifts are divinely given capacities to perform useful functions for God, especially in service" (74: 38). In addition, Merritt said, "The gifts were divine in origin, miraculous in manifestation, and supernatural in operation (36, p. 172).

CHAPTER TWENTY. QUESTIONS TO ANSWER;

What is the doctrine of the Holy Spirit?

What are the deity and personality of the Holy Spirit?

What is the work of the Holy Spirit?

Define the day of Pentecost and the baptism of the Holy Spirit?

When does, Christians receive the Holy Spirit?

Why did Jesus, receive the Holy Spirit?

What are the signs of the baptism of the Holy Spirit?

What are the gifts of the Holy Spirit? Did they cease or not?

What are the fruits of the Holy Spirit? Did they cease of not?

How does the Holy Spirit make us Christians?

BEDROOM OF ADAM AND EVE

CHAPTER 21

BIBLICAL PASSAGES FOR PRISON MINISTRY

Are there biblical passages that support prison ministries? To be honest the whole bible says something about prison ministries. I found these passages to be specific to the teaching of prison ministry, though not exhausted the list. In our prayers and social life, we should remember to pray for men and women behind bars in prison as the word of God says, "Remember those who are in prison, as though in prison with them, and those who are mistreated, since you also are in the body. Hebrew 13:3

The Lord Jesus Christ wants us to visit those in prison behind bars. Our lives are often busy with family and work issues, but this should not be excused not to share our blessings with those in oppression state, "For I was hungry and you gave me food, I was thirsty and you gave me drink, I was a stranger and you welcomed me, I was naked and you clothed me, I was sick and you visited me, I was in prison and you came to me.' Then the righteous will answer him, saying, 'Lord, when did we see you hungry and feed you, or thirsty and give you drink? And when did we see you a stranger and welcome you, or naked and clothe you? And when did we see you sick or in prison and visit you?' Matthew 25:35-46"

God in Christ through his Spirit frees prisoners, "The Spirit of the Lord is upon me, because he has anointed me to proclaim good news to the poor. He has sent me to proclaim liberty to the captives and recovering of sight to the blind, to set at liberty those who are oppressed. Isaiah 61: 1, Luke 4: 18. We may not be physically in prison, but in our lives, we are behind bars. We need our Lord Jesus Christ through his Spirit to free us all the time. He frees us from the issues and the pressures of life. He opens both our eyes as well as the eyes of the prisoners. He has the power "To open the eyes that are blind, to bring out the prisoners from the dungeon, from the prison those who sit in darkness. Isaiah 42:7. It is not good to laugh at prisoners because the Lord himself has the power to save them and even put them in high positions like Joseph in Egypt

And Joseph's master took him and put him into the prison, the place where the king's prisoners were confined, and he was there in prison. But the Lord was with Joseph and showed him steadfast love and gave him favor in the sight of the keeper of the prison. And the keeper of the prison put Joseph in charge of all the prisoners who were in the prison. Whatever was done there, he was the one who did it. The keeper of the prison paid no attention to anything that was in Joseph's charge, because the Lord was with him. And whatever he did, the Lord made it succeed. Genesis 39: 20-23.

The Lord hears them every day. He knows what they are going through and he can give them solutions. The bible says, "For the Lord hears the needy and does not despise his own people who are prisoners." Psalm 69:33. Elsewhere it is written, "To hear the groans of the prisoners, to set free those who were doomed to die. Psalm 102: 20. The Psalms asked, "Who executes justice for the oppressed, who gives food to the hungry? The Lord sets the prisoners free." Psalm 146:7.

Not all prisoners are law breakers; some are serving time for God to be revealed. Paul and Silas were in prison because of following and believing in Jesus Christ. But when her owners saw that their hope of gain was gone, they seized Paul and Silas and dragged them into the marketplace before the rulers. And when they had brought them to the magistrates, they said, "These men are Jews, and they are disturbing our city. They advocate customs that are not lawful for us as Romans to accept or practice." The crowd joined in attacking them, and the magistrates tore the garments off them and gave orders to beat them with rods. And when they had inflicted many blows upon them, they threw them into prison, ordering the jailer to keep them safely. Acts 16:19-4.

Prisoners have rights and can even speak in their defense about their cases while behind bars. Paul as a prisoner said, "I answered them that it was not the custom of the Romans to give up anyone before the accused met the accusers face to face and had the opportunity to make his defense concerning the charge laid against him Acts 25:16. Nothing is impossible to God. If he wants to free prisoners from serving time He can do it per his will and purpose. The bible says, "Now when Herod was about to bring him out, on that very night, Peter was sleeping between two soldiers, bound with two chains, and sentries before the door were guarding the prison. Acts 12:6.

If we believe that the Lord Jesus has the power to forgive all our sins and heal all our sickness, then we must also believe that he can do these acts of grace on prisoners too. He can even lift them up from their low. The Psalmists said, "Of David. Bless the Lord, O my soul, and all that is within me, bless his holy name! Bless the Lord, O my soul, and forget not all his benefits, who forgives all your iniquity, who heals all your diseases, who redeems your life from the pit, who crowns you with steadfast love and mercy, who satisfies you with good so that your youth is renewed like the eagles. Psalm 103:1-22.

The Lord Jesus can use prisoners to preach his gospel. Paul said, "Are they servants of Christ? I am a better one-I am talking like a madman-with far greater labors, far more imprisonments, with countless beatings, and often near death. 2 Corinthians 11: 23; It is also written, "Having received this order, he put them into the inner prison and fastened their feet in the stocks. About midnight Paul and Silas were praying and singing hymns to God, and the prisoners were listening to them, Acts 16:24-25. Elsewhere it is written, "Now when John heard in prison about the deeds of the Christ, he sent word by his disciples Matthew 11:2.

He sets the prisoners free even in the face of adversary.

And when he saw that it pleased the Jews, he proceeded to arrest Peter also. This was during the days of Unleavened Bread. And when he had seized him, he put him in prison, delivering him over to four squads of soldiers to guard him, intending after the Passover to bring him out to the people. So, Peter was kept in prison, but earnest prayer for him was made to God by the church.

Now when Herod was about to bring him out, on that very night, Peter was sleeping between two soldiers, bound with two chains, and sentries before the door were guarding the prison. And, behold, an angel of the Lord stood next to him, and a light shone in the cell. He struck Peter on the side and woke him, saying, "Get up quickly." And the chains fell off his hands. And the angel said to him, "Dress yourself and put on your sandals." And he did so. And he said to him, "Wrap your cloak around you and follow me." And he went out and followed him. He did not know that what was being done by the angel was real, but thought he was seeing a vision.

When they had passed the first and the second guard, they came to the iron gate leading into the city. It opened for them of its own accord, and they went out and went along one street, and immediately the angel left him. When Peter came to himself, he said, "Now I am sure that the Lord has sent his angel and rescued me from the hand of Herod and from all that the Jewish people were expecting" Acts 12:3-25.

The disciples of Jesus Christ were put in prison for preaching the good news. Christ sent his angel to free them from prison. If Christ did, that he can still do this even today. He does all things per his purpose. It is not just getting out of prison, but to be free in Jesus Christ and experience salvation.

But the high priest rose, and all who were with him (that is, the party of the Sadducees), and filled with jealousy they arrested the apostles and put them in the public prison. But during the night an angel of the Lord opened the prison doors and brought them out, and said, "Go and stand in the temple and speak to the people all the words of this Life." And when they heard this, they entered the temple at daybreak and began to teach. Now when the high priest came, and those who were with him, they called together the council and all the senate of the people of Israel and sent to the prison to have them brought. Acts 5:17-42. The prisoner was freed instead of Jesus Christ due to the divine will of God, "Now at the first he used to release for them one prisoner for whom they asked. Mark 15:6.

Not all prisoners get fired. Some die in prison due to sickness, fights, suicide, or natural causes. In the bible, we read one prisoner that died in prison for the will of God. John came to make the way of the Lord. After he completed his work he was beheaded. We might not know why some prisoners die in prison, but God knows.

For Herod, had seized John, and bound him and put him in prison for the sake of Herodias, his brother Philip's wife, because John had been saying to him, "It is not lawful for you to have her." And though he wanted to put him to death, he feared the people, because they held him to be a prophet. But when Herod's birthday came, the daughter of Herodias danced before the company and pleased Herod, so that he promised with an oath to give her whatever she might ask. Matthew 14:3-1.

Some prisoners never stay in one place while serving time. They move from facility to facility until the day of their judgment. Apostle Paul travelled from Jerusalem to Rome to appear before Cesar. "And when it was decided that we should sail for Italy, they delivered Paul and some other prisoners to a centurion of the Augustan Cohort named Julius. Acts 27:1.

True worshippers will always worship the Lord in truth and in spirit. Some prisoners are true worshippers. They love the Lord with all their hearts and mind.

They know that Jesus died for them. The bible says, "But the hour is coming, and is now here, when the true worshipers will worship the Father in spirit and truth, for the Father is seeking such people to worship him." John 4: 23. One of the famous verses in the bible says, "For God so loved the world, that he gave his only Son, that whoever believes in him should not perish but have eternal life." John 3: 16.

Some prisoners will be beaten for the right thing while others get some freedom, even while serving their time. Jeremiah was beaten and put in prison while Apostle Paul in prison had some freedom to speak and even preach the gospel. Incarceration is not the end of life. The bible says, "And the officials were enraged at Jeremiah, and they beat him and imprisoned him in the house of Jonathan the secretary, for it had been made a prison. Jeremiah 37:15.

In the book of Acts, it is written, "And when we came into Rome, Paul could stay by himself, with the soldier that guarded him Acts 28:16. All people have the right to a fair trial, including prisoners, "Paul argued in his defense, "Neither against the law of the Jews, nor against the temple, nor against Caesar have I committed any offense" Acts 25:8.

Some people are put in prison wrongly for selfish gains. Judas betrayed Jesus with a kiss for few coins of money. While he was still speaking, there came a crowd, and the man called Judas, one of the twelve, was leading them. He drew near to Jesus to kiss him, but Jesus said to him, "Judas, would you betray the Son of Man with a kiss?" And when those who were around him saw what would follow, they said, "Lord, shall we strike with the sword?" And one of them struck the servant of the high priest and cut off his right ear. But Jesus said, "No more of this!" And he touched his ear and healed him. Luke 22: 47-51.

We need to help one another and stop being final judges of each other. Jeremiah was put in prison to die, but God worked through other people and feed him.

When Ebed-melech the Ethiopian, a eunuch who was in the king's house, heard that they had put Jeremiah into the cistern-the king was sitting in the Benjamin Gate- Ebed-melech went from the king's house and said to the king, "My lord the king, these men have done evil in all that they did to Jeremiah the prophet by casting him into the cistern, and he will die there of hunger, for there is no bread left in the city." Then the king commanded Ebed-melech the Ethiopian, "Take thirty men with you from here, and lift Jeremiah the prophet out of the cistern before he dies." So Ebed-melech took the men with him and went to the house of the king, to a wardrobe in the storehouse, and took from there old rags and worn-out clothes, which he let down to Jeremiah in the cistern by ropes. Jeremiah 38: 7-28.

Some people devoted their time feeding prisoners. They bring them food, water and even medicine. One king said, "And say, 'Thus says the king, "Put this fellow in prison, and feed him meager rations of bread and water, until I come in peace."'" 1 Kings 22:27. The good part is that some prisoners find Jesus Christ in while in prison. Therefore, although in Christ I could be bold and order you to do what you ought to do, yet I prefer to appeal to you on the basis of love. As it is none other than Paul-an old man and now also a prisoner of Christ Jesus---that I appeal to you for my son Onesismus, who became my son while I was in chains. Formerly, he was useless to you, but now he has become useful both to you and to me. I am sending him-back to you. Philemon 8-12.

CHAPTER ONE. QUESTIONS TO ANSWER;

Mention some of the biblical passages for prison ministry?

Are all prisoners law breakers? Do prisoners have rights?

Can prisoners be forgiven of their sins by Jesus Christ?

Who sets prisoners free?

Who has the right to judge prisoners?

What do these statements mean to you;

FREE PEOPLE DO NOT RUN AWAY FROM PRISON, PRISONERS DO?

IF THE SON OF GOD SETS YOU FREE YOU ARE FREE INDEED?

Do you know a prisoner who is on fire for the Lord Jesus Christ?

Can you or your church warmly accept him or her in your family or church once released?

What would Jesus DO?

CHAPTER 22

SEVEN WAYS TEACHING REFORMED THEOLOGY IN USA PRISONS?

A. Seminary model

B. Pod model

C. Unit model

D. Chapel model

E. Chaplain mode

F. Volunteer model

G. Distance Learning Model (DVD and Mail)

There are many ways of teaching reformed theology in prisons across the United States, but in this chapter, there are seven suggestions that will be discussed. These seven sections consist of Seminary model, Pad and Unit model, Chapter model, Chaplain Model, Volunteer model and Distance learning model which includes (DVD and Mail).

A. Seminary Model

A seminar model is literally having a theological seminar inside the prison. When I graduated my high school from Chassa secondary school in Petauke Zambia in 1981 I went to study theology at Justo Mwale theological University College. I studied theology at this school from 1985 to 1989. After graduation, the School board sent me to a rural congregation at Msanga Reformed Church where I was ordained as a minister in 1989. After serving the Lord in this church God called me for further studies in the United States. In 1993 I arrived in the Sates and did my first undergraduate at Kuyper College, formerly known as the Reformed Bible College. I did my graduate school at Calvin Seminary and Cincinnati Christian University, where I got my masters in theology. I did my post graduate school at International theological seminary of California and Trinity College of the bible and a theological seminary.

I know a lot about theological schools and theological studies. I know how important theology is to my life. Christian theology involves the whole person's life of an individual. Therefore, it is very fitting for people behind bars study theology. They have plenty of time in prison to finish the study in time. Inmates in prison are removed from family issues, therefore if they choose to study theology they will be able to learn well. Moreover, I am a full-time chaplain in prison and I know what I am talking about. I have taught some theology to inmates already.

The first thing to keep in mind when starting a seminary in prison is the time served in prison. How long is the length or serving time of the inmates that are going to study theology? To be frank any prisoner serving time more than one year on the same facility will be a good candidate for attending seminary model.

The second thing to consider is the facility staff, which includes the warden. How willing are they to have a few of their inmates involved in theological seminary? What benefits will they get as far as safety and security is concerned? It is better to talk with the warden and his team and have their blessing on the project.

The third thing to be considered is the curriculum? Do you have enough courses already written down to start the program? Does the curriculum follow reformed tradition seminary programs and what is the end game after graduation? Are the inmates given full accredited diplomas or not? Are they able to use them when they leave the facility into the society? Does the curriculum prepare graduates to face the real world out of prison?

The fourth thing to have in mind when starting a seminary model in prison is supported from within and outside. Is the program supported by reliable organizations outside as far as finance and other materials are concerned? Is there enough staff willing to work with inmates in their struggles within close bars? This is where the seminary model becomes a challenge because very few good theological teachers would like to spend their talents with prisoners. Most people get scared to be inside prisons. They do not like to be around criminal's period.

There might be more steps to consider when starting seminary model in US Prisons but these four suggestions mentioned above are very important. These four steps must be part of the seminary model. Divine Hope Reformed Bible Seminary in Danville Correctional Center in Illinois in Chicago has embedded all the four steps of a seminary model. Though this facility housed only medium level men inmates, seminary model can work with all genders and levels as long all four steps are followed.

Seminary model is no different than education school in prison. Many states and private facilities offer educational programs to their inmates. The only difference is that they teach common education instead of theological studies. I cannot wait to see facilities across the United State get involved in a theological seminary education following the seminary model.

B and C Pod and Unit Model

The pod model means that reformed theology will be taught to inmates who are living in the specific pod only. Unit model means that reformed theology will be taught to inmates' living in the specific unit only. Many facilities across the United States have faith based or sometimes known as bible based programs in a pod or a unit. I know CCA, which stands for the Correction Corporation of America has many faiths based programs in many of its facilities. Therefore, pod or unit models are already familiar to many inmates in America. To start reforming theological teaching to inmates in a pod or the unit will not be a problem at all.

Many people who have never been in prison may not know the meaning of pod or unit. A pod is a group of cells and a unit is a group of pod together. A cell is a typical home of a prisoner. A pod can be described as the typical village of a prisoner. Someone described a pod this way;

Modern prison designs, particularly those of high-security prisons, have sought to increasingly restrict and control the movement of prisoners throughout the facility while minimizing the corrections staffing needed to monitor and control the population. As compared to the traditional landing-cellblock-hall designs, many newer prisons are designed in a decentralized "podular" layout with individual self-contained housing units, known as "pods" or "modules", arranged around centralized outdoor yards in a "campus". The pods contain tiers of cells laid out in an open pattern arranged around a central control station from which a single corrections officer can monitor all of the cells and the entire pod. Control of cell doors, communications and CCTV monitoring is conducted from the control station as well. Moving out of the pod to the exercise yard or work assignments can be restricted to individual pods at designated times, or else prisoners may be kept almost always within their pod or even their individual cells depending upon the level of security. Goods and services, such as meals, laundry, commissary, educational materials, religious services and medical care can increasingly be brought to individual pods or cells as well. This definition was taken from a Yahoo search for education and reference-words and word play by Yancychipper seven years ago,. Find online https://answers.yahoo.com/question/index?qid=20070924145902AAOkelv

A unit is made up of a group of pods. Chaplain Regina Beed who worked at Eloy Detention Center as a full-time chaplain used to be a faith based chaplain for five years. She taught faith based programs to inmates. The Eloy Detention center is run by CCA (Core Civic). I interviewed chaplain Beed about the faith based work she did at this facility. She told me that inmates who participated in the program signed their names first. Inmates were prepared to follow the rules set forth in the program. All faith and even none faith inmates could participate as long they followed and obeyed regulations put forth. Chaplain Beed taught courses herself, though sometimes religious volunteers helped her. CCA provided the curriculum taught in the faith based pods. I know CCA (Core civic) has collaborated with other organizations that make all faith based courses. Chaplain Beed said inmates were very happy and involving in all the programs. She also told me one thing she misses as a full-time chaplain is teaching inmates faith based programs.

Chaplain Beed said that all programs in the pod involve all inmates living in the pod. This means that all inmates live in the pod as they do their work. The Faith based schedule is written and strictly followed. Offices come in to help the chaplain in all the programs. Offices keep peace and security for the safety of all people in the pod. Chaplain Beed said that inmates that misbehaved were dealt with facility staff and sometimes sent to segregation for further disciplinary action. Inmates that successfully complete their work, were given certificates of completion. Chaplain Beed said these inmates are then removed from the pod and new ones come after signing their names to follow rules and regulations of faith pod.

I remember the time I was hired at the Florence Correctional Center in Florence Arizona, Warden Gay told me that I was going to oversee faith based programs. I did not what that meant at first though things did not work that way. I added up being a full-time chaplain for the facility. I would have loved to be a faith based chaplain too, because I like teaching especially reformed theology.

Pod model is easy to start in prisons across the land. All what is needed is dedicated teachers with reformed flavor to them. Teachers that know the bible very well and reformed teaching. The pod model needs teachers who are hungry for the gospel to inmates behind bars. The Pod model can eventually lead into a unit model that involves more than one pod. These two models must follow four steps discussed in the seminary model for good operation of the programs.

D, E and F Chapel Model/Chaplain Model/Volunteer Model

These three models are related to each other. Chapel model involves the chapel as the only place theology teachings are taught. Every volunteer as well as the chaplain can teach in the chapel reformed theology as long they are cleared to enter the facility. Chaplain model means that the chaplain will be the only one teaching reformed theology at the facility. The volunteer model simply means that reformed volunteers will be the only ones' teaching inmates reformed teaching at the specific pricing.

All theological teachings taught must be on the program or on the religious schedule of the facility. The chaplain or volunteers can teach reformed teachings to inmates per the schedule. All inmates desiring to attend the class must sign up in advance. Inmates will be coming to the chapel just as if they are going to education programs. At the end of the programs, diplomat will be given to all successful participants.

Chaplain Model involves the chaplain teaching all the programs per the schedule. The chaplain is not hired only for a specific group therefore all inmates that want to attend this program are welcome, provided they read and follow written regulations before signing their names. A chaplain model needs a reformed chaplain or someone that can teach reformed teachings. Remember the whole thesis is on the teaching of reformed theology in US Prisons.

Volunteer model will be taught by Christians that have a full understanding of the reformed teaching of grace and the sovereignty of God. At the Florence Correctional center facility in Florence, Arizona we have Prison fellowship volunteers. This group teaches some of the reformed doctrines to inmates. This group gives our certificates to all inmates that finish their course. Maria Alena Marin is the leader of this group. Maria Marin has both bachelors and masters from Trinity College of the Bible and Theological seminary. She has learned about reforming teaching.

Maria Marin and her husband Gustavo are very committed to the work of the Lord. Volunteer model is easy and great to implement in a prison facility. All inmates interested to come to the chapel get to learn what Prison Fellowship group teaches. There are many different religious groups that teach inmates in the chapel at FCC, but the only Prison Fellowship group gives out certificates at the end of each lesson. Inmates like the way this group teaches them.

All three models must have a systematic way of teaching the whole course of God according to the reformed faith. Chaplains and volunteers involved in these three models must have an end game. Inmates must be told in advance how the whole program will be and what they will get once they successfully complete their entire work. It is better to read and follow those four steps discussed in the seminary model and see which ones are applicable in these three models

G. Distance Learning Model (DVD and Mail model)

This model is the easiest of them all. Now that the world is in love with technology, it is best to teach inmates following this model. Inmates who want to learn more of theological teachings can enroll with any reformed theological seminary outside their prison walls. Lessons may be sent to them through mail, DVD, and CDs. In the chapel where I work, we have many DVDs and CDs sent in by Christian churches as donations. We also receive bibles and many Christian's books for inmates to use.

I remember some years ago, we had inmates doing distance theological education. The family paid for the courses while their job was to study and finish the course while serving time. Inmates are not allowed to have computers with internet in prison. The chaplain can assist them looking for more resources for their work on facility computers. The chaplain will also help these inmates with their courses in the chapel.

The chaplain can choose to go through the lesson together with inmates as a class. The distance learning model needs real committed and disciplined inmates to successfully complete the program. Inmates should be good and motivated at what they want to achieve in life. There are many things going on inside the prison that may disrupt inmates from doing their course work. There is literally no one to force them to complete their course, except their will inside of them. Students in the distance learning need clear focus on education alone if they must get what they are looking for.

In conclusion, we need to reform teachings in US Prisons today based on all or some of the seven basic teaching models discussed in this chapter.

CHAPTER TWENTY-TWO. QUESTIONS TO ANSWER;

What is the significance of reformed theology in US prisons or any prison?

Among reformed seminary if they are any?

Among reformed chaplains?

Among reformed prison volunteers?

Among USA prisons?

Among prisons that leant the teachings of reformed faith?

How do you understand prison ministry?

What are the challenges of prison ministry?

Who should do prison ministry?

CHAPTER 23

THE SIGNIFICANCE OF REFORMED THEOLOGY IN US PRISONS

A. Among reformed theological seminaries in US prison

What is the outcome of teachings of reformed theology in US prisons today? Reformed teachings are biblical as long as they remain true to the word of God in the bible. This issue had been discussed at length in chapter three of the dissertation. This means that reformed teachings convey the gospel message of our Lord and savior Jesus Christ to the public. When a reformed seminary is operating inside behind bars then it is proclaiming the message of hope in Jesus Christ to prisoners. This is the main significance of having a reformed seminary in US Prisons. Inmates will be able to study the word of God and have diplomas at graduation in their facilities. Inmates will have deep knowledge of the word of God for free.

Inmates that graduate and released will be able to share their life long experiences with the society and their families. Some of these inmates will be pastors, deacons. Others will be working as staff in the church or organizations. Inmates that graduate from seminaries inside prison will be ready to be useful to the people within and outside prison walls. Good example is Divine Hope Reformed Bible Seminary which has sent many seminary graduates back into the society. These graduates will continue supporting the facility and their families in prayers for life. We need many reformed seminaries in US Prisons to help inmates grown in faith and be useful to the facility and society when they graduate.

B. Among reformed prison chaplains

Reformed chaplains are those that believe in the sovereign grace of God. God is in control of all things and uphold all things. God in his own will and power chooses to intervene at will in this world and in the lives of people. God in his sovereign grace works out our salvation in Christ through the power of the Holy Spirit. Chaplains that believe in the sovereign word of God are called reformed chaplains and can bring forth the word of God to inmates in prisons according to the reformed tradition. This is very important because chaplains will bring forth nothing but the truth of the word of God to inmates who desire to learn more of the reformed faith. Chaplains will be taking part in the great commission. Mat. 28:16-20

C. Among reformed prison volunteers

Religious volunteers are individuals that bring hope and religious knowledge to inmates in prison. These volunteers are not paid to teach inmates the word of God. These volunteers sacrifice their lives and families to go into prisons and be with criminals. Very sad that some of the churches, denominations, and organizations which they represent never notice the work these volunteers do. Across United States they are millions and millions of religious volunteers that enter prisons doors to bring spiritual and material help to prisoners. Some of these volunteers come from reformed churches.

These reformed volunteers will bring the word of God per the reformed teaching. Inmates that attend reformed teachings will then have direct link to reformed resource through these volunteers. Volunteers will hence bring into the facilities reformed materials that help to make inmates faith grow deep in the knowledge of God. Chapel library will be full of reformed materials instead of other books and pamphlets that have nothing to do with solving issues of inmates' faith.

D. Among US Prisons

The question is what will have reformed teachings bring to prison facilities across United States of America? Before I answer this question let me reveal my theory about Christianity or any other religion inside a prison facility.

I have the conviction that among 500 inmates if 100 of them commit themselves to a studying their religion while serving time the rate of violence and misconduct in that prison will go down dramatically. If the facility has 1000 inmates 200 committed inmates to their faith will also help to scale down bad behavior inside prison walls. Religious help to move the focus of inmates away from their bad behavior into a positive one.

I have seen the impact of what religion can do on the lives of inmates in prison during my work with prions as far as religious programs are concerned. I came to America 1993 and in 1994 I started working with inmates as volunteer in jails and prisons in Grand Rapids, Michigan and Florence, Arizona.

Now that I have been a full-time chaplain prison for more than five years at Florence Correction Center in Florence, Arizona I have noticed how religion helped to change the mind of some committed inmates. Inmates that once were rooted into drugs, violence and bad behavior changed their lives because of their belief in a religion. Some of these religions are not even Christian in nature though they help inmates stay focus and not involved in bad ways. I am not going to give figures and names here in fear of breaking the trust of the inmates and the policy of the prison. In fact, this thesis is about teachings of reformed theology in prison and not a platform for criticizing other religions beliefs.

During my work with FCC I had three wardens so far, Gay, McDonald and Koehn. All three wardens fully supported religious programs. They knew the best way to correct an inmate is from the inside of the soul. Religious beliefs help to touch that inner being of the inmate and help change for the better.

Reformed faith is more than just a religion; it is the truth based on the infallible word of God. Inmates that study this truth find rest and hope in life. Jesus Christ alone is the author, provider, and finisher of salvation. He is the only one that gets the glory not reformed teachings or reformed chaplains and volunteers. Therefore, if 100 inmates out of 500 know the Lord Jesus Christ and study the word per reformed teachings, then these inmates will help bring peace in the facility where they are in. These inmates will eventually help promote good security and safety of the institution. These will be the ambassadors of peace and harmony among their friends and the staff as well.

I have the conviction therefore that if many inmates attend theological studies offered through seminary model, chaplain model, volunteer model, chapel model and distance model violence and misconduct in prison across US will be reduced. I did not say that bad behavior will be eradicated? This destruction of sin and evil is coming when Jesus Christ himself comes the second time. By preaching the truth of the word of God we help to restrain sin and evil. We help to stop the influence of the devil and its fallen demons on inmates in US prison when the truth of God is fearlessly proclaimed.

E. Among prisoners that took the teachings of reformed faith.

When I went to the website of Divine Hope Reformed Seminary I read the testimonies of inmates that graduated from the seminary and are now serving the Lord Jesus Christ outside prison walls. This is very encouraging to see the fruits of teaching reformed beliefs to inmates in prison. All the graduates get diplomas after completing the work just like those students that graduate from tradition seminaries.

The Lord Jesus Christ gets the final glory of all the inmates that study and graduate from Devine Hope seminary. In other words, all prisoners that study theology while in prison become the ambassadors of the Lord Jesus Christ in prison and outside prison. They have the truth which will be shared to families, friends, and the society during their life time. Some of them may become pastors, chaplains, volunteers or just a worker in the kingdom of God.

Inmates that were exposed to reformed teaching become appreciative to the institution, to themselves as well as to God in Christ Jesus. They give thanks to God and the institution for providing them second chance in life. These inmates develop a desire to serve the lord to the lost especially to their families and friends first. I know inmates that were in my theology class and have gone on with their lives as good productive solders of Christ in the kingdom. I cannot mention their names here but only let them read this thesis once it is done. I know they will be proud to hear that I think and pray for them occasionally till we meet again in heaven with the Lord Jesus Christ.

In conclusion, therefore, inmates that attend reformed seminary in prison become strong in their belief. They can know what they believe in and defend it. They know the need to listen to different religious beliefs without themselves breaking their own camp. This means they can listen to others beliefs at the same time remain conservative to theirs. These inmates that have studied reformed theology know the truth of the word of God and ready to teach it. They become the student of the word of God and not a critic. Their goal is to give to the society and not to take from it. Their lives have been changed for the better with Jesus alone. Most of these inmates will eventually form small bible study groups in the pods to help others with the word of God. Per Joel Osteen (2007, p.183) they start thinking to serve others.

F. Main Challenge for Prison Ministry

There is lack of support for prison ministry from many Christians. Prison ministry is categorized belonging to the few chosen and not all Christians. The big reason is that the Christian church has forgotten its main mission in the world. It has become blind to the great commission our Lord Jesus commanded us to do in the last chapter of the gospel per Matthew. Jesus commanded saying, "All authority in heaven and on earth has been given to me. Therefore, go and make disciples of all nations, baptizing them in the name of the father and of the Son and of the Holy Spirit, and teaching them to obey everything I have commanded you. And surely, I am with you always, to the very end of the age." Matt. 28:18-20. Also, the last words Jesus said to his disciples as he was being lifted into heaven were, "But you will receive power when the Holy Spirit comes on you; and you will be my witnesses in Jerusalem, and in all Judea and Samaria, and to the ends of the earth." Acts 1: 8

All of us have the duty to spread good news to all people including those behind bars. We know they are law breakers and they need judgment for what they have done. So are we when it comes to the law of God, we have broken the law. Praise the Lord someone shared the word to us and now we are Christians. But we still need his mercy and grace to walk with Jesus all the time. We still need someone to share scripture with us. People behind bars need people to help them with their walk with the Lord too. It is the duty of all believers in the Lord to carry this message of hope to them. The problem is that only few answer this call.

We become big mouth. We like talking about them because they are in prison and forget to help bring hope to them. We too need saving of being big mouth. Our mouth need saving too. Joyce Meyer (1997, 130) in her book Me and My Big Mouth says:

I remember when God spoke to my heart and said, Joyce, it is time for your mouth to be saved. That sound strange, but it was true. It is possible to be saved and not sound like it. An individual can be a child of God, and yet not talk like one. I know, because I was such a person. It is not enough to be saved, the must be saved also. That is part of the process which the Apostle Paul referred to as 'working out' one's own salvation.

Just as salvation message must be preached to all, all saints must practice Christian discipline. Pattison (2006, p. 85) in his book Poverty in the theology of John Calvin was right about Luther on this issue when he wrote:

Luther's attack on medieval ascetic practices in general and on monasticism in particular was not because of asceticism as such, nor even because of the abuses that had come into monastic life, but because much of the theology that lay behind them undercut the evangelical understanding of salvation. In addition to its distortion of the doctrine of salvation, the second reason Luther attacked monasticism was his conviction that all believers should practice the whole of Christian spirituality daily.

This means that the church during the time of Luther avoided its main mission of preaching the good news to all people including the poor. In our times, the poor can also mean the prisoners that are serving time in the prison for crimes committed.

John Calvin, chief architect of reformed teaching was convinced that the redemptive work of our Lord Jesus Christ revealed poverty and humility. Christ was born poor though belonged to the rich family of David. He lived a poor life and even died a poor man. He was buried in a borrowed grave. This is what Calvin said about Jesus birth as far as poverty was concerned:

We see here…the great poverty of Joseph …we see at the same time, what sort of beginning the life of the Son of God had, and in what candle He was placed. Such was his condition at his birth, because He had taken upon him our flesh for this purpose, that He might empty Himself on our account. When He was pushed into a stable, and was placed in a manger, and lodging refused Him among men, it was that heaven might be open to us, not as a temporary lodging, but as our eternal country and inheritance, and that angels might receive us into their abode. Read (Pringle, p. 112) Calvin Commentary on Luke. 2:7 CO 45, 72-73.

The outward signs of the life of Jesus Christ revealed his inner ward divine majesty. Pattison (2006, 156) said, "This is important for Calvin's Christology because he believes that Christ's ignominious birth can also serve to illumine the kind of king that Christ is and what kind of kingdom he rules. Christ is the king who was not only emptied of the splendor of heaven but also of the splendor of earth so that he could fill humankind with his spiritual riches."

If all Christians practice this kind of humility as our Lord showed us, we would be zealous to share the good news to all people including those behind bars. We bring nothing in this world and we take nothing when we leave this world. Our job is not to criticize but to help mend the broken hearts through the touch of Jesus. We need to see the world through the eyes of Jesus Christ. Jesus Christ brought no material wealthy with him but his word. Jesus Christ did not leave material wealth for us but his word and his Spirit. This is our charge now to take what he brought and left to all peoples of the world including prisoners behind bars.

In America, we have thousands upon thousands of men and women serving time behind bars. The nation has prisons built and run by both government and private enterprises. This has become the norm of our society. These prisons are built to help correct inmates to be better people in their lives. There is no better correction than the word of God. There we are all missionaries to all prisoners around us.

Sproul (1939, p. 20) in his book <u>Life views: Make a Christian Impact on Culture and Society</u>. Summarized it this way: In all of life's situation, we are to be His witnesses. Our job is to make the invisible reign of Jesus visible. The world is shrouded in darkness. Nothing is visible in the dark. No wonder then that we are called to be the light of the world. Every single one of us has a mission. We have all been sent to bear witness to Christ. That means simply that we are all missionaries…It's not enough simply to know the content of the gospel. It is also important that we understand the society in which we are acting out our role as missionary.

All Christians have the job to do not only the few. Our concept of stewardship and vocation need to be revisited and revised. Gardner (1960, p. 273) in his book <u>Biblical Faith and Social Ethics</u> wrote about the role of reformed teaching in the society which includes prisons.

The traditional biblical and protestant concepts of stewardship and vocation have become largely meaningless. For the layman---whether he be owner or employee-stewardship has come to be associated, not with the totality of life and resources of the earth, but with appeals for support of churches; and only those who are engaged in religious activities in a professional way think of themselves as having vocations.

CHAPTER TWENTY-THREE. QUESTIONS TO ANSWER;

Mention Seven ways of teaching theology in USA prisons?

Define seminary model?

Define pod model?

Define unit model?

Define chaplain model?

Define volunteer model?

Define volunteer model?

Define distance model?

What are the best models for you?

Is it right to have any of these models inside prisons?

CHAPTER 24

CONFESSIONS OF CHRISTIAN CHURCH

Those that believe in Jesus are now at home in the bedroom of Jesus Christ and therefore confess the true doctrine summarizes in the Creed below. They profess triune God: God the Father; God the Son; and God the Holy Spirit. It is good for a Christian to memorize the Apostolic Creed.

APSTOLIC CREED

I believe in God, the Father almighty, creator of heaven and earth.

I believe in Jesus Christ, his only Son, our Lord.
He was conceived by the power of the Holy Spirit
and born of the Virgin Mary.
He suffered under Pontius Pilate,
was crucified, died, and was buried.
He descended to the dead.
On the third day he rose again.
He ascended into heaven,

and is seated at the right hand of the Father.
He will come again to judge the living and the dead.

I believe in the Holy Spirit, the holy universal Christian Church, the communion of saints, the forgiveness of sins, the resurrection of the body, and the life everlasting. Amen.

Modern Christians should appreciate what is written in the Athanasian Creed. It is an expanded version of the Apostolic Creed. It gives more spiritual food and comfort to the members of the bedroom of Jesus Christ who once lived in the comfort of the bedroom of Adam and Eve. If the Athanasian Creed cannot be memorized, it can be confessed, studied and taught by the whole body of Christ living in every generation.

THE ATHANASIAN CREED

Whoever wants to be saved should above all cling to the Christian faith.

Whoever does not guard it whole and inviolable will doubtless perish eternally.

Now this is the Christian faith: We worship one God in trinity and the Trinity in unity, neither confusing the persons nor dividing the divine being.

For the Father is one person, the Son is another, and the Spirit is still another.

But the deity of the Father, Son, and Holy Spirit is one, equal in glory, coeternal in majesty.

What the Father is, the Son is, and so is the Holy Spirit.

Uncreated is the Father; uncreated is the Son; uncreated is the Spirit.

The Father is infinite; the Son is infinite; the Holy Spirit is infinite.

Eternal is the Father; eternal is the Son; eternal is the Spirit: And yet there are not three eternal beings, but one who is eternal; as there are not three uncreated and unlimited beings, but one who is uncreated and unlimited.

Almighty is the Father; almighty is the Son; almighty is the Spirit: And yet there are not three almighty beings, but one who is almighty.

Thus the Father is God; the Son is God; the Holy Spirit is God: And yet there are not three gods, but one God.

Thus the Father is Lord; the Son is Lord; the Holy Spirit is Lord: And yet there are not three lords, but one Lord.

As Christian truth compels us to acknowledge each distinct person as God and Lord, so catholic religion forbids us to say that there are three gods or lords.

The Father was neither made, nor created nor begotten; the Son was neither made, nor created, but was alone begotten of the Father; the Spirit was neither made nor created, but is proceeding from the Father and the Son.

Thus there is one Father, not three fathers; one Son, not three sons; one Holy Spirit, not three spirits.

And in this Trinity, no one is before or after, greater or less than the other; but all three persons are in themselves, coeternal and coequal; and so we must worship the Trinity in unity and the one God in three persons.

Whoever wants to be saved should think thus about the Trinity.

It is necessary for eternal salvation that one also faithfully believe that our Lord Jesus Christ became flesh.

For this is the true faith that we believe and confess: That our Lord Jesus Christ, God's Son, is both God and man.

He is God, begotten before all worlds from the being of the Father, and he is man, born in the world from the being of his mother -- existing fully as God, and fully as man with a rational soul and a human body; equal to the Father in divinity, subordinate to the Father in humanity.

Although he is God and man, he is not divided, but is one Christ.

He is united because God has taken humanity into himself; he does not transform deity into humanity.

He is completely one in the unity of his person, without confusing his natures.

For as the rational soul and body are one person, so the one Christ is God and man.

He suffered death for our salvation. He descended into hell and rose again from the dead.

He ascended into heaven and is seated at the right hand of the Father.

He will come again to judge the living and the dead.

At his coming all people shall rise bodily to give an account of their own deeds.

Those who have done good will enter eternal life, those who have done evil will enter eternal fire. This is the Christian faith.

One cannot be saved without believing this firmly and faithfully.

The Belgic Confession is truly one of the confessions the Christendom has used to proclaim its beliefs to its members and to the world at large. The church today must continue teaching this confession to its members especially new Christians that need a lot help understanding core Christian values. The Belgic Confession reveals true reformed beliefs as reflected in the Holy Scriptures.

EDWARD KAVIMBA LUNGU PHD
THE BELGIC CONFESSION

Article 1: The Only God

We all believe in our hearts
and confess with our mouths
that there is a single
and simple
spiritual being,
whom we call God-

eternal,
incomprehensible,
invisible,
unchangeable,
infinite,
almighty;

completely wise,
just,
and good,

and the overflowing source
of all good.

Article 2: The Means by Which We Know God

We know God by two means:

First, by the creation, preservation, and government
of the universe,
since that universe is before our eyes
like a beautiful book
in which all creatures,
great and small,
are as letters
to make us ponder
the invisible things of God:
God's eternal power and divinity,
as the apostle Paul says in Romans 1:20.

All these things are enough to convict humans
and to leave them without excuse.

Second, God makes himself known to us more clearly
by his holy and divine Word,
as much as we need in this life,
for God's glory
and for our salvation.

Article 3: The Written Word of God

We confess that this Word of God
was not sent nor delivered "by human will,"
but that "men and women moved by the Holy Spirit,
spoke from God,"
as Peter says.1

Afterward our God—
with special care
for us and our salvation—
commanded his servants, the prophets and apostles,

to commit this revealed Word to writing.
God, with his own finger,
wrote the two tables of the law.

Therefore, we call such writings
holy and divine Scriptures.

1 2 Pet. 1:21

Article 4: The Canonical Books

We include in the Holy Scripture the two volumes
of the Old and New Testaments.
They are canonical books
with which there can be no quarrel at all.

In the church of God the list is as follows:
In the Old Testament,
the five books of Moses—
Genesis, Exodus, Leviticus, Numbers, Deuteronomy;
the books of Joshua, Judges, and Ruth;
the two books of Samuel, and two of Kings;
the two books of Chronicles, called Paralipomenon;
the first book of Ezra; Nehemiah, Esther, Job;
the Psalms of David;
the three books of Solomon—
Proverbs, Ecclesiastes, and the Song;
the four major prophets—
Isaiah, Jeremiah*, Ezekiel, Daniel;
and then the other twelve minor prophets—
Hosea, Joel, Amos, Obadiah,
Jonah, Micah, Nahum, Habakkuk,
Zephaniah, Haggai, Zechariah, Malachi.

In the New Testament,
the four gospels—
Matthew, Mark, Luke, and John;
the Acts of the Apostles;
the fourteen letters of Paul—

to the Romans;
the two letters to the Corinthians;
to the Galatians, Ephesians, Philippians, and Colossians;
the two letters to the Thessalonians;
the two letters to Timothy;
to Titus, Philemon, and to the Hebrews;
the seven letters of the other apostles—
one of James;
two of Peter;
three of John;

one of Jude;
and the Revelation of the apostle John.

* "Jeremiah" here includes the Book of Lamentations as well as the Book of Jeremiah.

Article 5: The Authority of Scripture

We receive all these books
and these only
as holy and canonical,
for the regulating, founding, and establishing
of our faith.

And we believe
without a doubt
all things contained in them-
not so much because the church
receives and approves them as such
but above all because the Holy Spirit
testifies in our hearts
that they are from God,
and also because they
prove themselves
to be from God.

For even the blind themselves are able to see
that the things predicted in them
do happen.

Article 6: The Difference between Canonical and Apocryphal Books

We distinguish between these holy books
and the apocryphal ones,
which are the third and fourth books of Esdras;
the books of Tobit, Judith, Wisdom, Jesus Sirach, Baruch;
what was added to the Story of Esther;
the Song of the Three Children in the Furnace;
the Story of Susannah;
the Story of Bel and the Dragon;
the Prayer of Manasseh;
and the two books of Maccabees.

The church may certainly read these books
and learn from them
as far as they agree with the canonical books.
But they do not have such power and virtue
that one could confirm
from their testimony
any point of faith or of the Christian religion.
Much less can they detract
from the authority
of the other holy books.

Article 7: The Sufficiency of Scripture

We believe

that this Holy Scripture contains
the will of God completely
and that everything one must believe
to be saved
is sufficiently taught in it.

For since the entire manner of service
which God requires of us
is described in it at great length,
no one-
even an apostle
or an angel from heaven,

as Paul says2-
ought to teach other than
what the Holy Scriptures have
already taught us.

For since it is forbidden
to add to the Word of God,
or take anything away from it,3
it is plainly demonstrated
that the teaching is perfect
and complete in all respects.

Therefore, we must not consider human writings-
no matter how holy their authors may have been-
equal to the divine writings;
nor may we put custom,
nor the majority,
nor age,
nor the passage of times or persons,
nor councils, decrees, or official decisions
above the truth of God,
for truth is above everything else.

For all human beings are liars by nature
and more vain than vanity itself.

Therefore, we reject with all our hearts
everything that does not agree
with this infallible rule,
as we are taught to do by the apostles
when they say,
"Test the spirits
to see whether they are from God,"4
and also,
"Do not receive into the house
or welcome anyone
who comes to you
and does not bring this teaching."5

2 Gal. 1:8
3 Deut. 12:32; Rev. 22:18-19

4 1 John 4:1
5 2 John 10

Article 8: The Trinity

In keeping with this truth and Word of God
we believe in one God,
who is one single essence,
in whom there are three persons,
really, truly, and eternally distinct
according to their incommunicable properties-
namely,
Father,
Son,
and Holy Spirit.

The Father
is the cause,
origin,
and source of all things,
visible as well as invisible.

The Son
is the Word,
the Wisdom,
and the image
of the Father.

The Holy Spirit
is the eternal power
and might,
proceeding from the Father and the Son.

Nevertheless,
this distinction does not divide God into three,
since Scripture teaches us
that the Father, the Son, and the Holy Spirit

each has a distinct subsistence
distinguished by characteristics-
yet in such a way
that these three persons are
only one God.

It is evident then
that the Father is not the Son
and that the Son is not the Father,
and that likewise the Holy Spirit is
neither the Father nor the Son.

Nevertheless,
these persons,
thus distinct,
are neither divided
nor fused or mixed together.

For the Father did not take on flesh,
nor did the Spirit,
but only the Son.

The Father was never
without the Son,
nor without the Holy Spirit,
since all these are equal from eternity,
in one and the same essence.

There is neither a first nor a last,
for all three are one
in truth and power,
in goodness and mercy.

Article 9: The Scriptural Witness on the Trinity

All these things we know
from the testimonies of Holy Scripture

as well as from the effects of the persons,
especially from those we feel within ourselves.

The testimonies of the Holy Scriptures, which teach us to believe in this Holy Trinity,
are written in many places of the Old Testament,
which need not be enumerated
but only chosen with discretion.

In the book of Genesis God says,
"Let us make humankind in our image,
according to our likeness."
So "God created humankind in his image"-
indeed, "male and female he created them."[6]
"See, the man has become like one of us."[7]

It appears from this
that there is a plurality of persons
within the Deity,
when God says,
"Let us make humankind in our image"-
and afterward God indicates the unity
in saying,
"God created."

It is true that God does not say here
how many persons there are-
but what is somewhat obscure to us
in the Old Testament
is very clear in the New.

For when our Lord was baptized in the Jordan,
the voice of the Father was heard saying,
"This is my Son, the Beloved;"[8]
the Son was seen in the water;
and the Holy Spirit appeared in the form of a dove.

So, in the baptism of all believers
this form was prescribed by Christ:

Baptize all people "in the name
of the Father
and of the Son
and of the Holy Spirit."9

In the Gospel according to Luke
the angel Gabriel says to Mary,
the mother of our Lord:

"The Holy Spirit will come upon you,
and the power of the Most High will overshadow you;
therefore the child to be born will be holy;
he will be called Son of God."10

And in another place it says:
"The grace of the Lord Jesus Christ,
the love of God,
and the communion of the Holy Spirit
be with all of you."11

["There are three that testify in heaven,
the Father, the Word, and the Holy Spirit,
and these three are one."]12

In all these passages we are fully taught
that there are three persons
in the one and only divine essence.
And although this doctrine surpasses human understanding,
we nevertheless believe it now,
through the Word,
waiting to know and enjoy it fully
in heaven.

Furthermore,
we must note the particular works and activities
of these three persons in relation to us.
The Father is called our Creator,
by reason of his power.
The Son is our Savior and Redeemer,

his blood.
The Holy Spirit is our Sanctifier,
by living in our hearts.

This doctrine of the holy Trinity
has always been maintained in the true church,
from the time of the apostles until the present,
against Jews, Muslims,
and certain false Christians and heretics,
such as Marcion, Mani,
Praxeas, Sabellius, Paul of Samosata, Arius,
and others like them,

who were rightly condemned by the holy fathers.

And so,
in this matter we willingly accept
the three ecumenical creeds-
the Apostles', Nicene, and Athanasian-
as well as what the ancient fathers decided
in agreement with them.

6 Gen. 1:26-27
7 Gen. 3:22
8 Matt. 3:17
9 Matt. 28:19
10 Luke 1:35
11 2 Cor. 13:14
12 1 John 5:7-following the better Greek texts, the NRSV and other modern translations place this verse in a footnote.

Article 10: The Deity of Christ

We believe that Jesus Christ,
according to his divine nature,
is the only Son of God-
eternally begotten,
not made or created,
for then he would be a creature.

He is one in essence with the Father;
coeternal;
the exact image of the person of the Father
and the "reflection of God's glory,"13
being like the Father in all things.

Jesus Christ is the Son of God
not only from the time he assumed our nature
but from all eternity,
as the following testimonies teach us
when they are taken together.

Moses says that God created the world;14
and John says that all things were created through the Word,15
which he calls God.
The apostle says that God created the world through the Son.16
He also says that God created all things through Jesus Christ.17

And so it must follow
that the one who is called God, the Word, the Son, and Jesus Christ
already existed before creating all things.
Therefore the prophet Micah says
that Christ's origin is "from ancient days."18
And the apostle says
that the Son has "neither beginning of days
nor end of life."19

So then,

he is the true eternal God,
the Almighty,
whom we invoke,
worship,
and serve.

13 Col. 1:15; Heb. 1:3
14 Gen. 1:1
15 John 1:3
16 Heb. 1:2
17 Col. 1:16

18 Mic. 5:2
19 Heb. 7:3

Article 11: The Deity of the Holy Spirit

We believe and confess also
that the Holy Spirit proceeds eternally
from the Father and the Son-
neither made,
nor created,
nor begotten,
but only proceeding
from the two of them.

In regard to order,
the Spirit is the third person of the Trinity-
of one and the same essence,
and majesty,
and glory,
with the Father and the Son,
being true and eternal God,
as the Holy Scriptures teach us.

Article 12: The Creation of All Things

We believe that the Father,
when it seemed good to him,
created heaven and earth and all other creatures
from nothing,
by the Word-
that is to say,
by the Son.

God has given all creatures
their being, form, and appearance
and their various functions
for serving their Creator.

Even now
God also sustains and governs them all,

according to his eternal providence
and by his infinite power,
that they may serve humanity,

in order that humanity may serve God.

God has also created the angels good,
that they might be messengers of God
and serve the elect.

Some of them have fallen
from the excellence in which God created them
into eternal perdition;
and the others have persisted and remained
in their original state,
by the grace of God.

The devils and evil spirits are so corrupt
that they are enemies of God
and of everything good.
They lie in wait for the church
and every member of it
like thieves,
with all their power,
to destroy and spoil everything
by their deceptions.

So then,
by their own wickedness
they are condemned to everlasting damnation,
daily awaiting their torments.

For that reason,
we detest the error of the Sadducees,
who deny that there are spirits and angels,
and also the error of the Manicheans,
who say that the devils originated by themselves,
being evil by nature,
without having been corrupted.

Article 13: The Doctrine of God's Providence

We believe that this good God,
after creating all things,
did not abandon them to chance or fortune
but leads and governs them
according to his holy will,
in such a way that nothing happens in this world
without God's orderly arrangement.

Yet God is not the author of,
and cannot be charged with,
the sin that occurs.
For God's power and goodness
are so great and incomprehensible
that God arranges and does his works very well and justly
even when the devils and the wicked act unjustly.

We do not wish to inquire

with undue curiosity
into what God does that surpasses human understanding
and is beyond our ability to comprehend.
But in all humility and reverence
we adore the just judgments of God,
which are hidden from us,
being content to be Christ's disciples,
so as to learn only what God shows us in the Word,
without going beyond those limits.

This doctrine gives us unspeakable comfort
since it teaches us
that nothing can happen to us by chance
but only by the arrangement of our gracious
heavenly Father,
who watches over us with fatherly care,
sustaining all creatures under his lordship,
so that not one of the hairs on our heads
(for they are all numbered)
nor even a little bird

can fall to the ground
without the will of our Father.20

In this thought we rest,
knowing that God holds in check
the devils and all our enemies,
who cannot hurt us
without divine permission and will.

For that reason, we reject the damnable error of the Epicureans,
who say that God does not get involved in anything and leaves everything to chance.

20 Matt. 10:29-30

Article 14: The Creation and Fall of Humanity

even though for a time
it may appear very small
to human eyes-
as though it were snuffed out.

For example,
during the very dangerous time of Ahab
the Lord preserved for himself seven thousand
who did not bend their knees to Baal.75

And so this holy church
is not confined,
bound,
or limited to a certain place or certain people.
But it is spread and dispersed
throughout the entire world,
though still joined and united
in heart and will,

in one and the same Spirit,
by the power of faith.

75 1 Kings 19:18

Article 28: The Obligations of Church Members

We believe that
since this holy assembly and congregation
is the gathering of those who are saved
and there is no salvation apart from it,
people ought not to withdraw from it,
content to be by themselves,
regardless of their status or condition.

But all people are obliged
to join and unite with it,
keeping the unity of the church
by submitting to its instruction and discipline,

by bending their necks under the yoke of Jesus Christ,
and by serving to build up one another,
according to the gifts God has given them
as members of each other
in the same body.

And to preserve this unity more effectively,
it is the duty of all believers,
according to God's Word,
to separate themselves
from those who do not belong to the church,
in order to join this assembly
wherever God has established it,
even if civil authorities and royal decrees forbid
and death and physical punishment result.

And so,
all who withdraw from the church
or do not join it
act contrary to God's ordinance.

Article 29: The Marks of the True Church

We believe that we ought to discern
diligently and very carefully,
by the Word of God,
what is the true church-
for all sects in the world today
claim for themselves the name of "the church."

We are not speaking here of the company of hypocrites
who are mixed among the good in the church
and who nonetheless are not part of it,
even though they are physically there.
But we are speaking of distinguishing
the body and fellowship of the true church

from all sects that call themselves "the church."

The true church can be recognized
if it has the following marks:
The church engages in the pure preaching
of the gospel;
it makes use of the pure administration of the sacraments
as Christ instituted them;
it practices church discipline
for correcting faults.

In short, it governs itself
according to the pure Word of God,
rejecting all things contrary to it
and holding Jesus Christ as the only Head.
By these marks one can be assured
of recognizing the true church-
and no one ought to be separated from it.

As for those who can belong to the church,
we can recognize them by the distinguishing marks of Christians:
namely by faith,
and by their fleeing from sin and pursuing righteousness,
once they have received the one and only Savior,
Jesus Christ.
They love the true God and their neighbors,
without turning to the right or left,
and they crucify the flesh and its works.

Though great weakness remains in them,
they fight against it
by the Spirit
all the days of their lives,
appealing constantly
to the blood, suffering, death, and obedience of the Lord Jesus, in whom they have forgiveness of their sins,
through faith in him.

As for the false church,
it assigns more authority to itself and its ordinances
than to the Word of God;

it does not want to subject itself
to the yoke of Christ;
it does not administer the sacraments
as Christ commanded in his Word;
it rather adds to them or subtracts from them
as it pleases;
it bases itself on humans,
more than on Jesus Christ;
it persecutes those
who live holy lives according to the Word of God
and who rebuke it for its faults, greed, and idolatry.

These two churches
are easy to recognize
and thus to distinguish
from each other.

Article 30: The Government of the Church

We believe that this true church
ought to be governed according to the spiritual order
that our Lord has taught us in his Word.
There should be ministers or pastors
to preach the Word of God
and administer the sacraments.
There should also be elders and deacons,
along with the pastors,
to make up the council of the church.

By this means
true religion is preserved;
true doctrine is able to take its course;
and evil people are corrected spiritually and held in check,
so that also the poor
and all the afflicted
may be helped and comforted
according to their need.

By this means
everything will be done well
and in good order
in the church,
when such persons are elected
who are faithful
and are chosen according to the rule
that Paul gave to Timothy.76

76 1 Tim. 3

Article 31: The Officers of the Church

We believe that
ministers of the Word of God, elders, and deacons
ought to be chosen to their offices
by a legitimate election of the church,
with prayer in the name of the Lord,
and in good order,
as the Word of God teaches.

So all must be careful
not to push themselves forward improperly,
but must wait for God's call,
so that they may be assured of their calling
and be certain that they are
chosen by the Lord.

As for the ministers of the Word,

they all have the same power and authority,
no matter where they may be,
since they are all servants of Jesus Christ,
the only universal bishop,
and the only head of the church.

Moreover,
to keep God's holy order
from being violated or despised,
we say that everyone ought,

as much as possible,
to hold the ministers of the Word and elders of the church
in special esteem,
because of the work they do,
and be at peace with them,
without grumbling, quarreling, or fighting.

Article 32: The Order and Discipline of the Church

We also believe that
although it is useful and good
for those who govern the churches
to establish and set up
a certain order among themselves
for maintaining the body of the church,
they ought always to guard against deviating
from what Christ,
our only Master,
has ordained
for us.

Therefore, we reject all human innovations
and all laws imposed on us,
in our worship of God,
which bind and force our consciences
in any way.

So we accept only what is proper
to maintain harmony and unity
and to keep all in obedience
to God.

To that end excommunication,
with all it involves,
according to the Word of God,
is required.

Article 33: The Sacraments

We believe that our good God,
mindful of our crudeness and weakness,
has ordained sacraments for us
to seal his promises in us,
to pledge good will and grace toward us,

and also to nourish and sustain our faith.

God has added these to the Word of the gospel
to represent better to our external senses
both what God enables us to understand by the Word
and what he does inwardly in our hearts,
confirming in us
the salvation he imparts to us.

For they are visible signs and seals
of something internal and invisible,
by means of which God works in us
through the power of the Holy Spirit.
So they are not empty and hollow signs
to fool and deceive us,
for their truth is Jesus Christ,
without whom they would be nothing.

Moreover,
we are satisfied with the number of sacraments
that Christ our Master has ordained for us.
There are only two:
the sacrament of baptism
and the Holy Supper of Jesus Christ.

Article 34: The Sacrament of Baptism

We believe and confess that Jesus Christ,
in whom the law is fulfilled,
has by his shed blood
put an end to every other shedding of blood,

which anyone might do or wish to do
in order to atone or satisfy for sins.

Having abolished circumcision,
which was done with blood,
Christ established in its place
the sacrament of baptism.

By it we are received into God's church
and set apart from all other people and alien religions,
that we may wholly belong to him
whose mark and sign we bear.
Baptism also witnesses to us
that God, being our gracious Father,
will be our God forever.

Therefore, Christ has commanded
that all those who belong to him
be baptized with pure water
"in the name of the Father
and of the Son
and of the Holy Spirit."[77]

In this way God signifies to us

that just as water washes away the dirt of the body
when it is poured on us
and also is seen on the bodies of those who are baptized
when it is sprinkled on them,
so too the blood of Christ does the same thing internally,
in the soul,
by the Holy Spirit.
It washes and cleanses it from its sins
and transforms us from being the children of wrath
into the children of God.

This does not happen by the physical water
but by the sprinkling of the precious blood of the Son of God,
who is our Red Sea,
through which we must pass

to escape the tyranny of Pharaoh,
who is the devil,
and to enter the spiritual land
of Canaan.

So ministers,
as far as their work is concerned,
give us the sacrament and what is visible,
but our Lord gives what the sacrament signifies-
namely the invisible gifts and graces;
washing, purifying, and cleansing our souls
of all filth and unrighteousness;
renewing our hearts and filling them
with all comfort;
giving us true assurance
of his fatherly goodness;
clothing us with the "new self"
and stripping off the "old self
with its practices."[78]

For this reason, we believe that
anyone who aspires to reach eternal life
ought to be baptized only once
without ever repeating it-
for we cannot be born twice.
Yet this baptism is profitable
not only when the water is on us
and when we receive it
but throughout our
entire lives.

For that reason, we reject the error of the Anabaptists
who are not content with a single baptism
once received
and also condemn the baptism
of the children of believers.
We believe our children ought to be baptized

and sealed with the sign of the covenant,

as little children were circumcised in Israel
on the basis of the same promises
made to our children.

And truly,
Christ has shed his blood no less
for washing the little children of believers
than he did for adults.

Therefore, they ought to receive the sign and sacrament
of what Christ has done for them,
just as the Lord commanded in the law that
by offering a lamb for them
the sacrament of the suffering and death of Christ
would be granted them
shortly after their birth.
This was the sacrament of Jesus Christ.

Furthermore,
baptism does for our children
what circumcision did for the Jewish people.
That is why Paul calls baptism
the "circumcision of Christ."[79]

77 Matt. 28:19
78 Col.3:9
79 Col. 2:11

Article 35: The Sacrament of the Lord's Supper

We believe and confess
that our Savior Jesus Christ
has ordained and instituted the sacrament of the Holy Supper
to nourish and sustain those
who are already regenerated and ingrafted
into his family,
which is his church.

Now those who are born again have two lives in them.
The one is physical and temporal-

they have it from the moment of their first birth,
and it is common to all.
The other is spiritual and heavenly,
and is given them in their second birth-
it comes through the Word of the gospel
in the communion of the body of Christ;
and this life is common to God's elect only.

Thus, to support the physical and earthly life
God has prescribed for us
an appropriate earthly and material bread,
which is as common to all people
as life itself.

But to maintain the spiritual and heavenly life
that belongs to believers,
God has sent a living bread
that came down from heaven:
namely Jesus Christ,
who nourishes and maintains
the spiritual life of believers
when eaten-
that is, when appropriated
and received spiritually
by faith.

To represent to us
this spiritual and heavenly bread
Christ has instituted
an earthly and visible bread as the sacrament of his body
and wine as the sacrament of his blood.
He did this to testify to us that
just as truly as we take and hold the sacrament in our hands
and eat and drink it with our mouths,
by which our life is then sustained,
so truly we receive into our souls,
for our spiritual life,
the true body and true blood of Christ,
our only Savior.

We receive these by faith,
which is the hand and mouth of our souls.

Now it is certain
that Jesus Christ did not prescribe
his sacraments for us in vain,
since he works in us all he represents
by these holy signs,
although the manner in which he does it
goes beyond our understanding
and is incomprehensible to us,
just as the operation of God's Spirit
is hidden and incomprehensible.

Yet we do not go wrong when we say
that what is eaten is Christ's own natural body
and what is drunk is his own blood-
but the manner in which we eat it
is not by the mouth, but by the Spirit
through faith.

In that way Jesus Christ remains always seated
at the right hand of God the Father
in heaven-
but he never refrains on that account
to communicate himself to us
through faith.

BEDROOM OF ADAM AND EVE

This banquet is a spiritual table
at which Christ communicates himself to us
with all his benefits.
At that table he makes us enjoy himself
as much as the merits of his suffering and death,
as he nourishes, strengthens, and comforts
our poor, desolate souls
by the eating of his flesh,
and relieves and renews them
by the drinking of his blood.

Moreover,
though the sacraments and what they signify are joined together,
not all receive both of them.
The wicked certainly take the sacrament,
to their condemnation,
but do not receive the truth of the sacrament,
just as Judas and Simon the Sorcerer both indeed
received the sacrament,
but not Christ,
who was signified by it.
He is communicated only to believers.

Finally,
with humility and reverence
we receive the holy sacrament
in the gathering of God's people,
as we engage together,
with thanksgiving,
in a holy remembrance
of the death of Christ our Savior,
and as we thus confess
our faith and Christian religion.
Therefore none should come to this table
without examining themselves carefully,
lest by eating this bread
and drinking this cup
they "eat and drink judgment against themselves."80

In short,
by the use of this holy sacrament
we are moved to a fervent love
of God and our neighbors.

Therefore, we reject
as desecrations of the sacraments
all the muddled ideas and condemnable inventions
that people have added and mixed in with them.
And we say that we should be content with the procedure

that Christ and the apostles have taught us
and speak of these things
as they have spoken of them.

80 1 Cor. 11:29

Article 36: The Civil Government

We believe that
because of the depravity of the human race,
our good God has ordained kings, princes, and civil officers.
God wants the world to be governed by laws and policies
so that human lawlessness may be restrained
and that everything may be conducted in good order
among human beings.

For that purpose, God has placed the sword
in the hands of the government,
to punish evil people
and protect the good.

And the government's task is not limited
to caring for and watching over the public domain
but extends also to upholding the sacred ministry,
with a view to removing and destroying
all idolatry and false worship of the Antichrist;
to promoting the kingdom of Jesus Christ;
and to furthering the preaching of the gospel everywhere;
to the end that God may be honored and served by everyone,
as he requires in his Word.

Moreover, everyone,
regardless of status, condition, or rank,
must be subject to the government,
and pay taxes,
and hold its representatives in honor and respect,
and obey them in all things that are not in conflict
with God's Word,
praying for them

that the Lord may be willing to lead them
in all their ways
and that we may live a peaceful and quiet life
in all piety and decency.

And on this matter we reject the Anabaptists, anarchists,
and in general all those who want
to reject the authorities and civil officers
and to subvert justice
by introducing common ownership of goods
and corrupting the moral order
that God has established among human beings.

Article 37: The Last Judgment

Finally, we believe,
according to God's Word,
that when the time appointed by the Lord is come
(which is unknown to all creatures)

and the number of the elect is complete,
our Lord Jesus Christ will come from heaven,
bodily and visibly,
as he ascended,
with great glory and majesty,
to declare himself the judge
of the living and the dead.
He will burn this old world,
in fire and flame,
in order to cleanse it.

Then all human creatures will appear in person
before the great judge-
men, women, and children,
who have lived from the beginning until the end
of the world.

They will be summoned there
"with the archangel's call
and with the sound of God's trumpet."81

For all those who died before that time
will be raised from the earth,
their spirits being joined and united
with their own bodies
in which they lived.
And as for those who are still alive,
they will not die like the others
but will be changed "in the twinkling of an eye"
from perishable to imperishable.82

Then the books (that is, the consciences) will be opened,
and the dead will be judged
according to the things they did in the world,83
whether good or evil.
Indeed, all people will give account
of all the idle words they have spoken,84
which the world regards
as only playing games.
And then the secrets and hypocrisies of all people
will be publicly uncovered
in the sight of all.

Therefore,
with good reason
the thought of this judgment
is horrible and dreadful
to wicked and evil people.
But it is very pleasant
and a great comfort
to the righteous and elect,
since their total redemption
will then be accomplished.

They will then receive the fruits of their labor
and of the trouble they have suffered;

their innocence will be openly recognized by all;
and they will see the terrible vengeance
that God will bring on the evil ones
who tyrannized, oppressed, and tormented them
in this world.

The evil ones will be convicted
by the witness of their own consciences,
and shall be made immortal-
but only to be tormented
in "the eternal fire
prepared for the devil and his angels."[85]

In contrast,
the faithful and elect will be crowned
with glory and honor.

The Son of God will profess their names[86]
before God his Father and the holy and elect angels;
all tears will be wiped from their eyes;[87]
and their cause-
at present condemned as heretical and evil
by many judges and civil officers-
will be acknowledged as the cause of the Son of God.

And as a gracious reward
the Lord will make them possess a glory
such as the human heart
could never imagine.

So we look forward to that great day with longing
in order to enjoy fully
the promises of God in Christ Jesus,
our Lord.

81 1 Thess. 4:16
82 1 Cor. 15:51-53
83 Rev. 20:12
84 Matt. 12:36

85 Matt. 25:41
86 Matt. 10:32
87 Rev. 7:17

BEDROOM OF ADAM AND EVE
CONFESSION OF BELHAR

Racism has no place in the body of Christ or in the world at large. For the local church to learn more of how to avoid falling into a racism trap must study and teach this Belmar confession to its members. This confession is a product of Uniting Reformed Church in Southern African (URCSA) which was fed up of South Africa, Apartheid system supported by the Dutch Reformed Church for a long time.

Unconfessed hatred towards one another, sometimes bleeds injustice and racism. Racism views one race being pure and superior over the rest. Racism disrespects and undermines the true teaching of the word of God, which says all human beings are created equal before their creator. The word of God is plain clear that all human beings are made in the image of God (Genesis 1:26). Racism is and must be a zero-tolerance policy in all races and culture. Hatred in any form is a crime against humanity. We-Them Distinction must not be elevated in people's lives. We-Them Distinction simply means we are better than them. This distinction destroys the biblical teaching that says we are all made in the image of our creator (Genesis 1:26).

Terrorism in any form is also a crime against humanity. Terrorism breeds and brings the fear of man and not God. This is ungodly and contrary to biblical teaching which says the fear of God is the beginning of wisdom. Not the fear of man.

Therefore, Racism, hatred and terrorism breed from deprived human condition called the bedroom of Adam and Eve. The cure to all these social and racial injustices is the blood of Jesus Christ. Tooth for a tooth is not a solution to social and racial injustice but love in the name of Jesus Christ. Here is the Belhar Confession;

We believe in the triune God, Father, Son and Holy Spirit, who gathers, protects and cares for the church through Word and Spirit. Thus, God has done since the beginning of the world and will do to the end.

We believe in one holy, universal Christian church, the communion of saints called from the entire human family.

We believe -that Christ's work of reconciliation is made manifest in the church as the community of believers who have been reconciled with God and with one another (Eph. 2:11-22); -that unity is, therefore, both a gift and an obligation for the church of Jesus Christ; that through the working of God's Spirit it is a binding force, yet simultaneously a reality which must be earnestly pursued and sought: one which the people of God must continually be built up to attain (Eph. 4:1-16); -that this unity must become visible so that the world may believe that separation, enmity and hatred between people and groups is sin which Christ has already conquered, and accordingly that anything which threatens this unity may have no place in the church and must be resisted (John 17:20-23);

-hat this unity of the people of God must be manifested and be active in a variety of ways: in that we love one another; that we experience, practice and pursue community with one another; that we are obligated to give ourselves willingly and joyfully to be of benefit and blessing to one another; that we share one faith, have one calling, are of one soul and one mind; have one God and Father, are filled with one Spirit, are baptized with one baptism, eat of one bread and drink of one cup, confess one name, are obedient to one Lord, work for one cause, and share one hope; together come to know the height and the breadth and the depth of the love of Christ; together are built up to the stature of Christ, to the new humanity; together know and bear one another's burdens, thereby fulfilling the law of Christ that we need one another and upbuild one another, admonishing and comforting one another; that we suffer with one another for the sake of righteousness; pray together; together serve God in this world; and together fight against all which may threaten or hinder this unity (Phil. 2:1-5; 1 Cor. 12:4-31; John 13:1-17; 1 Cor. 1:10-13; Eph. 4:1-6; Eph. 3:14-20; 1 Cor. 10:16-17; 1 Cor. 11:17-34; Gal. 6:2; 2 Cor. 1:3-4);

-that this unity can be established only in freedom and not under constraint; that the variety of spiritual gifts, opportunities, backgrounds, convictions, as well as the various languages and cultures, are by virtue of the reconciliation in Christ, opportunities for mutual service and enrichment within the one visible people of God (Rom. 12:3-8; 1 Cor. 12:1-11; Eph. 4:7-13; Gal. 3:27-28; James 2:1-13);

-that true faith in Jesus Christ is the only condition for membership of this church.

Therefore, we reject any doctrine

=which absolutizes either natural diversity or the sinful separation of people in such a way that this absolutization hinders or breaks the visible and active unity of the church, or even leads to the establishment of a separate church formation;

=which professes that this spiritual unity is truly being maintained in the bond of peace while believers of the same confession are in effect alienated from one another for the sake of diversity and in despair of reconciliation;

=which denies that a refusal earnestly to pursue this visible unity as a priceless gift is sin;

=which explicitly or implicitly maintains that descent or any other human or social factor should be a consideration in determining membership of the church.

We believe -that God has entrusted the church with the message of reconciliation in and through Jesus Christ, that the church is called to be the salt of the earth and the light of the world, that the church is called blessed because it is a peacemaker, that the church is witness both by word and by deed to the new heaven and the new earth in which righteousness dwells (2 Cor. 5:17-21; Matt. 5:13-16; Matt. 5:9; 2 Peter 3:13; Rev. 21-22).

-That God's life-giving Word and Spirit has conquered the powers of sin and death, and therefore also of ire-reconciliation and hatred, bitterness and enmity, that God's life-giving Word and Spirit will enable the church to live in a new obedience which can open new possibilities of life for society and the world (Eph. 4:17-6:23, Rom. 6; Col. 1:9-14; Col. 2:13-19; Col. 3:1-4:6);

-That the credibility of this message is seriously affected and its beneficial work obstructed when it is proclaimed in a land which professes to be Christian, but in which the enforced separation of people on a racial basis promotes and perpetuates alienation, hatred and enmity;

-That any teaching which attempts to legitimate such forced separation by appeal to the gospel, and is not prepared to venture on the road of obedience and reconciliation, but rather, out of prejudice, fear, selfishness and unbelief, denies in advance the reconciling power of the gospel, must be considered ideology and false doctrine.

Therefore, we reject any doctrine which, in such a situation, sanctions in the name of the gospel or of the will of God the forced separation of people on the grounds of race and color and thereby in advance obstructs and weakens the ministry and experience of reconciliation in Christ.

We believe

-That God has revealed himself as the one who wishes to bring about justice and true peace among people;

-That God, in a world full of injustice and enmity, is in a special way the God of the destitute, the poor and the wronged;

-That God calls the church to follow him in this, for God brings justice to the oppressed and gives bread to the hungry;

-That God frees the prisoner and restores sight to the blind;

-That God supports the downtrodden, protects the stranger, helps orphans and widows and blocks the path of the ungodly;

-That for God pure and undefiled religion is to visit the orphans and the widows in their suffering;

-That God wishes to teach the church to do what is good and to seek the right (Deut. 32:4; Luke 2:14; John 14:27; Eph. 2:14; Isa. 1:16-17; James 1:27; James 5:1-6; Luke 1:46-55; Luke 6:20-26; Luke 7:22; Luke 16:19-31; Ps. 146; Luke 4:16-19; Rom. 6:13-18; Amos 5);

-That the church must therefore stand by people in any form of suffering and need, which implies, among other things, that the church must witness against and strive against any form of injustice, so that justice may roll down like waters, and righteousness like an ever-flowing stream;

-That the church as the possession of God must stand where the Lord stands, namely against injustice and with the wronged; that in following Christ the church must witness against all the powerful and privileged who selfishly seek their own interests and thus control and harm others.

Therefore, we reject any ideology which would legitimate forms of injustice and any doctrine which is unwilling to resist such an ideology in the name of the gospel.

We believe that, in obedience to Jesus Christ, its only head, the church is called to confess and to do all these things, even though the authorities and human laws might forbid them and punishment and suffering be the consequence (Eph. 4:15-16; Acts 5:29-33; 1 Peter 2:18-25; 1 Peter 3:15-18).

Jesus is Lord.

To the one and only God, Father, Son and Holy Spirit, be the honor and the glory for ever and ever.

Note: This is a translation of the original Afrikaans text of the confession as it was adopted by the synod of the Dutch Reformed Mission Church in South Africa in 1986. In 1994 the Dutch Reformed Mission Church and the Dutch Reformed Church in Africa united to form the Uniting Reformed Church in Southern Africa (URCSA). This inclusive language text was prepared by the Office of Theology and Worship, Presbyterian Church (U.S.A.).

Every Christian has a creed. A creed is a belief or statement of faith. A Christian Creed is a belief or statement of faith about God, Christ, the Holy Spirit or any maters of faith. All Christian local churches or Christian denominations hold to sacred beliefs which become the canon of faith as far as they remain true to the word of God.

Reformed denomination at large holds to the Canons of Dort. These articles are hard to understand. To avoid repeating doctrinal heresy pointed out by the reformers at Dort, the church should confess and teach these beliefs through the eyes of the Holy Bible.

BEDROOM OF ADAM AND EVE

CANONS OF DORT

Formally Titled
The Decision of the Synod of Dort on the Five Main Points of Doctrine in Dispute in the Netherlands

The First Main Point of Doctrine
Divine Election and Reprobation

The Judgment Concerning Divine Predestination Which the Synod Declares to Be in Agreement with the Word of God and Accepted Till Now in the Reformed Churches, Set Forth in Several Articles

Article 1: God's Right to Condemn All People
Since all people have sinned in Adam and have come under the sentence of the curse and eternal death, God would have done no one an injustice if it had been his will to leave the entire human race in sin and under the curse, and to condemn them on account of their sin. As the apostle says: "The whole world is liable to the condemnation of God" (Rom. 3:19), "All have sinned and are deprived of the glory of God" (Rom. 3:23), and "The wages of sin is death" (Rom. 6:23).

Article 2: The Manifestation of God's Love
But this is how God showed his love: he sent his only begotten Son into the world, so that whoever believes in him should not perish but have eternal life (1 John 4:9, John 3:16).

Article 3: The Preaching of the Gospel
In order that people may be brought to faith, God mercifully sends messengers of this very joyful message to the people and at the time he wills. By this ministry people are called to repentance and faith in Christ crucified. For "how shall they believe in him of whom they have not heard? And how shall they hear without someone preaching? And how shall they preach unless they have been sent?" (Rom. 10:14-15).

Article 4: A Twofold Response to the Gospel
God's wrath remains on those who do not believe this gospel. But those who do accept it and embrace Jesus the Savior with a true and living faith are delivered through him from God's wrath and from destruction, and receive the gift of eternal life.

Article 5: The Sources of Unbelief and of Faith
The cause or blame for this unbelief, as well as for all other sins, is not at all in God, but in humanity. Faith in Jesus Christ, however, and salvation through him is a free gift of God. As Scripture says, "It is by grace you have been saved, through faith, and this not from yourselves; it is a gift of God" (Eph. 2:8). Likewise: "It has been freely given to you to believe in Christ" (Phil. 1:29).

Article 6: God's Eternal Decree
The fact that some receive from God the gift of faith within time, and that others do not, stems from his eternal decree. For "all his works are known to God from eternity" (Acts 15:18; Eph. 1:11). In accordance with this decree God graciously softens the hearts, however hard, of the elect and inclines them to believe, but by a just judgment, God leaves in their wickedness and hardness of heart those who have not been chosen. And in this especially is disclosed to us God's act-unfathomable, and as merciful as it is just-of distinguishing between people equally lost. This is the well-known decree of election and reprobation revealed in God's Word. The wicked, impure, and unstable distort this decree to their own ruin, but it provides holy and godly souls with comfort beyond words.

Article 7: Election

The election is God's unchangeable purpose by which he did the following: Before the foundation of the world, by sheer grace, according to the free good pleasure of his will, God chose in Christ to salvation a definite number of particular people out of the entire human race, which had fallen by its own fault from its original innocence into sin and ruin. Those chosen were neither better nor more deserving than the others, but lay with them in the common misery. God did this in Christ, whom he also appointed from eternity to be the mediator, the head of all those chosen, and the foundation of their salvation.

And so God decreed to give to Christ those chosen for salvation, and to call and draw them effectively into Christ's fellowship through the Word and Spirit. In other words, God decreed to grant them true faith in Christ, to justify them, to sanctify them, and finally, after powerfully preserving them in the fellowship of the Son, to glorify them.

God did all this in order to demonstrate his mercy, to the praise of the riches of God's glorious grace.

As Scripture says, "God chose us in Christ, before the foundation of the world, so that we should be holy and blameless before him with love; he predestined us whom he adopted as his children through Jesus Christ, in himself, according to the good pleasure of his will, to the praise of his glorious grace, by which he freely made us pleasing to himself in his beloved" (Eph. 1:4-6). And elsewhere, "Those whom he predestined, he also called; and those whom he called, he also justified; and those whom he justified, he also glorified" (Rom. 8:30).

Article 8: A Single Decree of Election

This election is not of many kinds, but one and the same for all who were to be saved in the Old and the New Testament. For Scripture declares that there is a single good pleasure, purpose, and plan of God's will, by which he chose us from eternity both to grace and to glory, both to salvation and to the way of salvation, which God prepared in advance for us to walk in.

Article 9: Election Not Based on Foreseen Faith

This same election took place, not on the basis of foreseen faith, of the obedience of faith, of holiness, or of any other good quality and disposition, as though it were based on a prerequisite cause or condition in the person to be chosen, but rather for the purpose of faith, of the obedience of faith, of holiness, and so on. Accordingly, election is the source of every saving good. Faith, holiness, and the other saving gifts, and at last eternal life itself, flow forth from election as its fruits and effects. As the apostle says, "He chose us" (not because we were, but) "so that we should be holy and blameless before him in love" (Eph. 1:4).

Article 10: Election Based on God's Good Pleasure

But the cause of this undeserved election is exclusively the good pleasure of God. This does not involve God's choosing certain human qualities or actions from among all those possible as a condition of salvation, but rather involves adopting certain particular persons from among the common mass of sinners as God's own possession. As Scripture says, "When the children were not yet born, and had done nothing either good or bad…she (Rebecca) was told, "The older will serve the younger." As it is written, "Jacob I loved, but Esau I hated" (Rom. 9:11-13). Also, "All who were appointed for eternal life believed" (Acts 13:48).

Article 11: Election Unchangeable

Just as God is most wise, unchangeable, all-knowing, and almighty, so the election made by him can neither be suspended nor altered, revoked, or annulled; neither can God's chosen ones be cast off, nor their number reduced.

Article 12: The Assurance of Election

Assurance of their eternal and unchangeable election to salvation is given to the chosen in due time, though by various stages and in differing measure. Such assurance comes not by inquisitive searching into the hidden and deep things of God, but by noticing within themselves, with spiritual joy and holy delight, the unmistakable fruits of election pointed out in God's Word-such as, a true faith in Christ, a childlike fear of God, a godly sorrow for their sins, a hunger and thirst for righteousness, and so on.

Article 13: The Fruit of This Assurance
In their awareness and assurance of this election, God's children daily find greater cause to humble themselves before God, to adore the fathomless depth of God's mercies, to cleanse themselves, and to give fervent love in return to the One who first so greatly loved them. This is far from saying that this teaching concerning election, and reflection upon it, make God's children lax in observing his commandments or carnally self-assured. By God's just judgment this does usually happen to those who casually take for granted the grace of election or engage in idle and brazen talk about it but are unwilling to walk in the ways of the chosen.

Article 14: Teaching Election Properly
By God's wise plan, this teaching concerning divine election was proclaimed through the prophets, Christ himself, and the apostles, in Old and New Testament times. It was subsequently committed to writing in the Holy Scriptures. So also today in God's church, for which it was specifically intended, this teaching must be set forth with a spirit of discretion, in a godly and holy manner, at the appropriate time and place, without inquisitive searching into the ways of the Most High. This must be done for the glory of God's most holy name, and for the lively comfort of God's people.

Article 15: Reprobation
Moreover, Holy Scripture most especially highlights this eternal and undeserved grace of our election and brings it out more clearly for us, in that it further bears witness that not all people have been chosen but that some have not been chosen or have been passed by in God's eternal election-those, that is, concerning whom God, on the basis of his entirely free, most just, irreproachable, and unchangeable good pleasure, made the following decree:

to leave them in the common misery into which, by their own fault, they have plunged themselves; not to grant them saving faith and the grace of conversion; but finally to condemn and eternally punish those who have been left in their own ways and under God's just judgment, not only for their unbelief but also for all their other sins, in order to display his justice.

And this is the decree of reprobation, which does not at all make God the author of sin (a blasphemous thought!) but rather its fearful, irreproachable, just judge and avenger.

Article 16: Responses to the Teaching of Reprobation
Those who do not yet actively experience within themselves a living faith in Christ or an assured confidence of heart, peace of conscience, a zeal for childlike obedience, and a glorying in God through Christ, but who nevertheless use the means by which God has promised to work these things in us-such people ought not to be alarmed at the mention of reprobation, nor to count themselves among the reprobate; rather they ought to continue diligently in the use of the means, to desire fervently a time of more abundant grace, and to wait for it in reverence and humility. On the other hand, those who seriously desire to turn to God, to be pleasing to God alone, and to be delivered from the body of death, but are not yet able to make such progress along the way of godliness and faith as they would like-such people ought much less to stand in fear of the teaching concerning reprobation, since our merciful God has promised not to snuff out a smoldering wick or break a bruised reed*

However, those who have forgotten God and their Savior Jesus Christ and have abandoned themselves wholly to the cares of the world and the pleasures of the flesh-such people have every reason to stand in fear of this teaching, as long as they do not seriously turn to God.

*Isaiah 42:3

Article 17: The Salvation of the Infants of Believers
Since we must make judgments about God's will from his Word, which testifies that the children of believers are holy, not by nature but by virtue of the gracious covenant in which they together with their parents are included, godly parents ought not to doubt the election and salvation of their children whom God calls out of this life in infancy.

Article 18: The Proper Attitude Toward Election and Reprobation
To those who complain about this grace of an undeserved election and about the severity of a just reprobation, we reply with the words of the apostle, "Who are you, O man, to talk back to God?" (Rom. 9:20), and with the words of our Savior, "Have I no right to do what I want with my own?" (Matt. 20:15). We, however, with reverent adoration of these secret things, cry out with the apostle: "Oh, the depths of the riches both of the wisdom and the knowledge of God! How unsearchable are his judgments, and his ways beyond tracing out! For who has known the mind of the Lord? Or who has been his counselor? Or who has first given to God, that God should repay him? For from him and through him and to him are all things. To him be the glory forever! Amen" (Rom. 11:33-36).

The Second Main Point of Doctrine
Christ's Death and Human Redemption Through It

Article 1: The Punishment Which God's Justice Requires
God is not only supremely merciful, but also supremely just. This justice requires (as God has revealed in the Word) that the sins we have committed against his infinite majesty be punished with both temporal and eternal punishments, of soul as well as body. We cannot escape these punishments unless satisfaction is given to God's justice.

Article 2: The Satisfaction Made by Christ
Since, however, we ourselves cannot give this satisfaction or deliver ourselves from God's wrath, God in boundless mercy has given us as a guarantee his only begotten Son, who was made to be sin and a curse for us, in our place, on the cross, in order that he might give satisfaction for us.

Article 3: The Infinite Value of Christ's Death
This death of God's Son is the only and entirely complete sacrifice and satisfaction for sins; it is of infinite value and worth, more than sufficient to atone for the sins of the whole world.

Article 4: Reasons for This Infinite Value
This death is of such great value and worth for the reason that the person who suffered it is-as was necessary to be our Savior-not only a true and perfectly holy human, but also the only begotten Son of God, of the same eternal and infinite essence with the Father and the Holy Spirit. Another reason is that this death was accompanied by the experience of God's wrath and curse, which we by our sins had fully deserved.

Article 5: The Mandate to Proclaim the Gospel to All
Moreover, it is the promise of the gospel that whoever believes in Christ crucified shall not perish but have eternal life. This promise, together with the command to repent and believe, ought to be announced and declared without differentiation or discrimination to all nations and people, to whom God in his good pleasure sends the gospel.

Article 6: Unbelief, a Human Responsibility
However, that many who have been called through the gospel do not repent or believe in Christ but perish in unbelief is not because the sacrifice of Christ offered on the cross is deficient or insufficient, but because they themselves are at fault.

Article 7: Faith God's Gift
But all who genuinely believe and are delivered and saved by Christ's death from their sins and from destruction receive this favor solely from God's grace-which God owes to no one-given to them in Christ from eternity.

Article 8: The Saving Effectiveness of Christ's Death
For it was the entirely free plan and very gracious will and intention of God the Father that the enlivening and saving effectiveness of his Son's costly death should work itself out in all the elect, in order that God might grant justifying faith to them only and thereby lead them without fail to salvation. In other words, it was God's will that Christ through the blood of the cross (by which he confirmed the new covenant) should effectively redeem from every people, tribe, nation, and language all those and only those who were chosen from eternity to salvation and given to him by the Father; that Christ should grant them faith (which, like the Holy Spirit's other saving gifts, he acquired for them by his death). It was also God's will that Christ should cleanse them by his blood from all their sins, both original and actual, whether committed before or after their coming to faith; that he should faithfully preserve them to the very end; and that he should finally present them to himself, a glorious people, without spot or wrinkle.

Article 9: The Fulfillment of God's Plan
This plan, arising out of God's eternal love for the elect, from the beginning of the world to the present time has been powerfully carried out and will also be carried out in the future, the gates of hell seeking vainly to prevail against it. As a result, the elect are gathered into one, all in their own time, and there is always a church of believers founded on Christ's blood, a church which steadfastly loves, persistently worships, and here and in all eternity praises him as her Savior who laid down his life for her on the cross, as a bridegroom for his bride.

The Third and Fourth Main Points of Doctrine
Human Corruption, Conversion to God, and the Way It Occurs

Article 1: The Effect of the Fall on Human Nature
Human beings were originally created in the image of God and were furnished in mind with a true and sound knowledge of the Creator and things spiritual, in will and heart with righteousness, and in all emotions with purity; indeed, the whole human being was holy. However, rebelling against God at the devil's instigation and by their own free will, they deprived themselves of these outstanding gifts. Rather, in their place they brought upon themselves blindness, terrible darkness, futility, and distortion of judgment in their minds; perversity, defiance, and hardness in their hearts and wills; and finally impurity in all their emotions.

Article 2: The Spread of Corruption
Human beings brought forth children of the same nature as themselves after the fall. That is to say, being corrupt, they brought forth corrupt children. The corruption spread, by God's just judgment, from Adam and Eve to all their descendants-except for Christ alone-not by way of imitation (as in former times the Pelagians would have it) but by way of the propagation of their perverted nature.

Article 3: Total Inability
Therefore, all people are conceived in sin and bear the children of wrath, unfit for any saving good, inclined to evil, dead in their sins, and slaves to sin. Without the grace of the regenerating Holy Spirit, they are neither willing nor able to return to God, to reform their distorted nature, or even to dispose themselves to such reform.

Article 4: The Inadequacy of the Light of Nature
There is, to be sure, a certain light of nature remaining in all people after the fall, by virtue of which they retain some notions about God, natural things, and the difference between what is

moral and immoral, and demonstrate a certain eagerness for virtue and for good outward behavior. But this light of nature is far from enabling humans to come to a saving knowledge of God and conversion to him-so far, in fact, that they do not use it rightly even in matters of nature and society. Instead, in various ways they completely distort this light, whatever its precise character, and suppress it in unrighteousness. In doing so all people render themselves without excuse before God.

Article 5: The Inadequacy of the Law
In this respect, what is true of the light of nature is true also of the Ten Commandments given by God through Moses specifically to the Jews. Since humans cannot obtain saving grace through the Decalogue, because, although it does expose the magnitude of their sin and increasingly convict them of their guilt, yet it does not offer a remedy or enable them to escape from human misery, and, indeed, weakened as it is by the flesh, leaves the offender under the curse.

Article 6: The Saving Power of the Gospel
What, therefore, neither the light of nature nor the law can do, God accomplishes by the power of the Holy Spirit, through the Word or the ministry of reconciliation. This is the gospel about the Messiah, through which it has pleased God to save believers, in both the Old and the New Testaments.

Article 7: God's Freedom in Revealing the Gospel
In the Old Testament, God revealed this secret of his will to a small number; in the New Testament (now without any distinction between peoples) God discloses it to a large number. The reason for this difference must not be ascribed to the greater worth of one nation over another, or to a better use of the light of nature, but to the free good pleasure and undeserved love of God. Therefore, those who receive so much grace, beyond and in spite of all they deserve, ought to acknowledge it with humble and thankful hearts. On the other hand, with the apostle they ought to adore (but certainly not inquisitively search into) the severity and justice of God's judgments on the others, who do not receive this grace.

Article 8: The Earnest Call of the Gospel
Nevertheless, all who are called through the gospel are called earnestly. For urgent and most genuinely God makes known in the Word what is pleasing to him: that those who are called should come to God. God also earnestly promises rest for their souls and eternal life to all who do come and believe.

Article 9: Human Responsibility for Rejecting the Gospel
The fact that many who are called through the ministry of the gospel do not come and are not brought to conversion must not be blamed on the gospel, nor on Christ, who is offered through the gospel, nor on God, who calls them through the gospel and even bestows various gifts on them, but on the people themselves who are called. Some in self-assurance do not even entertain the Word of life; others do entertain it, but do not take it to heart, and for that reason, after the fleeting joy of a temporary faith, they relapse; others choke the seed of the Word with the thorns of life's cares and with the pleasures of the world and bring forth no fruits. This our Savior teaches in the parable of the sower (Matt. 13).

Article 10: Conversion as the Work of God
The fact that others who are called through the ministry of the gospel do come and are brought to conversion must not be credited to human effort, as though one distinguishes oneself by free choice from others who are furnished with equal or sufficient grace for faith and conversion (as the proud heresy of Pelagius maintains). No, it must be credited to God: just as from eternity God chose his own in Christ, so within time God effectively calls them, grants them faith and repentance, and, having rescued them from the dominion of darkness, brings them into the kingdom of

his Son, in order that they may declare the wonderful deeds of the One who called them out of darkness into this marvelous light, and may boast not in themselves, but in the Lord, as apostolic words frequently testify in Scripture.

Article 11: The Holy Spirit's Work in Conversion
Moreover, when God carries out this good pleasure in the elect, or works true conversion in them, God not only sees to it that the gospel is proclaimed to them outwardly, and enlightens their minds powerfully by the Holy Spirit so that they may rightly understand and discern the things of the Spirit of God, but, by the effective operation of the same regenerating Spirit, God also penetrates into the inmost being, opens the closed heart, softens the hard heart, and circumcises the heart that is uncircumcised. God infuses new qualities into the will, making the dead will alive, the evil one good, the unwilling one willing, and the stubborn one compliant. God activates and strengthens the will so that, like a good tree, it may be enabled to produce the fruits of good deeds.

Article 12: Regeneration a Supernatural Work
And this is the regeneration, the new creation, the raising from the dead, and the making alive so clearly proclaimed in the Scriptures, which God works in us without our help. But this certainly does not happen only by outward teaching, by moral persuasion, or by such a way of working that, after God's work is done, it remains in human power whether or not to be reborn or converted. Rather, it is an entirely supernatural work, one that is at the same time most powerful and most pleasing, a marvelous, hidden, and inexpressible work, which is not less than or inferior in power to that of creation or of raising the dead, as Scripture (inspired by the author of this work) teaches. As a result, all those in whose hearts God works in this marvelous way are, certainly, unfailingly, and effectively reborn and do actually believe. And then the will, now renewed, is not only activated and motivated by God, but in being activated by God is also itself active. For this reason, people, themselves, by that grace which they have received, are also rightly said to believe and to repent.

Article 13: The Incomprehensible Way of Regeneration
In this life believers cannot fully understand the way this work occurs; meanwhile, they rest content with knowing and experiencing that, by this grace of God, they do believe with the heart and love their Savior.

Article 14: The Way God Gives Faith
In this way, therefore, faith is a gift of God, not in the sense that it is offered by God for people to choose, but that it is in actual fact bestowed on them, breathed and infused into them. Nor is it a gift in the sense that God bestows only the potential to believe, but then awaits assent-the act of believing-by human choice; rather, it is a gift in the sense that God who works both willing and acting and, indeed, works all things in all people and produces in them both the will to believe and the belief itself.

Article 15: Responses to God's Grace
God does not owe this grace to anyone. For what could God owe to those who have nothing to give that can be paid back? Indeed, what could God owe to those who have nothing of their own to give but sin and falsehood? Therefore, those who receive this grace owe and give eternal thanks to God alone; those who do not receive it either do not care at all about these spiritual things and are satisfied with themselves in their condition, or else in self-assurance foolishly boast about having something which they lack. Furthermore, following the example of the apostles, we are to think and to speak in the most favorable way about those who outwardly profess their faith and better their lives, for the inner chambers of the heart are unknown to us. But for others who have not yet been called, we are to pray to the God who calls things that do not exist as though they did. In no way, however, are we to pride ourselves as better than they, as though

we had distinguished ourselves from them.

Article 16: Regeneration's Effect

However, just as by the fall humans did not cease to be human, endowed with intellect and will, and just as sin, which has spread through the whole human race, did not abolish the nature of the human race but distorted and spiritually killed it, so also this divine grace of regeneration does not act in people as if they were blocks and stones; nor does it abolish the will and its properties or coerce a reluctant will by force, but spiritually revives, heals, reforms, and-in a manner at once pleasing and powerful-bends it back.

As a result, a ready and sincere obedience of the Spirit now begins to prevail where before the rebellion and resistance of the flesh were completely dominant. In this the true and spiritual restoration and freedom of our will consists. Thus, if the marvelous Maker of every good thing were not dealing with us, we would have no hope of getting up from our fall by our own free choice, by which we plunged ourselves into ruin when still standing upright.

Article 17: God's Use of Means in Regeneration

Just as the almighty work by which God brings forth and sustains our natural life does not rule out but requires the use of means, by which God, according to his infinite wisdom and goodness, has wished to exercise that divine power, so also the aforementioned supernatural work by which God regenerates us in no way rules out or cancels the use of the gospel, which God in great wisdom has appointed to be the seed of regeneration and the food of the soul. For this reason, the apostles and the teachers who followed them taught the people in a godly manner about this grace of God, to give God the glory and to humble all pride, and yet did not neglect meanwhile to keep the people, by means of the holy admonitions of the gospel, under the administration of the Word, the sacraments, and discipline. So even today it is out of the question that the teachers or those taught in the church should presume to test God by separating what God in his good pleasure has wished to be closely joined together. For grace is bestowed through admonitions, and the more readily we perform our duty, the more lustrous the benefit of God working in us usually is, and the better that work advances. To God alone, both for the means and for their saving fruit and effectiveness, all glory is owed forever. Amen.

The Fifth Main Point of Doctrine
The Perseverance of the Saints

Article 1: The Regenerate Not Entirely Free from Sin

Those people whom God according to his purpose calls into fellowship with his Son Jesus Christ our Lord and regenerates by the Holy Spirit, God also sets free from the dominion and slavery of sin, though not entirely from the flesh and from the body of sin as long as they are in this life.

Article 2: The Believer's Reaction to Sins of Weakness

Hence daily sins of weakness arise, and blemishes cling to even the best works of saints, giving them continual cause to humble themselves before God, to flee for refuge to Christ crucified, to put the flesh to death more and more by the Spirit of supplication and by holy exercises of godliness, and to strain toward the goal of perfection, until they are freed from this body of death and reign with the Lamb of God in heaven.

Article 3: God's Preservation of the Converted

Because of these remnants of sin dwelling in them and also because of the temptations of the world and Satan, those who have been converted could not remain standing in this grace if left to their own resources. But God is faithful, mercifully strengthening them in the grace once conferred on them and powerfully preserving them in it to the end.

Article 4: The Danger of True Believers' Falling into Serious Sins

The power of God strengthening and preserving true believers in grace is more than a match for the flesh. Yet those converted are not always so activated and motivated by God that in certain specific actions they cannot by their own fault depart from the leading of grace, be led astray by the desires of the flesh, and give in to them. For this reason, they must constantly watch and pray that they may not be led into temptations. When they fail to do this, not only can they be carried away by the flesh, the world, and Satan into sins, even serious and outrageous ones, but also by God's just permission they sometimes are so carried away-witness the sad cases, described in Scripture, of David, Peter, and other saints falling into sins.

Article 5: The Effects of Such Serious Sins

By such monstrous sins, however, they greatly offend God, deserve the sentence of death, grieve the Holy Spirit, suspend the exercise of faith, severely wound the conscience, and sometimes lose the awareness of grace for a time-until, after they have returned to the right way by genuine repentance, God's fatherly face again shines upon them.

Article 6: God's Saving Intervention

For God, who is rich in mercy, according to the unchangeable purpose of election does not take the Holy Spirit from his own completely, even when they fall grievously. Neither does God, let them fall down so far that they forfeit the grace of adoption and the state of justification, or commit the sin which leads to death (the sin against the Holy Spirit), and plunge themselves, entirely forsaken by God, into eternal ruin.

Article 7: Renewal to Repentance

For, in the first place, God preserves in those saints when they fall the imperishable seed from which they have been born again, lest it perish or be dislodged. Secondly, by his Word and Spirit, God certainly and effectively renews them to repentance so that they have a heartfelt and godly sorrow for the sins they have committed; seek and obtain, through faith and with a contrite heart, forgiveness in the blood of the Mediator; experience again the grace of a reconciled God; through faith adore God's mercies; and from then on more eagerly work out their own salvation with fear and trembling.

Article 8: The Certainty of This Preservation

So it is not by their own merits or strength but by God's undeserved mercy that they neither forfeit faith and grace totally nor remain in their downfalls to the end and are lost. With respect to themselves this not only easily could happen, but also undoubtedly would happen; but with respect to God it cannot possibly happen. God's plan cannot be changed; God's promise cannot fail; the caller according to God's purpose cannot be revoked; the merit of Christ as well as his interceding and preserving cannot be nullified; and the sealing of the Holy Spirit can neither be invalidated nor wiped out.

Article 9: The Assurance of This Preservation

Concerning this preservation of those chosen to salvation and concerning the perseverance of true believers in faith, believers themselves can and do become assured in accordance with the measure of their faith. By this faith they firmly believe that they are and always will remain true and living members of the church, and that they have the forgiveness of sins and eternal life.

Article 10: The Ground of This Assurance

Accordingly, this assurance does not derive from some private revelation beyond or outside the Word, but from faith in the promises of God, which are very plentiful revealed in the Word for our comfort, from the testimony of "the Holy Spirit testifying with our spirit that we are God's children and heirs" (Rom. 8:16-17), and finally from a serious and holy pursuit of a clear conscience and of good works. If God's chosen ones in this world did not have this well-founded comfort that the victory will be theirs and this reliable guarantee of eternal glory, they would be of all people most miserable.

Article 11: Doubts Concerning This Assurance
Meanwhile, Scripture testifies that believers have to contend in this life with various doubts of the flesh, and that under severe temptation they do not always experience this full assurance of faith and certainty of perseverance. But God, the Father of all comfort, "does not let them be tempted beyond what they can bear, but with the temptation he also provides a way out" (1 Cor. 10:13), and by the Holy Spirit revives in them the assurance of their perseverance.

Article 12: This Assurance as an Incentive to Godliness
This assurance of perseverance, however, so far from making true believers proud and carnally self-assured, is rather the true root of humility, of childlike respect, of genuine godliness, of endurance in every conflict, of fervent prayers, of steadfastness in cross bearing and in confessing the truth, and of well-founded joy in God. Reflecting on this benefit provides an incentive to a serious and continual practice of thanksgiving and good works, as is evident from the testimonies of Scripture and the examples of the saints.

Article 13: Assurance No Inducement to Carelessness
Neither does the renewed confidence of perseverance produce immorality or lack of concern for godliness in those put back on their feet after a fall, but it produces a much greater concern to observe carefully the ways which the Lord prepared in advance. They observe these ways in order that by walking in them they may maintain the assurance of their perseverance, lest, by their abuse of God's fatherly goodness, the face of the gracious God (for the godly, looking upon that face is sweeter than life, but its withdrawal is more bitter than death) turn away from them again, with the result that they fall into greater anguish of spirit.

Article 14: God's Use of Means in Perseverance
And, just as it has pleased God to begin this work of grace in us by the proclamation of the gospel, so God preserves, continues, and completes this work by the hearing and reading of the gospel, by meditation on it, by its exhortations, threats, and promises, and also by the use of the sacraments.

Article 15: Contrasting Reactions to the Teaching of Perseverance
This teaching about the perseverance of true believers and saints, and about their assurance of it-a teaching which God has very richly revealed in the Word for the glory of his name and for the comfort of the godly, and which God impresses on the hearts of believers-is something which the flesh does not understand, Satan hates, the world ridicules, the ignorant and the hypocrites abuse, and the spirits of error attack. The bride of Christ, on the other hand, has always loved this teaching very tenderly and defended it steadfastly as a priceless treasure; and God, against whom no plan can avail and no strength can prevail, will ensure that the church will continue to do this. To this God alone, Father, Son, and Holy Spirit, be honor and glory forever. Amen.

Conclusion
Rejection of False Accusations

And so this is the clear, simple, and straightforward explanation of the orthodox teaching on the five articles in dispute in the Netherlands, as well as the rejection of the errors by which the Dutch churches have for some time been disturbed. This explanation and rejection the Synod declares to be derived from God's Word and in agreement with the confessions of the Reformed churches. Hence it clearly appears that those of whom one could hardly expect it have shown no truth, equity, and charity at all in wishing to make the public believe:

-That the teaching of the Reformed churches on predestination and on the points associated with it by its very nature and tendency draws the minds of people away from all godliness and religion, is an opiate of the flesh and the devil, and is a stronghold where Satan lies in wait for all people, wounds most of them, and fatally pierces many of them with the arrows of both despair and self-assurance;

-That this teaching makes God the author of sin, unjust, a tyrant, and a hypocrite; and is nothing but a refurbished Stoicism, Manicheism, Libertinism, and Turkism;

-That this teaching makes people carnally self-assured, since it persuades them that nothing endangers the salvation of the elect, no matter how they live, so that they may commit the most outrageous crimes with self-assurance; and that on the other hand nothing is of use to the reprobate for salvation even if they have truly performed all the works of the saints;

-That this teaching means that God predestined and created, by the bare and unqualified choice of his will, without the least regard or consideration of any sin, the greatest part of the world to eternal condemnation; that in the same manner in which election is the source and cause of faith and good works, reprobation is the cause of unbelief and ungodliness; that many infant children of believers are snatched in their innocence from their mothers' breasts and cruelly cast into hell so that neither the blood of Christ nor their baptism nor the prayers of the church at their baptism can be of any use to them; and very many other slanderous accusations of this kind which the Reformed churches not only disavow but even denounce with their whole heart.

Therefore this Synod of Dort in the name of the Lord pleads with all who devoutly call on the name of our Savior Jesus Christ to form their judgment about the faith of the Reformed churches, not on the basis of false accusations gathered from here or there, or even on the basis of the personal statements of a number of ancient and modern authorities-statements which are also often either quoted out of context or misquoted and twisted to convey a different meaning-but on the basis of the churches' own official confessions and of the present explanation of the orthodox teaching which has been endorsed by the unanimous consent of the members of the whole Synod, one and all.

Moreover, the Synod earnestly warns the false accusers themselves to consider how heavy a judgment of God awaits those who give false testimony against so many churches and their confessions, trouble the consciences of the weak, and seek to prejudice the minds of many against the fellowship of true believers.

Finally, this Synod urges all fellow ministers in the gospel of Christ to deal with this teaching in a godly and reverent manner, in the academic institutions as well as in the churches; to do so, both in their speaking and writing, with a view to the glory of God's name, holiness of life, and the comfort of anxious souls; to think and also speak with Scripture according to the analogy of faith; and, finally, to refrain from all those ways of speaking which go beyond the bounds set for us by the genuine sense of the Holy Scriptures and which could give impertinent sophists a just occasion to scoff at the teaching of the Reformed churches or even to bring false accusations against it.

May God's Son Jesus Christ, who sits at the right hand of God and gives gifts to humanity, sanctify us in the truth, lead to the truth those who err, silence the mouths of those who lay false accusations against sound teaching, and equip faithful ministers of God's Word with a spirit of wisdom and discretion, that all they say may be to the glory of God and the building up of their hearers. Amen.

It is wise for every Christian to learn, teach and practice the teachings of the reformed Heidelberg Catechism. Having said this, it is not right to take these writings to be equal or be substitute to the Holy Scriptures. However, Heidelberg Catechism can provide true biblical teaching to a newly born Christian in a course of one year.

EDWARD KAVIMBA LUNGU PHD

HEIDELBERG CATECHISM
INTRODUCTION

Lord's Day 1

Q&A 1
Q. What is your only comfort in life and in death?
A. That I am not my own,1 but belong-body and soul, in life and in death2-to my faithful Savior, Jesus Christ.3

He has fully paid for all my sins with his precious blood,4 and has set me free from the tyranny of the devil.5 He also watches over me in such a way6 that not a hair can fall from my head without the will of my Father in heaven;7 in fact, all things must work together for my salvation.8

Because I belong to him, Christ, by his Holy Spirit, assures me of eternal life9 and makes me wholeheartedly willing and ready from now on to live for him.10

1 1 Cor. 6:19-20
2 Rom. 14:7-9
3 1 Cor. 3:23; Titus 2:14
4 1 Pet. 1:18-19; 1 John 1:7-9; 2:2
5 John 8:34-36; Heb. 2:14-15; 1 John 3:1-11
6 John 6:39-40; 10:27-30; 2 Thess. 3:3; 1 Pet. 1:5
7 Matt. 10:29-31; Luke 21:16-18
8 Rom. 8:28
9 Rom. 8:15-16; 2 Cor. 1:21-22; 5:5; Eph. 1:13-14
10 Rom. 8:1-17

Q&A 2
Q. What must you know to live and die in the joy of this comfort?
A. Three things: first, how great my sin and misery are;1 second, how I am set free from all my sins and misery;2 third, how I am to thank God for such deliverance.3

1 Rom. 3:9-10; 1 John 1:10
2 John 17:3; Acts 4:12; 10:43
3 Matt. 5:16; Rom. 6:13; Eph. 5:8-10; 2 Tim. 2:15; 1 Pet. 2:9-10

PART I: MISERY

Lord's Day 2

Q&A 3
Q. How do you come to know your misery?
A. The law of God tells me.1

1 Rom. 3:20; 7:7-25

Q&A 4
Q. What does God's law require of us?
A. Christ teaches us this in summary in Matthew 22:37-40:

"'You shall love the Lord your God with all your heart, and with all your soul, and with all your mind.'1 This is the greatest and first commandment.

BEDROOM OF ADAM AND EVE

"And a second is like it: 'You shall love your neighbor as yourself.'2

"On these two commandments hang all the law and the prophets."

1 Deut. 6:5
2 Lev. 19:18

Q&A 5
Q. Can you live up to all this perfectly?
A. No.1 I have a natural tendency to hate God and my neighbor.2

1 Rom. 3:9-20, 23; 1 John 1:8, 10
2 Gen. 6:5; Jer. 17:9; Rom. 7:23-24; 8:7; Eph. 2:1-3; Titus 3:3

Lord's Day 3

Q&A 6
Q. Did God create people so wicked and perverse?
A. No. God created them good1 and in his own image,2 that is, in true righteousness and holiness,3 so that they might truly know God their creator,4 love him with all their heart, and live with God in eternal happiness, to praise and glorify him.5

1 Gen. 1:31
2 Gen. 1:26-27
3 Eph. 4:24
4 Col. 3:10
5 Ps. 8

Q&A 7
Q. Then where does this corrupt human nature come from?
A. The fall and disobedience of our first parents, Adam and Eve, in Paradise.1 This fall has so poisoned our nature2 that we are all conceived and born in a sinful condition.3

1 Gen. 3
2 Rom. 5:12, 18-19
3 Ps. 51:5

Q&A 8
Q. But are we so corrupt that we are totally unable to do any good and inclined toward all evil?
A. Yes,1 unless we are born again by the Spirit of God.2

1 Gen. 6:5; 8:21; Job 14:4; Isa. 53:6
2 John 3:3-5

Lord's Day 4

Q&A 9
Q. But doesn't God do us an injustice by requiring in his law what we are unable to do?
A. No, God created human beings with the ability to keep the law.1 They, however, provoked by the devil2 in willful disobedience,3 robbed themselves and all their descendants of these gifts.4

1 Gen. 1:31; Eph. 4:24
2 Gen. 3:13; John 8:44
3 Gen. 3:6
4 Rom. 5:12, 18, 19

Q&A 10
Q. Does God permit such disobedience and rebellion to go unpunished?
A. Certainly not. God is terribly angry with the sin we are born with as well as the sins we per-

sonally commit.

As a just judge, God will punish them both now and in eternity,1 having declared: "Cursed is everyone who does not observe and obey all the things written in the book of the law."2

1 Ex. 34:7; Ps. 5:4-6; Nah. 1:2; Rom. 1:18; Eph. 5:6; Heb. 9:27
2 Gal. 3:10; Deut. 27:26

Q&A 11
Q. But isn't God also merciful?
A. God is certainly merciful,1 but also just.2 God's justice demands that sin, committed against his supreme majesty, be punished with the supreme penalty-eternal punishment of body and soul.3

1 Ex. 34:6-7; Ps. 103:8-9
2 Ex. 34:7; Deut. 7:9-11; Ps. 5:4-6; Heb. 10:30-31
3 Matt. 25:35-46

PART II: DELIVERANCE

Lord's Day 5

Q&A 12
Q. According to God's righteous judgment we deserve punishment both now and in eternity: how then can we escape this punishment and return to God's favor?
A. God requires that his justice be satisfied, 1 therefore the claims of this justice must be paid in full, either by ourselves or by another.2

1 Ex. 23:7; Rom. 2:1-11
2 Isa. 53:11; Rom. 8:3-4

Q&A 13
Q. Can we make this payment ourselves?
A. Certainly not. Actually, we increase our debt every day.1

1 Matt. 6:12; Rom. 2:4-5

Q&A 14
Q. Can another creature-any at all-pay this debt for us?
A. No. To begin with, God will not punish any other creature for what a human is guilty of.1 Furthermore, no mere creature can bear the weight of God's eternal wrath against sin and deliver others from it.2

1 Ezek. 18:4, 20; Heb. 2:14-18
2 Ps. 49:7-9; 130:3

Q&A 15
Q. What kind of mediator and deliverer should we look for then?

A. One who is a true1 and righteous2 human, yet more powerful than all creatures, that is, one who is also true God.3

1 Rom. 1:3; 1 Cor. 15:21; Heb. 2:17
2 Isa. 53:9; 2 Cor. 5:21; Heb. 7:26
3 Isa. 7:14; 9:6; Jer. 23:6; John 1:1

Lord's Day 6

Q&A 16
Q. Why must the mediator be a true and righteous human?

BEDROOM OF ADAM AND EVE

A. God's justice demands that human nature, which has sinned, must pay for sin;1 but a sinful human could never pay for others.2

1 Rom. 5:12, 15; 1 Cor. 15:21; Heb. 2:14-16
2 Heb. 7:26-27; 1 Pet. 3:18

Q&A 17
Q. Why must the mediator also be true God?
A. So that the mediator, by the power of his divinity, might bear the weight of God's wrath in his humanity and earn for us and restore to us righteousness and life.1

1 Isa. 53; John 3:16; 2 Cor. 5:21

Q&A 18
Q. Then who is this mediator-true God and at the same time a true and righteous human?
A. Our Lord Jesus Christ,1 who was given to us to completely deliver us and make us right with God.2

1 Matt. 1:21-23; Luke 2:11; 1 Tim. 2:5
2 1 Cor. 1:30

Q&A 19
Q. How do you come to know this?
A. The holy gospel tells me. God began to reveal the gospel already in Paradise;1 later God proclaimed it by the holy patriarchs2 and prophets3 and foreshadowed it by the sacrifices and other ceremonies of the law;4 and finally God fulfilled it through his own beloved Son.5

1 Gen. 3:15
2 Gen. 22:18; 49:10

3 Isa. 53; Jer. 23:5-6; Mic. 7:18-20; Acts 10:43; Heb. 1:1-2
4 Lev. 1-7; John 5:46; Heb. 10:1-10
5 Rom. 10:4; Gal. 4:4-5; Col. 2:17

Lord's Day 7

Q&A 20
Q. Are all people then saved through Christ just as they were lost through Adam?
A. No. Only those are saved who through true faith are grafted into Christ and accept all his benefits.1

1 Matt. 7:14; John 3:16, 18, 36; Rom. 11:16-21

Q&A 21
Q. What is true faith?
A. True faith is not only a sure knowledge by which I hold as true all that God has revealed to us in Scripture;1 it is also a wholehearted trust,2 which the Holy Spirit creates in me3 by the gospel,4 that God has freely granted, not only to others but to me also,5 forgiveness of sins, eternal righteousness, and salvation.6 These are gifts of sheer grace, granted solely by Christ's merit.7

1 John 17:3, 17; Heb. 11:1-3; James 2:19
2 Rom. 4:18-21; 5:1; 10:10; Heb. 4:14-16
3 Matt. 16:15-17; John 3:5; Acts 16:14
4 Rom. 1:16; 10:17; 1 Cor. 1:21
5 Gal. 2:20
6 Rom. 1:17; Heb. 10:10
7 Rom. 3:21-26; Gal. 2:16; Eph. 2:8-10

Q&A 22
Q. What then must a Christian believe?
A. All that is promised us in the gospel,1 a summary of which is taught us in the articles of our universal and undisputed Christian faith.

1 Matt. 28:18-20; John 20:30-31

Q&A 23
Q. What are these articles?
A. I believe in God, the Father almighty, creator of heaven and earth.

I believe in Jesus Christ, his only begotten Son, our Lord, who was conceived by the Holy Spirit and born of the virgin Mary. He suffered under Pontius Pilate, was crucified, died, and was buried; he descended to hell. The third day he rose again from the dead. He ascended to heaven and is seated at the right hand of God the Father almighty. From there he will come to judge the living and the dead.

I believe in the Holy Spirit, the holy catholic church, the communion of saints, the forgiveness of sins, the resurrection of the body, and the life everlasting. Amen.

Lord's Day 8

Q&A 24
Q. How are these articles divided?
A. Into three parts: God the Father and our creation; God the Son and our deliverance; and God the Holy Spirit and our sanctification.

Q&A 25
Q. Since there is only one divine being,1 why do you speak of three: Father, Son, and Holy Spirit?
A. Because that is how God has revealed himself in his Word:2 these three distinct persons are one, true, eternal God.

1 Deut. 6:4; 1 Cor. 8:4, 6
2 Matt. 3:16-17; 28:18-19; Luke 4:18 (Isa. 61:1); John 14:26; 15:26; 2 Cor. 13:14; Gal. 4:6; Titus 3:5-6

GOD THE FATHER

Lord's Day 9

Q&A 26
Q. What do you believe when you say, "I believe in God, the Father almighty, creator of heaven and earth"?
A. That the eternal Father of our Lord Jesus Christ, who out of nothing created heaven and earth and everything in them,1 who still upholds and rules them by his eternal counsel and providence,2 is my God and Father because of Christ the Son.3

I trust God so much that I do not doubt he will provide whatever I need for body and soul,4 and will turn to my good whatever adversity he sends upon me in this sad world.5

God is able to do this because he is almighty God,6 and desires to do this because he is a faithful Father.7

1 Gen. 1-2; Ex. 20:11; Ps. 33:6; Isa. 44:24; Acts 4:24; 14:15
2 Ps. 104; Matt. 6:30; 10:29; Eph. 1:11
3 John 1:12-13; Rom. 8:15-16; Gal. 4:4-7; Eph. 1:5

BEDROOM OF ADAM AND EVE

4 Ps. 55:22; Matt. 6:25-26; Luke 12:22-31

5 Rom. 8:28
6 Gen. 18:14; Rom. 8:31-39
7 Matt. 7:9-11

Lord's Day 10

Q&A 27
Q. What do you understand by the providence of God?
A. The almighty and ever present power of God1 by which God upholds, as with his hand, heaven and earth and all creatures,2 and so rules them that leaf and blade, rain and drought, fruitful and lean years, food and drink, health and sickness, prosperity and poverty-3 all things, in fact, come to us not by chance4 but by his fatherly hand.5

1 Jer. 23:23-24; Acts 17:24-28
2 Heb. 1:3
3 Jer. 5:24; Acts 14:15-17; John 9:3; Prov. 22:2
4 Prov. 16:33
5 Matt. 10:29

Q&A 28
Q. How does the knowledge of God's creation and providence help us?
A. We can be patient when things go against us,1 thankful when things go well,2 and for the future we can have good confidence in our faithful God and Father that nothing in creation will separate us from his love.3 For all creatures are so completely in God's hand that without his will they can neither move nor be moved.4

1 Job 1:21-22; James 1:3
2 Deut. 8:10; 1 Thess. 5:18
3 Ps. 55:22; Rom. 5:3-5; 8:38-39
4 Job 1:12; 2:6; Prov. 21:1; Acts 17:24-28

GOD THE SON

Lord's Day 11

Q&A 29
Q. Why is the Son of God called "Jesus," meaning "savior"?
A. Because he saves us from our sins,1 and because salvation should not be sought and cannot be found in anyone else.2

1 Matt. 1:21; Heb. 7:25
2 Isa. 43:11; John 15:5; Acts 4:11-12; 1 Tim. 2:5

Q&A 30
Q. Do those who look for their salvation in saints, in themselves, or elsewhere really believe in the only savior Jesus?
A. No. Although they boast of being his, by their actions they deny the only savior, Jesus.1

Either Jesus is not a perfect savior, or those who in true faith accept this savior have in him all they need for their salvation.2

1 1 Cor. 1:12-13; Gal. 5:4
2 Col. 1:19-20; 2:10; 1 John 1:7

Lord's Day 12

Q&A 31
Q. Why is he called "Christ," meaning "anointed"?
A. Because he has been ordained by God the Father and has been anointed with the Holy Spirit1 to be our chief prophet and teacher2 who fully reveals to us the secret counsel and will of God concerning our deliverance;3 our only high priest4 who has delivered us by the one sacrifice of his body,5 and who continually pleads our cause with the Father;6 and our eternal king7 who governs us by his Word and Spirit, and who guards us and keeps us in the freedom he has won for us.8

1 Luke 3:21-22; 4:14-19 (Isa. 61:1); Heb. 1:9 (Ps. 45:7)
2 Acts 3:22 (Deut. 18:15)
3 John 1:18; 15:15
4 Heb. 7:17 (Ps. 110:4)
5 Heb. 9:12; 10:11-14
6 Rom. 8:34; Heb. 9:24
7 Matt. 21:5 (Zech. 9:9)
8 Matt. 28:18-20; John 10:28; Rev. 12:10-11

Q&A 32
Q. But why are you called a Christian?
A. Because by faith I am a member of Christ1 and so I share in his anointing.2 I am anointed to confess his name,3 to present myself to him as a living sacrifice of thanks,4 to strive with a free conscience against sin and the devil in this life,5 and afterward to reign with Christ over all creation for eternity.6

1 1 Cor. 12:12-27
2 Acts 2:17 (Joel 2:28); 1 John 2:27
3 Matt. 10:32; Rom. 10:9-10; Heb. 13:15
4 Rom. 12:1; 1 Pet. 2:5, 9
5 Gal. 5:16-17; Eph. 6:11; 1 Tim. 1:18-19
6 Matt. 25:34; 2 Tim. 2:12

Lord's Day 13

Q&A 33
Q. Why is he called God's "only begotten Son" when we also are God's children?
A. Because Christ alone is the eternal, natural Son of God.1 We, however, are adopted children of God-adopted by grace through Christ.2

1 John 1:1-3, 14, 18; Heb. 1
2 John 1:12; Rom. 8:14-17; Eph. 1:5-6

Q&A 34
Q. Why do you call him "our Lord"?
A. Because-not with gold or silver, but with his precious blood1- he has set us free from sin and from the tyranny of the devil,2 and has bought us, body and soul, to be his very own.3

1 1 Pet. 1:18-19
2 Col. 1:13-14; Heb. 2:14-15
3 1 Cor. 6:20; 1 Tim. 2:5-6

Lord's Day 14

Q&A 35
Q. What does it mean that he "was conceived by the Holy Spirit and born of the virgin Mary"?
A. That the eternal Son of God, who is and remains true and eternal God,1 took to himself,

through the working of the Holy Spirit,2 from the flesh and blood of the virgin Mary,3 a truly human nature so that he might also become David's true descendant,4 like his brothers and sisters in every way5 except for sin.6

1 John 1:1; 10:30-36; Acts 13:33 (Ps. 2:7); Col. 1:15-17; 1 John 5:20
2 Luke 1:35
3 Matt. 1:18-23; John 1:14; Gal. 4:4; Heb. 2:14
4 2 Sam. 7:12-16; Ps. 132:11; Matt. 1:1; Rom. 1:3
5 Phil. 2:7; Heb. 2:17
6 Heb. 4:15; 7:26-27

Q&A 36
Q. How does the holy conception and birth of Christ benefit you?
A. He is our mediator1 and, in God's sight, he covers with his innocence and perfect holiness my sinfulness in which I was conceived.2

1 1 Tim. 2:5-6; Heb. 9:13-15
2 Rom. 8:3-4; 2 Cor. 5:21; Gal. 4:4-5; 1 Pet. 1:18-19

Lord's Day 15

Q&A 37
Q. What do you understand by the word "suffered"?
A. That during his whole life on earth, but especially at the end, Christ sustained in body and soul the wrath of God against the sin of the whole human race.1

This he did in order that, by his suffering as the only atoning sacrifice,2 he might deliver us, body and soul, from eternal condemnation,3 and gain for us God's grace, righteousness, and eternal life.4

1 Isa. 53; 1 Pet. 2:24; 3:18
2 Rom. 3:25; Heb. 10:14; 1 John 2:2; 4:10
3 Rom. 8:1-4; Gal. 3:13
4 John 3:16; Rom. 3:24-26

Q&A 38
Q. Why did he suffer "under Pontius Pilate" as judge?
A. So that he, though innocent, might be condemned by an earthly judge,1 and so free us from the severe judgment of God that was to fall on us.2

1 Luke 23:13-24; John 19:4, 12-16
2 Isa. 53:4-5; 2 Cor. 5:21; Gal. 3:13

Q&A 39
Q. Is it significant that he was "crucified" instead of dying some other way?
A. Yes. By this I am convinced that he shouldered the curse which lay on me, since death by crucifixion was cursed by God.1

1 Gal. 3:10-13 (Deut. 21:23)

Lord's Day 16

Q&A 40
Q. Why did Christ have to suffer death?

A. Because God's justice and truth require it:1 nothing else could pay for our sins except the death of the Son of God.2

1 Gen. 2:17
2 Rom. 8:3-4; Phil. 2:8; Heb. 2:9

Q&A 41
Q. Why was he "buried"?
A. His burial testifies that he really died.1

1 Isa. 53:9; John 19:38-42; Acts 13:29; 1 Cor. 15:3-4

Q&A 42
Q. Since Christ has died for us, why do we still have to die?
A. Our death does not pay the debt of our sins.1 Rather, it puts an end to our sinning and is our entrance into eternal life.2

1 Ps. 49:7
2 John 5:24; Phil. 1:21-23; 1 Thess. 5:9-10

Q&A 43
Q. What further benefit do we receive from Christ's sacrifice and death on the cross?
A. By Christ's power our old selves are crucified, put to death, and buried with him,1 so that the evil desires of the flesh may no longer rule us,2 but that instead we may offer ourselves as a sacrifice of gratitude to him.3

1 Rom. 6:5-11; Col. 2:11-12
2 Rom. 6:12-14
3 Rom. 12:1; Eph. 5:1-2

Q&A 44
Q. Why does the creed add, "He descended to hell"?
A. To assure me during attacks of deepest dread and temptation that Christ my Lord, by suffering unspeakable anguish, pain, and terror of soul, on the cross, but also earlier, has delivered me from hellish anguish and torment.1

1 Isa. 53; Matt. 26:36-46; 27:45-46; Luke 22:44; Heb. 5:7-10

Lord's Day 17

Q&A 45
Q. How does Christ's resurrection benefit us?
A. First, by his resurrection he has overcome death, so that he might make us share in the righteousness he obtained for us by his death.1

Second, by his power we too are already raised to a new life.2

Third, Christ's resurrection is a sure pledge to us of our blessed resurrection.3

1 Rom. 4:25; 1 Cor. 15:16-20; 1 Pet. 1:3-5
2 Rom. 6:5-11; Eph. 2:4-6; Col. 3:1-4
3 Rom. 8:11; 1 Cor. 15:12-23; Phil. 3:20-21

Lord's Day 18

Q&A 46
Q. What do you mean by saying, "He ascended to heaven"?
A. That Christ while his disciples watched, was taken up from the earth into heaven1 and remains there on our behalf2 until he comes again to judge the living and the dead.3

1 Luke 24:50-51; Acts 1:9-11
2 Rom. 8:34; Eph. 4:8-10; Heb. 7:23-25; 9:24

BEDROOM OF ADAM AND EVE

3 Acts 1:11

Q&A 47
Q. But isn't Christ with us until the end of the world as he promised us?1
A. Christ is truly human and truly God. In his human nature Christ is not now on earth;2 but in his divinity, majesty, grace, and Spirit he is never absent from us.3

1 Matt. 28:20
2 Acts 1:9-11; 3:19-21
3 Matt. 28:18-20; John 14:16-19

Q&A 48
Q. If his humanity is not present wherever his divinity is, then aren't the two natures of Christ separated from each other?
A. Certainly not. Since divinity is not limited and is present everywhere,1 it is evident that Christ's divinity is surely beyond the bounds of the humanity that has been taken on, but at the same time his divinity is in and remains personally united to his humanity.2

1 Jer. 23:23-24; Acts 7:48-49 (Isa. 66:1)
2 John 1:14; 3:13; Col. 2:9

Q&A 49
Q. How does Christ's ascension to heaven benefit us?
A. First, he is our advocate in heaven in the presence of his Father.1

Second, we have our own flesh in heaven as a sure pledge that Christ our head will also take us, his members, up to himself.2

Third, he sends his Spirit to us on earth as a corresponding pledge.3 By the Spirit's power we seek not earthly things, but the things above, where Christ is, sitting at God's right hand.4

1 Rom. 8:34; 1 John 2:1
2 John 14:2; 17:24; Eph. 2:4-6
3 John 14:16; 2 Cor. 1:21-22; 5:5
4 Col. 3:1-4

Lord's Day 19

Q&A 50
Q. Why the next words: "and is seated at the right hand of God"?
A. Because Christ ascended to heaven to show there that he is head of his church,1 the one through whom the Father rules all things.2

1 Eph. 1:20-23; Col. 1:18 2 Matt. 28:18; John 5:22-23

Q&A 51
Q. How does this glory of Christ our head benefit us?
A. First, through his Holy Spirit, he pours out gifts from heaven upon us his members.1

Second, by his power he defends us and keeps us safe from all enemies.2

1 Acts 2:33; Eph. 4:7-12
2 Ps. 110:1-2; John 10:27-30; Rev. 19:11-16

Q&A 52
Q. How does Christ's return "to judge the living and the dead" comfort you?
A. In all distress and persecution, with uplifted head I confidently await the very judge who has already offered himself to the judgment of God in my place and removed the whole curse from me.1 Christ will cast all his enemies and mine into everlasting condemnation, but will take me

and all his chosen ones to himself into the joy and glory of heaven.2

1 Luke 21:28; Rom. 8:22-25; Phil. 3:20-21; Titus 2:13-14
2 Matt. 25:31-46; 2 Thess. 1:6-10

GOD THE HOLY SPIRIT

Lord's Day 20

Q&A 53
Q. What do you believe concerning "the Holy Spirit"?
A. First, that the Spirit, with the Father and the Son, is eternal God.1

Second, that the Spirit is given also to me,2 so that, through true faith, he makes me share in Christ and all his benefits3 through true faith, comforts me,4 and will remain with me forever.5

1 Gen. 1:1-2; Matt. 28:19; Acts 5:3-4
2 1 Cor. 6:19; 2 Cor. 1:21-22; Gal. 4:6
3 Gal. 3:14
4 John 15:26; Acts 9:31
5 John 14:16-17; 1 Pet. 4:14

Lord's Day 21

Q&A 54
Q. What do you believe concerning "the holy catholic church"?
A. I believe that the Son of God through his Spirit and Word,1 out of the entire human race,2 from the beginning of the world to its end,3 gathers, protects, and preserves for himself a community chosen for eternal life4 and united in true faith.5 And of this community I am6 and always will be7 a living member.

1 John 10:14-16; Acts 20:28; Rom. 10:14-17; Col. 1:18
2 Gen. 26:3b-4; Rev. 5:9
3 Isa. 59:21; 1 Cor. 11:26
4 Matt. 16:18; John 10:28-30; Rom. 8:28-30; Eph. 1:3-14
5 Acts 2:42-47; Eph. 4:1-6
6 1 John 3:14, 19-21
7 John 10:27-28; 1 Cor. 1:4-9; 1 Pet. 1:3-5

Q&A 55
Q. What do you understand by "the communion of saints"?

A. First, that believers one and all, as members of this community, share in Christ and in all his treasures and gifts.1

Second, that each member should consider it a duty to use these gifts readily and joyfully for the service and enrichment of the other members.2

1 Rom. 8:32; 1 Cor. 6:17; 12:4-7, 12-13; 1 John 1:3
2 Rom. 12:4-8; 1 Cor. 12:20-27; 13:1-7; Phil. 2:4-8

Q&A 56
Q. What do you believe concerning "the forgiveness of sins"?
A. I believe that God, because of Christ's satisfaction, will no longer remember any of my sins1 or my sinful nature which I need to struggle against all my life.2

Rather, by grace God grants me the righteousness of Christ to free me forever from judgment.3

BEDROOM OF ADAM AND EVE

1 Ps. 103:3-4, 10, 12; Mic. 7:18-19; 2 Cor. 5:18-21; 1 John 1:7; 2:2
2 Rom. 7:21-25
3 John 3:17-18; Rom. 8:1-2

Lord's Day 22

Q&A 57
Q. How does "the resurrection of the body" comfort you?
A. Not only will my soul be taken immediately after this life to Christ its head,1 but also my very flesh will be raised by the power of Christ, reunited with my soul and made like Christ's glorious body.2

1 Luke 23:43; Phil. 1:21-23
2 1 Cor. 15:20, 42-46, 54; Phil. 3:21; 1 John 3:2

Q&A 58
Q. How does the article concerning "life everlasting" comfort you?
A. Even as I already now experience in my heart the beginning of eternal joy,1 so after this life I will have perfect blessedness such as no eye has seen, no ear has heard, no human heart has ever imagined: a blessedness in which to praise God forever.2

1 Rom. 14:17
2 John 17:3; 1 Cor. 2:9

Lord's Day 23

Q&A 59
Q. What good does it do you, however, to believe all this?
A. In Christ I am righteous before God and heir to life everlasting.1

1 1 John 3:36; Rom. 1:17 (Hab. 2:4); Rom. 5:1-2

Q&A 60
Q. How are you righteous before God?
A. Only by true faith in Jesus Christ.1

Even though my conscience accuses me of having grievously sinned against all God's commandments, of never having kept any of them,2 and of still being inclined toward all evil,3 nevertheless, without any merit of my own,4 out of sheer grace,5 God grants and credits to me the perfect satisfaction, righteousness, and holiness of Christ,6 as if I had never sinned nor been a sinner, and as if I had been as perfectly obedient as Christ was obedient for me.7

All I need to do is accept this gift with a believing heart.8

1 Rom. 3:21-28; Gal. 2:16; Eph. 2:8-9; Phil 3:8-11
2 Rom. 3:9-10
3 Rom. 7:23
4 Titus 3:4-5
5 Rom. 3:24; Eph. 2:8
6 Rom. 4:3-5 (Gen. 15:6); 2 Cor. 5:17-19; 1 John 2:1-2
7 Rom. 4:24-25; 2 Cor. 5:21
8 John 3:18; Acts 16:30-31

Q&A 61
Q. Why do you say that through faith alone you are righteous?
A. Not because I please God by the worthiness of my faith. It is because only Christ's satisfaction, righteousness, and holiness make me righteous before God,1 and because I can accept this righteousness and make it mine in no other way than through faith.2

1 1 Cor. 1:30-31
2 Rom. 10:10; 1 John 5:10-12

Lord's Day 24

Q&A 62
Q. Why can't our good works be our righteousness before God, or at least a part of our righteousness?
A. Because the righteousness which can pass God's judgment must be entirely perfect and must in every way measure up to the divine law.1 But even our best works in this life are imperfect and stained with sin.2

1 Rom. 3:20; Gal. 3:10 (Deut. 27:26)
2 Isa. 64:6

Q&A 63
Q. How can our good works be said to merit nothing when God promises to reward them in this life and the next?1
A. This reward is not earned; it is a gift of grace.2

1 Matt. 5:12; Heb. 11:6
2 Luke 17:10; 2 Tim. 4:7-8

Q&A 64
Q. But doesn't this teaching make people indifferent and wicked?
A. No. It is impossible for those grafted into Christ through true faith not to produce fruits of gratitude.1

1 Luke 6:43-45; John 15:5

THE HOLY SACRAMENTS

Lord's Day 25

Q&A 65
Q. It is through faith alone that we share in Christ and all his benefits: where then does that faith come from?
A. The Holy Spirit produces it in our hearts1 by the preaching of the holy gospel,2 and confirms it by the use of the holy sacraments.3

1 John 3:5; 1 Cor. 2:10-14; Eph. 2:8
2 Rom. 10:17; 1 Pet. 1:23-25
3 Matt. 28:19-20; 1 Cor. 10:16

Q&A 66
Q. What are sacraments?

A. Sacraments are visible, holy signs and seals. They were instituted by God so that by our use of them he might make us understand more clearly the promise of the gospel, and seal that promise.1

And this is God's gospel promise: to grant us forgiveness of sins and eternal life by grace because of Christ's one sacrifice accomplished on the cross.2

1 Gen. 17:11; Deut. 30:6; Rom. 4:11
2 Matt. 26:27-28; Acts 2:38; Heb. 10:10

Q&A 67

Q. Are both the word and the sacraments then intended to focus our faith on the sacrifice of Jesus Christ on the cross as the only ground of our salvation?
A. Yes! In the gospel the Holy Spirit teaches us and by the holy sacraments confirms that our entire salvation rests on Christ's one sacrifice for us on the cross.1

1 Rom. 6:3; 1 Cor. 11:26; Gal. 3:27

Q&A 68
Q. How many sacraments did Christ institute in the New Testament?
A. Two: holy baptism and the holy supper.1

1 Matt. 28:19-20; 1 Cor. 11:23-26

HOLY BAPTISM

Lord's Day 26

Q&A 69
Q. How does holy baptism remind and assure you that Christ's one sacrifice on the cross benefits you personally?
A. In this way: Christ instituted this outward washing1 and with it promised that, as surely as water washes away the dirt from the body, so certainly his blood and his Spirit wash away my soul's impurity, that is, all my sins.2

1 Acts 2:38
2 Matt. 3:11; Rom. 6:3-10; 1 Pet. 3:21

Q&A 70
Q. What does it mean to be washed with Christ's blood and Spirit?
A. To be washed with Christ's blood means that God, by grace, has forgiven our sins because of Christ's blood poured out for us in his sacrifice on the cross.1

To be washed with Christ's Spirit means that the Holy Spirit has renewed and sanctified us to be members of Christ, so that more and more we become dead to sin and live holy and blameless lives.2

1 Zech. 13:1; Eph. 1:7-8; Heb. 12:24; 1 Pet. 1:2; Rev. 1:5
2 Ezek. 36:25-27; John 3:5-8; Rom. 6:4; 1 Cor. 6:11; Col. 2:11-12

Q&A 71
Q. Where does Christ promise that we are washed with his blood and Spirit as surely as we are washed with the water of baptism?
A. In the institution of baptism, where he says:

"Go therefore and make disciples of all nations, baptizing them in the name of the Father and of the Son and of the Holy Spirit."1

"The one who believes and is baptized will be saved; but the one who does not believe will be condemned."2

This promise is repeated when Scripture calls baptism "the water of rebirth"3 and the washing away of sins.4

1 Matt. 28:19
2 Mark 16:16
3 Titus 3:5
4 Acts 22:16

Lord's Day 27

Q&A 72
Q. Does this outward washing with water itself wash away sins?
A. No, only Jesus Christ's blood and the Holy Spirit cleanse us from all sins.1

1 Matt. 3:11; 1 Pet. 3:21; 1 John 1:7

Q&A 73
Q. Why then does the Holy Spirit call baptism the washing of rebirth and the washing away of sins?
A. God has good reason for these words. To begin with, God wants to teach us that the blood and Spirit of Christ take away our sins just as water removes dirt from the body.1

But more important, God wants to assure us, by this divine pledge and sign, that we are as truly washed of our sins spiritually as our bodies are washed with water physically.2

1 1 Cor. 6:11; Rev. 1:5; 7:14
2 Acts 2:38; Rom. 6:3-4; Gal. 3:27

Q&A 74
Q. Should infants also be baptized?
A. Yes, Infants as well as adults are included in God's covenant and people,1 and they, no less than adults, are promised deliverance from sin through Christ's blood and the Holy Spirit who produces faith.2

Therefore, by baptism, the sign of the covenant, they too should be incorporated into the Christian church and distinguished from the children of unbelievers.3 This was done in the Old Testament by circumcision,4 which was replaced in the New Testament by baptism.5

1 Gen. 17:7; Matt. 19:14
2 Isa. 44:1-3; Acts 2:38-39; 16:31
3 Acts 10:47; 1 Cor. 7:14
4 Gen. 17:9-14
5 Col. 2:11-13

THE HOLY SUPPER OF JESUS CHRIST

Lord's Day 28

Q&A 75
Q. How does the holy supper remind and assure you that you share in Christ's one sacrifice on the cross and in all his benefits?
A. In this way: Christ has commanded me and all believers to eat this broken bread and to drink this cup in remembrance of him. With this command come these promises:1

First, as surely as I see with my eyes the bread of the Lord broken for me and the cup shared with me, so surely his body was offered and broken for me and his blood poured out for me on the cross.

Second, as surely as I receive from the hand of the one who serves, and taste with my mouth the bread and cup of the Lord, given me as sure signs of Christ's body and blood, so surely he nourishes and refreshes my soul for eternal life with his crucified body and poured-out blood.

1 Matt. 26:26-28; Mark 14:22-24; Luke 22:19-20; 1 Cor. 11:23-25

Q&A 76
Q. What does it mean to eat the crucified body of Christ and to drink his poured-out blood?
A. It means to accept with a believing heart the entire suffering and death of Christ and thereby to receive forgiveness of sins and eternal life.1

But it means more. Through the Holy Spirit, who lives, both in Christ and in us, we are united more and more to Christ's blessed body.2 And so, although he is in heaven3 and we are on earth, we are flesh of his flesh and bone of his bone.4 And we forever live on and are governed by one Spirit, as the members of our body are by one soul.5

1 John 6:35, 40, 50-54
2 John 6:55-56; 1 Cor. 12:13
3 Acts 1:9-11; 1 Cor. 11:26; Col. 3:1
4 1 Cor. 6:15-17; Eph. 5:29-30; 1 John 4:13
5 John 6:56-58; 15:1-6; Eph. 4:15-16; 1 John 3:24

Q&A 77
Q. Where does Christ promise to nourish and refresh believers with his body and blood as surely as they eat this broken bread and drink this cup?
A. In the institution of the Lord's Supper:

"The Lord Jesus, on the night when he was betrayed took a loaf of bread, and when he had given thanks, he broke it and said, 'This is my body that is [broken]* for you. Do this in remembrance of me.' In the same way he took the cup also, after supper, saying, 'This cup is the new covenant in my blood. Do this, as often as you drink it, in remembrance of me.' For as often as you eat this bread and drink the cup, you proclaim the Lord's death until he comes."1

This promise is repeated by Paul in these words:

"The cup of blessing that we bless, is it not a sharing in the blood of Christ? The bread that we break, is it not a sharing in the body of Christ? Because there is one bread, we who are many, are one body, for we all partake of the one bread."2

1 1 Cor. 11:23-26
2 1 Cor. 10:16-17

*The word "broken" does not appear in the NRSV text, but it was present in the original German of the Heidelberg Catechism

Lord's Day 29

Q&A 78
Q. Do the bread and wine become the real body and blood of Christ?
A. No. Just as the water of baptism is not changed into Christ's blood and does not itself wash away sins, but is simply a divine sign and assurance1 of these things, so too the holy bread of the Lord's Supper does not become the actual body of Christ,2 even though it is called the body of Christ3 in keeping with the nature and language of sacraments.4

1 Eph. 5:26; Titus 3:5
2 Matt. 26:26-29
3 1 Cor. 10:16-17; 11:26-28
4 Gen. 17:10-11; Ex. 12:11, 13; 1 Cor. 10:1-4

Q&A 79
Q. Why then does Christ call the bread his body and the cup his blood, or the new covenant in his blood, and Paul use the words, a participation in Christ's body and blood?
A. Christ has good reason for these words. He wants to teach us that just as bread and wine nourish the temporal life, so too his crucified body and poured-out blood are the true food and drink of our souls for eternal life.1

But more important, he wants to assure us, by this visible sign and pledge, that we, through the

Holy Spirit's work, share in his true body and blood as surely as our mouths receive these holy signs in his remembrance,2 and that all of his suffering and obedience are as definitely ours as if we personally had suffered and made satisfaction for our sins.3

1 John 6:51, 55
2 1 Cor. 10:16-17; 11:26
3 Rom. 6:5-11

Lord's Day 30

Q&A 80*
Q. How does the Lord's Supper differ from the Roman Catholic Mass?
A. The Lord's Supper declares to us that all our sins are completely forgiven through the one sacrifice of Jesus Christ, which he himself accomplished on the cross once for all.1 It also declares to us that the Holy Spirit grafts us into Christ, 2 who with his true body is now in heaven at the right hand of the Father3 where he wants us to worship him.4

But the Mass teaches that the living and the dead do not have their sins forgiven through the suffering of Christ unless Christ is still offered for them daily by the priests. It also teaches that Christ is bodily present under the form of bread and wine where Christ is therefore to be worshiped. Thus the Mass is basically nothing but a denial of the one sacrifice and suffering of Jesus Christ and a condemnable idolatry.

1 John 19:30; Heb. 7:27; 9:12, 25-26; 10:10-18
2 1 Cor. 6:17; 10:16-17
3 Acts 7:55-56; Heb. 1:3; 8:1
4 Matt. 6:20-21; John 4:21-24; Phil. 3:20; Col. 3:1-3

*Q&A 80 was altogether absent from the first edition of the catechism, but was present in a shorter form in the second edition. The translation here given is of the expanded text of the third edition.

Q&A 81

Q. Who should come to the Lord's Table?
A. Those who are displeased with themselves because of their sins, but who nevertheless trust that their sins are pardoned and that their remaining weakness is covered by the suffering and death of Christ, and who also desire more and more to strengthen their faith and to lead a better life.

Hypocrites and those who are unrepentant, however, eat and drink judgment on themselves.1

1 1 Cor. 10:19-22; 11:26-32

Q&A 82
Q. Should those be admitted to the Lord's Supper who show by what they profess and how they live that they are unbelieving and ungodly?
A. No, that would dishonor God's covenant and bring down God's wrath upon the entire congregation.1 Therefore, according to the instruction of Christ and his apostles, the Christian church is duty-bound to exclude such people, by the official use of the keys of the kingdom, until they reform their lives.

1 1 Cor. 11:17-32; Ps. 50:14-16; Isa. 1:11-17

Lord's Day 31

Q&A 83
Q. What are the keys of the kingdom?

A. The preaching of the holy gospel and Christian discipline toward repentance. Both of them open the kingdom of heaven to believers and close it to unbelievers.1

1 Matt. 16:19; John 20:22-23

Q&A 84
Q. How does preaching the holy gospel open and close the kingdom of heaven?
A. According to the command of Christ, the kingdom of heaven is opened by proclaiming and publicly declaring to all believers, each and every one, that, as often as they accept the gospel promise in true faith, God, because of Christ's merit, truly forgives all their sins.

The kingdom of heaven is closed, however, by proclaiming and publicly declaring to unbelievers and hypocrites that, as long as they do not repent, the wrath of God and eternal condemnation rest on them. God's judgment, both in this life and in the life to come, is based on this gospel testimony.1

1 Matt. 16:19; John 3:31-36; 20:21-23

Q&A 85
Q. How is the kingdom of heaven closed and opened by Christian discipline?
A. According to the command of Christ: Those who, though called Christians, profess unchristian teachings or live unchristian lives, and who after repeated personal and loving admonitions, refuse to abandon their errors and evil ways, and who after being reported to the church, that is, to those ordained by the church for that purpose, fail to respond also to the church's admonitions- such persons the church excludes from the Christian community by withholding the sacraments from them, and God also excludes them from the kingdom of Christ.1 Such persons, when promising and demonstrating genuine reform, are received again as members of Christ and of his church.2

1 Matt. 18:15-20; 1 Cor. 5:3-5, 11-13; 2 Thess. 3:14-15
2 Luke 15:20-24; 2 Cor. 2:6-11

PART III: GRATITUDE

Lord's Day 32

Q&A 86
Q. Since we have been delivered from our misery by grace through Christ without any merit of our own, why then should we do good works?
A. Because Christ, having redeemed us by his blood, is also restoring us by his Spirit into his image, so that with our whole lives, we may show that we are thankful to God for his benefits,1 so that he may be praised through us,2 so that we may be assured of our faith by its fruits,3 and so that by our godly living our neighbors may be won over to Christ.4

1 Rom. 6:13; 12:1-2; 1 Pet. 2:5-10
2 Matt. 5:16; 1 Cor. 6:19-20
3 Matt. 7:17-18; Gal. 5:22-24; 2 Pet. 1:10-11
4 Matt. 5:14-16; Rom. 14:17-19; 1 Pet. 2:12; 3:1-2

Q&A 87
Q. Can those be saved who do not turn to God from their ungrateful and unrepentant ways?
A. By no means. Scripture tells us that no unchaste person, no idolater, adulterer, thief, no covetous person, no drunkard, slanderer, robber, or the like will inherit the kingdom of God.1

1 1 Cor. 6:9-10; Gal. 5:19-21; Eph. 5:1-20; 1 John 3:14

Lord's Day 33

Q&A 88
Q. What is involved in genuine repentance or conversion?
A. Two things: the dying-away of the old self, and the rising-to-life of the new.1

1 Rom. 6:1-11; 2 Cor. 5:17; Eph. 4:22-24; Col. 3:5-10

Q&A 89
Q. What is the dying-away of the old self?
A. To be genuinely sorry for sin and more and more to hate and run away from it.1

1 Ps. 51:3-4, 17; Joel 2:12-13; Rom. 8:12-13; 2 Cor. 7:10

Q&A 90
Q. What is the rising-to-life of the new self?
A. Wholehearted joy in God through Christ1 and a love and delight to live according to the will of God by doing every kind of good work.2

1 Ps. 51:8, 12; Isa. 57:15; Rom. 5:1; 14:17
2 Rom. 6:10-11; Gal. 2:20

Q&A 91
Q. What are good works?
A. Only those which are done out of true faith,1 conform to God's law,2 and are done for God's glory;3 and not those based on our own opinion or human tradition.4

1 John 15:5; Heb. 11:6
2 Lev. 18:4; 1 Sam. 15:22; Eph. 2:10
3 1 Cor. 10:31
4 Deut. 12:32; Isa. 29:13; Ezek. 20:18-19; Matt. 15:7-9

THE TEN COMMANDMENTS

Lord's Day 34

Q&A 92
Q. What is God's law?
A. God spoke all these words:

THE FIRST COMMANDMENT
"I am the LORD your God, who brought you out of the land of Egypt, out of the house of slavery; you shall have no other gods before me."

THE SECOND COMMANDMENT
"You shall not make for yourself an idol, whether in form of anything that is in heaven above, or that is on the earth beneath, or that is in the water under the earth. You shall not bow down to them or worship them; for I the LORD your God am a jealous God, punishing children for the iniquity of parents, to the third and the fourth generation of those who reject me, but showing love to the thousandth generation of those who love me and keep my commandments."

THE THIRD COMMANDMENT
"You shall not make wrongful use of the name of the LORD your God, for the LORD will not acquit anyone who misuses his name."

THE FOURTH COMMANDMENT
"Remember the sabbath day, end keep it holy. Six days you shall labor and do all your work. But the seventh day is a sabbath to the LORD your God; you shall not do any work-you, your son or your daughter, your male or female slave, your livestock, or the alien resident in your towns.

BEDROOM OF ADAM AND EVE

For in six days the LORD made heaven and earth, the sea, and all that is in them, but rested the seventh day; therefore, the LORD blessed the sabbath day and consecrated it."

THE FIFTH COMMANDMENT
"Honor your father and your mother, so that your days may be long in the land that the LORD your God is giving to you."

THE SIXTH COMMANDMENT
"You shall not murder."

THE SEVENTH COMMANDMENT
"You shall not commit adultery."

THE EIGHTH COMMANDMENT
"You shall not steal."

THE NINTH COMMANDMENT
"You shall not bear false witness against your neighbor."

THE TENTH COMMANDMENT
"You shall not covet your neighbor's house; you shall not covet your neighbor's wife, or male or female slave, or ox, or donkey, or anything that belongs to your neighbor."1

1 Ex. 20:1-17; Deut. 5:6-21

Q&A 93
Q. How are these commandments divided?
A. Into two tables. The first has four commandments, teaching us how we ought to live in relation to God. The second has six commandments, teaching us what we owe our neighbor.1

1 Matt. 22:37-39

Q&A 94
Q. What does the Lord require in the first commandment?
A. That I, not wanting to endanger my own salvation, avoid and shun all idolatry,1 sorcery, superstitious rites,2 and prayer to saints or to other creatures.3

That I rightly know the only true God,4 trust him alone,5 and look to God for every good thing6 humbly7 and patiently,8 and love,9 fear,10 and honor11 God with all my heart.

In short, that I give up anything rather than go against God's will in any way.12

1 1 Cor. 6:9-10; 10:5-14; 1 John 5:21
2 Lev. 19:31; Deut. 18:9-12
3 Matt. 4:10; Rev. 19:10; 22:8-9
4 John 17:3
5 Jer. 17:5, 7
6 Ps. 104:27-28; James 1:17
7 1 Pet. 5:5-6
8 Col. 1:11; Heb. 10:36
9 Matt. 22:37 (Deut. 6:5)
10 Prov. 9:10; 1 Pet. 1:17
11 Matt. 4:10 (Deut. 6:13)
12 Matt. 5:29-30; 10:37-39

Q&A 95
Q. What is idolatry?
A. Idolatry is having or inventing something in which one trusts in place of or alongside of the

only true God, who has revealed himself in the Word.1

1 1 Chron. 16:26; Gal. 4:8-9; Eph. 5:5; Phil. 3:19

Lord's Day 35

Q&A 96
Q. What is God's will for us in the second commandment?
A. That we in no way make any image of God1 nor worship him in any other way than has been commanded in God's Word.2

1 Deut. 4:15-19; Isa. 40:18-25; Acts 17:29; Rom. 1:22-23
2 Lev. 10:1-7; 1 Sam. 15:22-23; John 4:23-24

Q&A 97
Q. May we then not make any image at all?
A. God cannot and may not be visibly portrayed in any way.

Although creatures may be portrayed, yet God forbids making or having such images if one's intention is to worship them or to serve God through them.1

1 Ex. 34:13-14, 17; 2 Kings 18:4-5

Q&A 98
Q. But may not images be permitted in churches in place of books for the unlearned?
A. No, we should not try to be wiser than God. God wants the Christian community instructed by the living preaching of his Word1-not by idols that cannot even talk.2

1 Rom. 10:14-15, 17; 2 Tim. 3:16-17; 2 Pet. 1:19
2 Jer. 10:8; Hab. 2:18-20

Lord's Day 36

Q&A 99
Q. What is the aim of the third commandment?
A. That we neither blaspheme nor misuse the name of God by cursing,1 perjury,2 or unnecessary oaths,3 nor share in such horrible sins by being silent bystanders.4

In summary, we should use the holy name of God only with reverence and awe,5 so that we may properly confess God,6 pray to God,7 and glorify God in all our words and works.8

1 Lev. 24:10-17
2 Lev. 19:12
3 Matt. 5:37; James 5:12
4 Lev. 5:1; Prov. 29:24
5 Ps. 99:1-5; Jer. 4:2
6 Matt. 10:32-33; Rom. 10:9-10

7 Ps. 50:14-15; 1 Tim. 2:8
8 Col. 3:17

Q&A 100
Q. Is blasphemy of God's name by swearing and cursing really such serious sin that God is angry also with those who do not do all they can to help prevent and forbid it?
A. Yes, indeed;1 No sin is greater or provokes God's wrath more than blaspheming his name. That is why God commanded it to be punished with death.2

1 Lev. 5:1
2 Lev. 24:10-17

BEDROOM OF ADAM AND EVE

Lord's Day 37

Q&A 101
Q. But may we swear an oath in God's name if we do it reverently?
A. Yes, when the government demands it, or when necessity requires it, in order to maintain and promote truth and trustworthiness for God's glory and our neighbor's good.

Such oaths are grounded in God's Word1 and were rightly used by the people of God in the Old and New Testaments.2

1 Deut. 6:13; 10:20; Jer. 4:1-2; Heb. 6:16
2 Gen. 21:24; Josh. 9:15; 1 Kings 1:29-30; Rom. 1:9; 2 Cor. 1:23

Q&A 102
Q. May we also swear by saints or other creatures?
A. No. A legitimate oath means calling upon God as the only one who knows my heart to witness to my truthfulness and to punish me if I swear falsely.1 No creature is worthy of such honor.2

1 Rom. 9:1; 2 Cor. 1:23
2 Matt. 5:34-37; 23:16-22; James 5:12

Lord's Day 38

Q&A 103
Q. What is God's will for you in the fourth commandment?
A. First, that the gospel ministry and education for it be maintained,1 and that, especially on the festive day of rest, I diligently attend the assembly of God's people2 to learn what God's Word teaches,3 to participate in the sacraments,4 to pray to God publicly,5 and to bring Christian offerings for the poor.6

Second, that every day of my life I rest from my evil ways, let the Lord work in me through his Spirit, and so begin in this life the eternal Sabbath.7

1 Deut. 6:4-9, 20-25; 1 Cor. 9:13-14; 2 Tim. 2:2; 3:13-17; Titus 1:5
2 Deut. 12:5-12; Ps. 40:9-10; 68:26; Acts 2:42-47; Heb. 10:23-25
3 Rom. 10:14-17; 1 Cor. 14:31-32; 1 Tim. 4:13
4 1 Cor. 11:23-25
5 Col. 3:16; 1 Tim. 2:1
6 Ps. 50:14; 1 Cor. 16:2; 2 Cor. 8-9
7 Isa. 66:23; Heb. 4:9-11

Lord's Day 39

Q&A 104
Q. What is God's will for you in the fifth commandment?
A. That I honor, love, and be loyal to my father and mother and all those in authority over me; that I submit myself with proper obedience to all their good teaching and discipline;1 and also that I be patient with their failings2-for through them God chooses to rule us.3

1 Ex. 21:17; Prov. 1:8; 4:1; Rom. 13:1-2; Eph. 5:21-22; 6:1-9; Col. 3:18-4:1
2 Prov. 20:20; 23:22; 1 Pet. 2:18
3 Matt. 22:21; Rom. 13:1-8; Eph. 6:1-9; Col. 3:18-21

Lord's Day 40

Q&A 105
Q. What is God's will for you in the sixth commandment?
A. I am not to belittle, hate, insult, or kill my neighbor-not by my thoughts, my words, my look

or gesture, and certainly not by actual deeds-and I am not to be party to this in others;1 rather, I am to put away all desire for revenge.2

I am not to harm or recklessly endanger myself either.3

Prevention of murder is also why government is armed with the sword.4

1 Gen. 9:6; Lev. 19:17-18; Matt. 5:21-22; 26:52
2 Prov. 25:21-22; Matt. 18:35; Rom. 12:19; Eph. 4:26
3 Matt. 4:7; 26:52; Rom. 13:11-14
4 Gen. 9:6; Ex. 21:14; Rom. 13:4

Q&A 106
Q. Does this commandment refer only to murder?
A. By forbidding murder God teaches us that he hates the root of murder: envy, hatred, anger, vindictiveness.1

In God's sight all such are disguised forms of murder.2

1 Prov. 14:30; Rom. 1:29; 12:19; Gal. 5:19-21; 1 John 2:9-11
2 1 John 3:15

Q&A 107
Q. Is it enough then that we do not murder our neighbor in any such way?
A. No. By condemning envy, hatred, and anger God wants us to love our neighbors as ourselves,1 to be patient, peace-loving, gentle, merciful, and friendly toward them,2 to protect them from harm as much as we can, and to do good even to our enemies.3

1 Matt. 7:12; 22:39; Rom. 12:10
2 Matt. 5:3-12; Luke 6:36; Rom. 12:10, 18; Gal. 6:1-2; Eph. 4:2; Col. 3:12; 1 Pet. 3:8
3 Ex. 23:4-5; Matt. 5:44-45; Rom. 12:20-21 (Prov. 25:21-22)

Lord's Day 41

Q&A 108
Q. What does the seventh commandment teach us?
A. That God condemns all unchastity,1 and that therefore we should thoroughly detest it2 and live decent and chaste lives,3 within or outside of the holy state of marriage.

1 Lev. 18:30; Eph. 5:3-5
2 Jude 22-23
3 1 Cor. 7:1-9; 1 Thess. 4:3-8; Heb. 13:4

Q&A 109
Q. Does God, in this commandment, forbid only such scandalous sins as adultery?
A. We are temples of the Holy Spirit, body and soul, and God wants both to be kept clean and holy. That is why God forbids all unchaste actions, looks, talk, thoughts, or desires,1 and whatever may incite someone to them.2

1 Matt. 5:27-29; 1 Cor. 6:18-20; Eph. 5:3-4
2 1 Cor. 15:33; Eph. 5:18

Lord's Day 42

Q&A 110
Q. What does God forbid in the eighth commandment?
A. God forbids not only outright theft and robbery, punishable by law.1

But in God's sight theft, also includes all scheming and swindling in order to get our neighbor's goods for ourselves, whether by force or means that appear legitimate,2 such as inaccurate measurements of weight, size, or volume; fraudulent merchandising; counterfeit money; excessive interest; or any other means forbidden by God.3

In addition, God forbids all greed4 and pointless squandering of his gifts.5

1 Ex. 22:1; 1 Cor. 5:9-10; 6:9-10
2 Mic. 6:9-11; Luke 3:14; James 5:1-6
3 Deut. 25:13-16; Ps. 15:5; Prov. 11:1; 12:22; Ezek. 45:9-12; Luke 6:35
4 Luke 12:15; Eph. 5:5
5 Prov. 21:20; 23:20-21; Luke 16:10-13

Q&A 111
Q. What does God require of you in this commandment?
A. That I do whatever I can for my neighbor's good, that I treat others as I would like them to treat me, and that I work faithfully so that I may share with those in need.1

1 Isa. 58:5-10; Matt. 7:12; Gal. 6:9-10; Eph. 4:28

Lord's Day 43

Q&A 112
Q. What is the aim of the ninth commandment?
A. That I never give false testimony against anyone, twist no one's words, not gossip or slander, nor join in condemning anyone rashly or without a hearing.1

Rather, in court and everywhere else, I should avoid lying and deceit of every kind; these are the very devices the devil uses, and they would call down on me God's intense wrath.2 I should love the truth, speak it candidly, and openly acknowledge it.3 And I should do what I can to guard and advance my neighbor's good name.4

1 Ps. 15; Prov. 19:5; Matt. 7:1; Luke 6:37; Rom. 1:28-32
2 Lev. 19:11-12; Prov. 12:22; 13:5; John 8:44; Rev. 21:8
3 1 Cor. 13:6; Eph. 4:25
4 1 Pet. 3:8-9; 4:8

Lord's Day 44

Q&A 113
Q. What is the aim of the tenth commandment?
A. That not even the slightest desire or thought contrary to any one of God's commandments should ever arise in our hearts.

Rather, with all our hearts we should always hate sin and take pleasure in whatever is right.1

1 Ps. 19:7-14; 139:23-24; Rom. 7:7-8

Q&A 114
Q. But can those converted to God, obey these commandments perfectly?
A. No. In this life even the holiest have only a small beginning of this obedience.1

Nevertheless, with all seriousness, of purpose, they do begin to live according to all, not only some, of God's commandments.2

1 Eccles. 7:20; Rom. 7:14-15; 1 Cor. 13:9; 1 John 1:8-10
2 Ps. 1:1-2; Rom. 7:22-25; Phil. 3:12-16

Q&A 115
Q. Since no one in this life can obey the Ten Commandments perfectly, why does God want them

to preach so pointedly?
A. First, so that the longer we live the more we may come to know our sinfulness and the more eagerly look to Christ for forgiveness of sins and righteousness.1

Second, so that we may never stop striving, and never stop praying to God for the grace of the Holy Spirit, to be renewed more and more after God's image, until after this life we reach our goal: perfection.2

1 Ps. 32:5; Rom. 3:19-26; 7:7, 24-25; 1 John 1:9
2 1 Cor. 9:24; Phil. 3:12-14; 1 John 3:1-3

THE LORD'S PRAYER

Lord's Day 45

Q&A 116
Q. Why do Christians need to pray?
A. Because prayer is the most important part of the thankfulness God requires of us.1 And also because God gives his grace and Holy Spirit only to those who pray continually and groan inwardly, asking God for these gifts and thanking God for them.2

1 Ps. 50:14-15; 116:12-19; 1 Thess. 5:16-18
2 Matt. 7:7-8; Luke 11:9-13

Q&A 117
Q. What is the kind of prayer that pleases God and that he listens to?
A. First, we must pray from the heart to no other than the one true God, revealed to us in his Word, asking for everything God has commanded us to ask for.1

Second, we must fully recognize our need and misery, so that we humble ourselves in God's majestic presence.2

Third, we must rest on this unshakable foundation: even though we do not deserve it, God will surely listen to our prayer because of Christ our Lord. That is what God promised us in his Word.3

1 Ps. 145:18-20; John 4:22-24; Rom. 8:26-27; James 1:5; 1 John 5:14-15
2 2 Chron. 7:14; Ps. 2:11; 34:18; 62:8; Isa. 66:2; Rev. 4
3 Dan. 9:17-19; Matt. 7:8; John 14:13-14; 16:23; Rom. 10:13; James 1:6

Q&A 118
Q. What did God command us to pray for?
A. Everything, we need, spiritually and physically,1 as embraced in the prayer Christ our Lord himself taught us.

1 James 1:17; Matt. 6:33

Q&A 119
Q. What is this prayer?
A. Our Father in heaven, hallowed be your name. Your kingdom come. Your will be done, on earth as it is in heaven. Give us this day our daily bread. And forgive us our debts, as we also have forgiven our debtors. And do not bring us to the time of trial, but rescue us from the evil one. * For the kingdom and the power and the glory are yours forever. Amen.1 **

1 Matt. 6:9-13; Luke 11:2-4

* This text of the Lord's Prayer is from the New Revised Standard Version in keeping with the use of the NRSV throughout this edition of the catechism. Most biblical scholars agree that it is

an accurate translation of the Greek text and carries virtually the same meaning as the more traditional text of the Lord's Prayer.

**Earlier and better manuscripts of Matthew 6 omit the words "For the kingdom and ... Amen."

Lord's Day 46

Q&A 120
Q. Why did Christ command us to call God "our Father"?
A. To awaken in us at the very beginning of our prayer what should be basic to our prayer-a childlike reverence and trust that through Christ God has become our Father, and that just as our parents do not refuse us the things of this life, even less will God our Father refuse to give us what we ask in faith.1

1 Matt. 7:9-11; Luke 11:11-13

Q&A 121
Q. Why the words "in heaven"?
A. These words teach us not to think of God's heavenly majesty as something earthly,1 and to expect everything needed for body and soul from God's almighty power.2

1 Jer. 23:23-24; Acts 17:24-25
2 Matt. 6:25-34; Rom. 8:31-32

Lord's Day 47

Q&A 122
Q. What does the first petition mean?
A. "Hallowed be your name" means: Help us to truly know you,1 to honor, glorify, and praise you for all your works and for all that shines forth from them: your almighty power, wisdom, kindness, justice, mercy, and truth.2

And it means, help us to direct all our living-what we think, say, and do-so that your name will never be blasphemed because of us but always honored and praised.3

1 Jer. 9:23-24; 31:33-34; Matt. 16:17; John 17:3
2 Ex. 34:5-8; Ps. 145; Jer. 32:16-20; Luke 1:46-55, 68-75; Rom. 11:33-36
3 Ps. 115:1; Matt. 5:16

Lord's Day 48

Q&A 123
Q. What does the second petition mean?
A. "Your kingdom come" means: Rule us by your Word and Spirit in such a way that more and more we submit to you.1

Preserve your church and make it grow.2

Destroy the devil's work; destroy every force which revolts against you and every conspiracy against your holy Word.3

Do this until your kingdom fully comes, when you will be all in all.4

1 Ps. 119:5, 105; 143:10; Matt. 6:33
2 Ps. 122:6-9; Matt. 16:18; Acts 2:42-47
3 Rom. 16:20; 1 John 3:8
4 Rom. 8:22-23; 1 Cor. 15:28; Rev. 22:17, 20

Lord's Day 49

Q&A 124
Q. What does the third petition mean?
A. "Your will be done, on earth as it is in heaven" means:

Help us and all people reject our own wills and to obey your will without any back talk. Your will alone is good.1

Help us one and all to carry out the work we are called to,2 as willingly and faithfully as the angels in heaven.3

1 Matt. 7:21; 16:24-26; Luke 22:42; Rom. 12:1-2; Titus 2:11-12
2 1 Cor. 7:17-24; Eph. 6:5-9
3 Ps. 103:20-21

Lord's Day 50

Q&A 125
Q. What does the fourth petition mean?
A. "Give us this day our daily bread" means:

Do take care of all our physical needs1 so that we come to know that you are the only source of everything good,2 and that neither our work and worry nor your gifts can do us any good without your blessing;3

And so help us to give up our trust in creatures and trust in you alone.4

1 Ps. 104:27-30; 145:15-16; Matt. 6:25-34
2 Acts 14:17; 17:25; James 1:17
3 Deut. 8:3; Ps. 37:16; 127:1-2; 1 Cor. 15:58
4 Ps. 55:22; 62; 146; Jer. 17:5-8; Heb. 13:5-6

Lord's Day 51

Q&A 126
Q. What does the fifth petition mean?
A. "Forgive us our debts, as we also have forgiven our debtors" means:

Because of Christ's blood, do not hold against us, poor sinners that we are, any of the sins we do or the evil that constantly clings to us.1

Forgive us just as we are fully determined, as evidence of your grace in us, to forgive our neighbors.2

1 Ps. 51:1-7; 143:2; Rom. 8:1; 1 John 2:1-2
2 Matt. 6:14-15; 18:21-35

Lord's Day 52

Q&A 127
Q. What does the sixth petition mean?
A. "And do not bring us to the time of trial, but rescue us from the evil one" means:

By ourselves we are too weak to hold our own even for a moment.1

And our sworn enemies-the devil,2 the world,3 and our own flesh4-never stop attacking us.

And so, Lord, uphold us and make us strong with the strength of your Holy Spirit, so that we may not go down to defeat in this spiritual struggle,5 but may firmly resist our enemies until we finally win the complete victory.6

1 Ps. 103:14-16; John 15:1-5

2 2 Cor. 11:14; Eph. 6:10-13; 1 Pet. 5:8
3 John 15:18-21
4 Rom. 7:23; Gal. 5:17
5 Matt. 10:19-20; 26:41; Mark 13:33; Rom. 5:3-5
6 1 Cor. 10:13; 1 Thess. 3:13; 5:23

Q&A 128
Q. What does your conclusion to this prayer mean?
A. "For the kingdom and the power and the glory are yours forever" means:

We have made all these petitions of you because, as our all-powerful king, you are both willing and able to give us all that is good;1 and because your holy name, and not we ourselves, should receive all the praise, forever.2

1 Rom. 10:11-13; 2 Pet. 2:9 2 Ps. 115:1; John 14:13

Q&A 129
Q. What does that little word "Amen" express?
A. "Amen" means:

This shall truly and surely be!

It is even more sure that God listens to my prayer than that I really desire what I pray for.1

1 Isa. 65:24; 2 Cor. 1:20; 2 Tim. 2:13

I did not include the historical facts that led to Christian creeds and confessions. It was a deliberate move. If you need to learn the history of the church from the time of Christ to present church, then take an online course or enroll in a traditional theological college for more information. In the Nicene Creed we learn that Jesus Christ is God. He has the same essence as God the Father and God the Holy Spirit. God the Father sent Jesus to us, but this does not suggest that Jesus was made or was inferior to the father. In the Creed we also learn that the Holy Spirit was sent by both the father and the son. This is in line with biblical truth confessed in scripture.

THE NICENE CREED

We believe in one God, the Father, the Almighty, maker of heaven and earth, of all that is, seen and unseen.

We believe in one Lord, Jesus Christ, the only Son of God, eternally begotten of the Father, God from God, Light from Light, true God from true God, begotten, not made, of one being with the Father; through him all things were made.
For us and for our salvation he came down from heaven: was incarnate of the Holy Spirit and the Virgin Mary, and became truly human.
For our sake he was crucified under Pontius Pilate; he suffered death and was buried.
On the third day he rose again in accordance with the Scriptures; he ascended into heaven and is seated at the right hand of the Father.
He will come again in glory to judge the living and the dead, and his kingdom will have no end.

We believe in the Holy Spirit, the Lord, the giver of life, who proceeds from the Father [and the Son], who with the Father and the Son is worshiped and glorified, who has spoken through the prophets.
We believe in one holy Catholic (universal Christian) Church and apostolic Church.
We acknowledge one baptism for the forgiveness of sins.
We look for the resurrection of the dead, and the life of the world to come. Amen.

CHAPTER 24 QUESTIONS TO ANSWER

How can we study creeds and confessions in our local churches?

Why should we read and study, church confessions?

Who made these church confessions?

What is the danger of Christian churches not studying church confessions?

Are the church confessions the word of God?

Can new members of the church study these church confessions as a requirement for membership?

BIBLIOGRAPHY

Harrison, Everett, Ed., (1960). Baker's Dictionary of Theology. Baker House: Grand Rapids, Michigan.

Berkhof, L. (1933). Manual of Christian Doctrine. Eerdmans: Grand Rapids, Michigan.

Bosma, M.J. (1927). Exposition of Reformed Doctrine. Zondervan: Grand Rapids, Michigan

Calvin, J. (1948). Commentary on the book of the Prophet Isaiah. Vol.4. Eerdmans: Grand Rapids, Michigan.

Calvin, J. (1960). Institute of the Christian Religion. 2 Vols. Edited by John T. McNeill. Translated by Ford Lewis Battles. Westminster: Philadelphia.

Gardner, E. C. (1960). Biblical faith and Social Ethics. Harper & Row: New York and Evanston.

Gore, R. J. Outline of Systematic Theology. Third Edition. Trinity College & Theological Seminary: Newburgh, Indiana.

Green, M. (1975). I Believe in the Holy Spirit. Eerdmans: Grand Rapids, Michigan.

Grudem, W. (1994). Systematic Theology. Inter-Varsity Press: Leicester, England.

Hertz, J.H. (1937). The Pentateuch and Haftorahs. 5 Vols. Oxford: England.

Hodge, A. A. (1928). Outlines of Theology. Eerdmans: Grand Rapids, Michigan.

Hodge, C. (1970). Systematic Theology. 3 Vols. 1871-73; reprint. Eerdmans: Grand Rapids.

House, H. W. (1992). Charts of Christian Theology & Doctrine. Zondervan: Grand Rapids, Michigan.

Pattison, B. (2006). Poverty in the Theology of John Calvin. Pickwick: Eugene, OR.

Sproul, R.C. (1995). Faith Alone. The Evangelical Doctrine of Justification. Baker: Grand Rapids, Michigan.

Jacob, E. (1817). Theology of the Old Testament. Harper & Row: New York and Evanston.

Lungu, E. K. (2010). The African Way. Struggles and Success of the Life of Lungu. Xlibris & Lungu Publishing: Florence, Arizona.

Meyer, J. (1997). Me and My Big Mouth. Your Answer is Right under Your Nose. Faith Words: New York.

Osteen, J. (2007). Becoming a better you. 7 Keys to improving your Life every day. Free Press: New York.

Sproul, R.C. (1986). Life views. Make a Christian Impact on Culture and Society. Power Books: Old Tappan, NJ.

Thornton, E. E. (1964). Theology and Pastoral Counseling. Fortress: Philadelphia.

Warfield, B. B. (2010). The Person and Work of the Holy Spirit. Solid Ground Christian Books: Birmingham, Alabama.

Online Websites Cited.

Hegeman. (2000). MINTS Course. In MINTS. Retrieved January 5, from www.mintsespanol.byethost12.com <http://www.mintsespanol.byethost12.com>.

Ligonier Press. (1647). Westminster confession of faith Chapter 14:11. In Learn. Retrieved April 4 from http://www.ligonier.org/learn/articles/westminster-confession-faith.

RCA Press. (1563). Heidelberg Catechism Question 21. In RCA. Retrieved May 9 from https://www.rca.org/heidelbergcatechism

Yancychipper. (2007). What's a Pod in Prison? In Yahoo.com. Retrieved May 8 from https://answers.yahoo.com/question/index?qid=20070924145902AAOkelv

Kelli Mahoney. (2015). Christian Teen Expert about Sex: Abortion of a cold. http://www.merriam-webster.com/medical/abortion

Creeds and Confessions from https://www.rca.org/resources/creeds-confessions

BEDROOM OF ADAM AND EVE

ANOTHER WORK BY DR. EK LUNGU

The African Way: Struggles and Success of the Life of Lungu
ISBN: Softcover 978-0-9830232-03 printed by Lungu Publishing Company Inc. 2010

CONTACT US

CONTACT US IN USA
Lungu Publishing Company, Inc.
P.O Box 2932
Florence Arizona 85132 USA

CONTACT US IN ZAMBIA
Lungu Publishing Company, Inc.
Kanyuka Village
Chief Ndake
P. O. Box 570119
Nyimba District
Zambia, Africa.

Website www.lungupci.com <http://www.lungupci.com>
info@lungupci.com <info@lungupci.com>
www.kanyukavillage.com <http://www.kanyukavillage.com>
www.bedroomadameve.com <http://www.bedroomadameve.com>
Contact the author by request only.

BEDROOM OF ADAM AND EVE

THE TARGET FOR THIS BOOK

Have you ever wondered what sin is and what it has done to you and the rest of the people? Does sin bother you? Or do you put the whole blame of sin solely on one man Adam?

This book -<u>Bedroom of Adam and Eve</u>-will help you understand that you and the rest of the people in the world are sleeping in the in the bedroom of Adam and eve. Yes, all people, including myself love to sleep comfortably in the bedroom of Adam and Eve. We naturally know what to do with sin from birth. Nobody tells us how to sin since sin has totally taken control of all our parts of the body. This is called total depravity and this is the Bedroom of Adam and Eve.

The only way humans can get out of the comfort of the bedroom of Adam and Eve is to live in the comfort of the bedroom of Jesus Christ. This is possible by the grace of God through faith in Jesus Christ.

This book tells how man and woman came to live in the bedroom of Adam and Eve and how some of the men and women found a way out and started to live in the bedroom of Christ. The bedroom of Adam and Eve also explains what people in the bedroom of Christ came to confess and proclaim throughout Christendom as they walked with the Lord Jesus Christ.

The target of this book is you who seek to know more about sin and salvation; it is the religious volunteers and chaplains working for the Lord everywhere in the world; It is the convicted people in prison serving time for the crime they have done. Yes, the target of this book is for those wanting to learn more of the protestant Christian values so that they can teach and practice them to their families, friends, and churches in the world.

By buying this book you are also contributing to building of Kanyuka Village Hospital in Kanyuka village in Zambia. One dollar from each book bought goes to the Moyo Africa Foundation for the same cause stated above.

ABOUT THE AUTHOR

Rev. Dr. Edward Kavimba Lungu was born January 01, 1962 at Kanyuka Village, Chief Ndake, Petauke (now Nyimba) District, Zambia. His parents were Yulu Bernard Kavimba and Malita Chisece Mumba. Later on, my mother got married to Stiphano (Steven) Lungu.

Dr. Lungu studied theological education at (JMTC) now Justo Mwale University in Zambia (1984-1988).

Dr. Lungu was an ordained minister of Msanga RCZ in Chipata at Gonda Barracks (1989-1993).

Dr. Lungu married Elizabeth Sakala Lungu (1989- 1994).

Dr. Lungu married Karoline Ann Lungu in 2004 Ten years after Elizabeth Sakala Lungu died.

Dr. Ek. Lungu Studied theology in USA at

-Reformed Bible College (Kuyper College) in Grand Rapids, MI (1993-1996 BRE)

-Calvin Theological Seminary in Grand Rapids, MI (1996-1998 M.T.S)

-Cincinnati Christian University (1999-20002 MATS)

-International theological school in California (2000 Th.D.)

-Cincinnati University (2003 Administration of Criminal Justice)

-Trinity Theological Seminary (1998-2013 Ph.D.)

Rev. Dr. Lungu worked at the CADC Florence Complex (CCA) in Florence Arizona.Now Core Civic (www.corecivic.com)

Rev. Dr. Lungu was;

The founder and pastor of Grace Bible, Reformed church in Florence Arizona (www.gracebiblereformedchurch.com).

The founder and president of Moyo Africa Foundation (www.moyoafricafoundation.org)

The founder and president of Lungu Publishing Company Inc. (www.lungupci.com)

The founder and president of Grace Bible Reformed University in Florence Arizona (www.gbru.org/www.gracebiblereformeduniversity.org)

The founder and president of Zambia Christian University (www.zambiachristianuniversity.com/www.zamcu.com)

DEDICATION

Bedroom of Adam and Eve is dedicated to Grace Bible Reformed University and Zambia Christian University. All students of Grace Bible Reformed University and Zambia Christian University are required to study this book during their school with the institutions. This means that when you buy and study this book, you are also involved in the studies taught at GBRU and ZAMCU. You may not get a diploma with us after reading this book, but you can teach these facts as you wish for your families, churches, and friends free of charge. God bless the Reformed Church in America for well stated Christian confessions that are included in this book.

FRIENDS OF REFORMED THEOLOGY

Pastors and professors that graduated from Justo Mwale University, are members of Reformed Church in zambia, working or worked in the Reformed Church in Zambia, lived, and worked in another country and still holds on to Reformed Faith.

Rev. Dr. Alfred Ngoma Minister at Reformed Church in Zambia (Australia).

Prison Chaplain in Australia).

Rev. Dr. Edward Kavimba Lungu Minister at Reformed Church in Zambia (USA).

Prison Chaplain at Core Civic and President of Grace Bible Reformed University.

Rev. Dr. Edwin Zulu Minister at Reformed Church in zambia (Zimbabwe).

Now serving the Lord as Associate Professor of Old Testament at Justo Mwale University, Lusaka zambia and the Moderator of the Reformed Church in zambia.

Rev. Dr. Japhet Ndhlovu Minister at Reformed Church in Zambia (Kenya, Canada).

Now serving the Lord as Program Coordinator South Asia/Southern Africa Church in Mission, The United Church of Canada.

Nedson Zulu Sr. Missionary minister of the word and sacraments in Malawi(Malawi).

HOW TO US THIS BOOK

As devotion book. Read one topic a month for a year and answer questions at the end of each chapter.

As resource for systematic theology. Teach the doctrines in Christian schools.

As church membership. Let new believers in the church study it before confirmed or baptized.

As bible study. Open the bible and follow each topic in this book as you do the study. Make sure that every topic is in line with the word of God. If you differ with many of these views in the book state your differences in love.

As research tool. You can critic the entire book in support of the author or not. Come up with your take on the book. Get PhD on it.

As charitable organization. You can choose to distributes many copies of the book to prisons and other places of your choice.

As special gift. You can buy the book and surprise your loved ones as gift at special occasions.

This book is not to be used as a tool to bash those who agree or disagree with the views of the author.

WHAT YOU NEED TO DO

When you buy, this book, ask yourself what you need to know from it. If you are already a believer read 8 steps how to use this book in the previous page. Choose your step and go for it. But if you are not a believer, here what you can do;

Ask help from God in whatever situation you are in. He is more than willing to help.

Ask this way, Lord Jesus, you know me better than myself. Help me knowing you. Forgive me my sins. Help me to love you more than myself. Write my name in your book of life. Amen.

If you find the Lord Jesus by praying this short prayer tell it to your loved ones.

BEDROOM OF ADAM AND EVE

www.ingramcontent.com/pod-product-compliance
Lightning Source LLC
Chambersburg PA
CBHW060512300426
44112CB00017B/2631